*"As a psychotherapist I found the chapter in your book **Stress Personalities** on Critical Judge to be particularly useful for depressed clients with low self esteem."*
—Wilmington, DE

ᗢᗣᗢᗣᗢᗣ

*"I was impressed with the universality of your book **Stress Personalities.**"*
—Bakersfield, CA

ᗢᗣᗢᗣᗢᗣ

*"I have a copy of your book **Stress Personalities** and I consider it one of the best publications I have ever read."*
—Calgary, Alberta

ᗢᗣᗢᗣᗢᗣ

*"I enjoyed reading the book **Stress Personalities** very much. It is very lucid, carries great conviction. It should help many stressed persons to understand themselves and modify stress behavior . . ."*
—Ray Rosenman, MD, Co-Author,
"Type A Behavior and Your Heart."

ᗢᗣᗢᗣᗢᗣ

"I'm enjoying your book and using something from it every day."
—Cupertino, CA

ᗢᗣᗢᗣᗢᗣ

Focal Point Services

We provide a variety of Human Resource services including; speeches, stress management and conflict resolution workshops, conference presentations, consultation, team building and the publication of a job stress newsletter. Our programs can be specifically designed for your organization or profession. We also provide on-going training and consultation for those interested in using Stress Personalities Training in their work. Materials available:

"Stress Personalities, A Look Inside Our Selves," text, 267 pgs., is an in-depth look at stress and it's effects on health work life and interpersonal relationships. $15.00

"A Guide to Your Stress Personalities," stress workbook, 53 pgs., a stress management program focused on stress behavior. $15.00

"Your Stress Personalities," 49 min, color video with humorous skits programmed to follow the stress workbook. $125.00

"Conflict at Work," conflict workbook, 67 pgs, a step by step process for managing conflict in work and life. $15.00

"Relaxation & Mind Clearing," audio tape, 45 min., includes progressive relaxation, mind clearing and short relaxation exercises. $20.00

"Focal Point on Stress, a humorous look at a serious topic" audio tape, 45 min., recorded live at the NAMI conference in San Francisco, includes skits featuring interactions with the Stress Personalities. $20.00

"Stress Personalities Follow-Up Workbook", 40 pgs., workbook designed to reinforce the Stress Personalities Model. $15.00

Focal Point on Job Stress, newsletter, to keep you up to date on the latest developments in job stress and an on-going follow-up to Stress Personalities Training.

ORDER FORM

❏ **YES,** please contact me about Focal Point services.

❏ **YES,** please send me _____ Book(s), "Stress Personalities, A Look Inside Our Selves" @ $15.00 ea.

❏ **YES,** please send me _____ Workbook(s), "A Guide To Your Stress Personalities" @ $15.00 ea.

❏ **YES,** please send me _____ Workbook(s), "Conflict At Work" @ $15.00 ea.

❏ **YES,** please send me _____ Workbook(s), "Stress Personalities Follow-Up Workbook" @ $15.00 ea.

❏ **YES,** please send me _____ Video(s), "Your Stress Personalities" @ $125.00 ea.

❏ **YES,** please send me _____ Relaxation & Mind Clearing Audio Tape(s) @ $20.00 ea.

❏ **YES,** please send me _____ "Focal Point on Stress, A humorous look at a serious topic" Audio Tape(s) @ $20.00 ea.

❏ **YES,** please send me the Focal Point on Job Stress Newsletter.

NAME   STREET ADDRESS

CITY   STATE/ZIP   PHONE (Optional)

1. Total from above: $ _____

2. California residents add applicable sales tax: $ _____

3. Shipping and Handling. Single orders: Add $1.00 (3rd) or $2.00 (1st class) for each workbook and/or tape. For multiple orders (over 10), add $6.00 for each order sent to the same address: $ _____

Total payment enclosed: $ _____

4. Make Check Payable to:

FOCAL POINT PROGRAMS
P.O. BOX 415
BOLINAS, CA   94924

Stress Personalities

A Look Inside Our Selves

Mary Dempcy & Rene Tihista

2nd edition, revised

Focal Point Press

Published by Focal Point Press
P.O. Box 415
Bolinas, CA 94924

Library of Congress Cataloguing in Publication Data

Dempcy, Mary, 1936—
        Stress Personalities.

Bibliography: p. 233
1. Stress (Psychology)   2. Personality.
3. Social role.   I.   Tihista, Rene, 1939— joint author
II. Title.
Library of Congress Catalog Card Number   91-76786
ISBN 0-9631277-4-8

Design by Scott Sorkin
Illustrations by Judy Trottier
Printed in the United States of America

For our parents Harold (Newt) Dempcy and Marie
Iparaguerre Tihista for giving us two of the best
stress reducers there are . . .
Love and Laughter.

—M.D.   R.T.

CONTENTS

Prologue
How the Stress Personalities Developed

In this book we present a dynamic theory of human behavior, The Stress Personalities Model. It's been developed and tested in our seminars, workshops, individual and group therapy practice since 1976.

It is based on the premise that within all human personalities there exist differing facets that are parts of the Self. We saw these different "Selves" emerge in psychotherapy when we treated clients who engaged in self-defeating behavior even after realizing it was self destructive. It was apparent they were unwittingly acting against their better judgement.

Unlike "Multiple Personalities" which are split off and unrecognized, a feature of abnormal psychology, Stress Personalities were readily apparent to our clients and recognized as normal. So the question was, why do we continue to activate parts of ourselves that hamper healthy functioning? The answer lay in the study of coping responses people use to handle stress. During high stress situations, people repeatedly attempt to cope by reacting with familiar, predictable and recognizable behavior patterns. These coping behaviors, or "Parts of the Self," are relied on even though they increase rather than decrease stress in a given situation.

For example, certain people in the process of learning a new task or skill, depend on an insistent, negative, kibitzing part of themselves which prevents them from taking in needed information and blocks learning. This creates self-doubt, erodes self esteem and contributes to depression. Any type of new learning situation invariably brings out the same negative response. The pattern is repeated and increases stress. It's this predictable internal voice that we recognized as a Stress Personality. It became easier in the therapy sessions to give this process a name, an identity on which the client could focus. Hence, the Stress

Personality we call Critical Judge was uncovered.

Gradually we recognized other common stress behavior patterns. The stress and anguish that came from nonassertive passivity identified Pleaser. Smoldering, passive-aggressive and angry outbursts marked the Sabertooth. As we shifted our focus from individuals and small groups, we investigated the phenomena of stress behavior in broader settings. What is it that people do in high stress situations that makes the stress worse instead of ameliorating it? How are the patterns different among us all, and how are they the same? From these beginnings we developed a psychology of normal behavior.

We had long explored evidence of the connection between stress behavior and disease. Of the many books on this subject, we were impressed with *Type A Behavior and Your Heart*, by cardiologists Meyer Friedman and Ray Rosenman. They presented convincing evidence that the high stress **Type A Personality** was implicated in the development of heart disease. Over the years, our work and research have corroborated one of the most important and overlooked discoveries of Friedman and Rosenman: time-pressured behavior, which they labeled "hurry sickness." It is the most widely displayed stress behavior we've seen in the many thousands of people who've been through our programs in the United States and Canada.

From *Type A Behavior and Your Heart* came our ideas for Internal Timekeeper and Striver, as well as our recognition of the Type A characteristics in Sabertooth. From those clients that displayed panicky, worried, and agitated outbursts of excitement in response to stress situations, came the idea for the Alarmist, which later became Worrier. Thus our first six Stress Personalities were born.

Traveling throughout the western United States we conducted workshops arranged through colleges, hospitals and health organizations. In small towns and large cities, we tested the effectiveness of the Stress Personalities Model as a way of helping people understand and cope with stress. We found enthusiastic acceptance of our concepts among people from all walks of life. Health practitioners began asking for training in the method. Organizations asked us to analyze and consult with them on the stress factors that created problems in their operational effectiveness. Individuals wanted to bring their spouses and children to our programs. Schools, hospitals, and professional groups of all kinds applied these concepts to their work.

Early on, we encouraged suggestions and ideas from those who attended our programs. Did they see stress behavior patterns unique to themselves that we hadn't included? Input from workshop participants made it clear our model had to address substance abuse; poor health habits; procrastination; and the unwillingness to deal with failing relationships. What they all had in common was the process of denial. We recognized this pattern as the seventh Stress Personality, Internal Con Artist. It refers to behavior people use when they con themselves in an attempt to cope with stress. Naming and identifying Stress Personalities was important to the development of the theory.

The next step was figuring out why people insist on using Stress Personalities even when they aren't effective in coping with stress. The answer came when we discovered "Faulty Perceptions." A Faulty Perception is a belief which becomes programmed into the Unconscious through self injunctions. These messages we tell ourselves determine our outlook and the behaviors we use. Since stress behavior is based on Faulty Perceptions, it became apparent that it's vital to counter with New Perceptions. A New Perception is a new and different way to frame a problem, situation or conflict. It allows for new behavioral choices. New Perceptions became an important part of the theory because they open a window to view problems from a completely different perspective. It provides another angle on the issue free of the Stress Personality's influence.

The next step in using the Model to change behavior was to find a way to get the Stress Personalities to cooperate. Since you never get rid of Stress Personalities, as it's an integral part of your

Self, you need to get the Stress Personality to work with you not against you. We developed a method of contracting for behavior change with the Stress Personality through Guided Dialoguing. It is adapted from Fritz Perls' Gestalt Therapy method and an effective way to create an interaction between parts of your Self. The result has been one of the most practical and successful methods of treating stress disorders.

People who have applied these concepts to their personal lives have found immediate and long lasting benefit. The Stress Personalities model is a success. Since the publication of the first edition in 1981 thousands have been through this training and read our book. They've found it a valuable tool for managing stress.

"I gave your book and workbook to a friend who's been going through heavy stress in his life," reported Ann, a software engineer. "He asked me to pass his feedback on to the two of you. He found these materials more helpful in learning how to handle stress than a whole year of therapy."

"This program not only lit up my life, it saved it," wrote a dentist's wife.

"Rene and Mary recently conducted a stress program for our administrative and supervisory personnel, a total of eighty participants," wrote the Department Head of a large Insurance Company. "One hundred percent found the workshop to be valuable and worthwhile." "The presentation of the concepts through the Stress Personalities is of particular note. You can see exactly what you're doing every day that causes stress and what to do about it."

"Over the course of my career I've taken many classes on abnormal behavior, like the psychology of serial killers," says a State Police Detective. "I must confess the Stress Personalities Model is the only program I've ever taken on normal psychology." He added, "It's valuable because in reality most of the people I deal with are normal."

Over the years since the publication of the first edition, more and more of the stress situations reported in our research have focused on conflict. It is a major source of stress. Many who've read the book find this practical approach useful in handling conflict.

A salesman comments, "The concept of Sabertooth as a part of myself that I can control has made a world of difference. I no longer feel like a prisoner of my temper. I also recognize the Sabertooth in others and have learned how to handle hot tempers, both at home and at work."

In developing the Stress Personalities Model, one common thread runs through our philosophy. No matter how miserable we feel or how shaky we are, one part of us that has our best interests at heart is always available and waiting to be called on; it's our Better Judgement. This is the part of us that is not influenced by the Stress Personalities.

We also believe that while it is absolutely vital to look seriously at ourselves and our behavior in order to live a happier, healthier life, we can do so with humor. The ability to laugh is itself a stress reducing power we all have within us. Our programs and concepts all contain liberal doses of humor and have always resulted in enthusiastically receptive audiences.

It's important to realize that the Stress Personalities you read about in these pages are normal coping patterns. We all act through Stress Personalities at one time or another, though not always to the Stress Point. For example, when you're learning a new job, Striver energy will motivate you. But if you become a workaholic, you've let Striver drive you to the Stress Point. The human species has an infinite capacity to change behavior, even the self-destructive kind. No one has to be a prisoner of one's self, or be unduly influenced by another person's Stress Personality. This book will help you understand and gain control of Stress Personalities so that you can maintain a healthy balance in your life.

In this prologue we would like to thank those who helped us put this book together. Many thanks to Scott Sorkin for his layout, cover design, editorial and production assistance. Thanks also to Robyn Watson whose extraordinary talent and eagle eye helped us organize and put the first edition of this book together, and to Sharon Griggs who was our original editorial consultant. Also thanks to Judy Trottier for the artful rendering of art, and to Thelma McMillan and David Walter for editorial assistance. Now, let us introduce the Stress Personalities.

Mary Dempcy
Rene Tihista
October, 1991
Bolinas, CA

INTRODUCTION

 Internal Timekeeper

Internal Timekeeper is the Stress Personality you see in people who have a compulsion to do several things at once: juggling a telephone between shoulder and ear, jotting notes on a pad, directing a secretary, and anxiously motioning a colleague to "Sit right down, be with you in just a minute." This frenzy of activity hurts your creativity. Your Internal Timekeeper will always keep you overscheduled. Either you'll tend to be late or pride yourself on always being exactly on time. Woe to those who keep you waiting. Internal Timekeeper will keep you busy, but not necessarily efficient. You'll be too busy to pay attention to your health. You will ignore the telltale signs of fatigue, a signal you're approaching the Stress Point.

 Pleaser

For Pleaser, the mere thought of saying "no" creates guilt and anxiety. If Pleaser runs your life you'll feel like a martyr, always doing for others and putting yourself last. Pleaser will make it difficult for you to express anger, and make you feel resentful when others don't return favors. Pleaser respects the opinions of others more than your own, and is intimidated by authority. If you are driven by Pleaser, you'll reach the Stress Point when you suffer from feelings of helplessness and set yourself up to be a victim of others who may take advantage of you.

 Sabertooth

Is the part of you that fumes when you have to wait in lines at banks or restaurants. This Stress Personality will have you steaming like a teakettle with no spout. Sabertooth imputes a hostile motive where none is intended. Anger then often seeps out indirectly through sarcasm, needling or arguments over trivialities. Sabertooth's anger spills out unpredictably or inappropriately. Children may catch it in the form of explosive outbursts of rage over a spilled glass of milk. At work a moody coworker can be civil one day and a raging beast the next for no apparent reason. Sabertooth is a protective behavior that's used to guard against the fear of manipulation. It can prevent intimacy by never allowing you to be vulnerable enough to love or be loved. When you are chronically irritable, hostile, and frustrated, you are reaching Sabertooth's Stress Point.

Critical Judge

When you hear an internal voice telling you that you did a sloppy job or made a stupid comment, you can bet you're listening to Critical Judge. Under the mistaken impression that you'll be best motivated by negative criticism, this Stress Personality never gives you the benefit of the doubt. If you do something well, Critical Judge will say, "Well, it's about time you finally got something right." If someone praises you, Critical Judge admonishes, "Don't let that go to your head. It's too big already." Critical Judge undermines your confidence by pointing out all of your failures and glosses over your success as "strokes of luck." The chief danger of this Stress Personality is the depression you feel when you can't live up to its standards of perfection. Psychological depression is a factor in depressing the immune system. When Critical Judge sentences you to self-loathing, discouragement, and despair, you become vulnerable to chronic colds, viruses and other immune disorders. When in balance, Critical Judge can be useful in pointing out errors for corrective action. When it erodes self esteem, it goes over the line and reaches the Stress Point.

Striver

Striver is the energy of our normal achievement drives. Out of balance, Striver sees life as an endless climb to the top of the achievement ladder. Striver measures life by accomplishments, status, and possessions. A strong need for recognition plunges

Striver into withdrawal and loss of motivation when your ambition is thwarted. Striver won't let you derive satisfaction from your accomplishments. Instead of enjoying the present, you'll start looking for the excitement of a new challenge. Soon that too will fail to sustain Striver's interest. You'll be plagued with boredom, restlessness, and a gnawing sense of dissatisfaction. This compulsive search for something better at the expense of what you already have will drive you toward serious health problems and render you vulnerable to burnout.

 Worrier

"What if I don't get the raise?" "Did I turn off the stove?" "Shouldn't I start thinking about retirement?" "Should I take my money out of the bank before the banks fail?" "What if I get laid off?" You may hear these worries reiterated day in and day out. Insomniacs hear them in the middle of the night. This anxious, apprehensive voice is Worrier. It's normal to worry sometimes. When it alerts us to potential problems it can be helpful. This Stress Personality is problematic when your worries become obsessive and you can't turn them off. Worrier is the Stress Personality that represents a fundamental lack of trust in yourself and your ability to manage your own life. For Worrier, life is a roller coaster of catastrophe. Worrier always expects the worst. The anxiety, fear and panic prompted by Worrier's Chicken Little view of the world are an attempt to convince you that these stress inducing emotions are essential to your survival. Unfortunately, such emotions are more likely to lead you to the Worrier Stress Point: insomnia, panic attacks and paralyzing self-doubt.

Internal Con Artist

Internal Con Artist is the voice of procrastination, causing you to put off until tomorrow what you could do today. This Stress Personality is implicated in all kinds of self-defeating behavior. Internal Con Artist talks you into reckless action. You'll be tempted to give in to impulsive whims. It's the part of you that fools you into believing all is well when it isn't. Internal Con Artist will cause you to deny the existence of problems, often until it's too late to do anything about them. This Stress Personality indulges your bad habits by telling you that you can't change or that your habits aren't really harmful. If you eat, drink, or smoke when you feel sad, depressed, or anxious, it may be Internal Con Artist's unsuccessful attempt to nourish you. The plus side of this Stress Personality is that it likes you to have fun and is ever vigilant that you're not overworking. But the Stress Point is reached when it robs you of motivation to achieve your goals. You will struggle constantly with problems of overindulgence and underachievement.

🐛 🐛 🐛

Now that you're familiar with the basic characteristics of the Stress Personalities, take a look at them in action and see how they cloud your perceptions of the world. Imagine you are walking along a deserted country road, lost in fantasy. Suddenly you become aware of a man in dark clothing approaching you. As you strain for some distinguishing feature, you begin to develop perceptions about him. If you see him through the eyes of a Stress Personality, your perceptions vary depending on the personality. Your Critical Judge admonishes you with a stern, "You shouldn't have come out here all by yourself, you fool. Now look what you've got us into." Sabertooth will make you bristle and say to yourself, "If that creep thinks he's going to hassle me, he'd better think twice." Internal Timekeeper will have you so busy thinking about a half dozen other things that you won't notice the stranger at all. If Pleaser emerges, you will smile apologetically and tell the man you are sorry for disturbing his walk. Internal Con Artist will see a good opportunity to ask the man for a cigarette, since he doesn't know you've announced to the whole world you've quit smoking. Your Striver will start figuring out a way to sell the man an insurance policy. If Worrier takes over, your heart will start to pound furiously, and breathing will become shallow as your body experiences panic. Worrier warns you, "He could be a killer. Let's get out of here fast." Then as the figure draws closer, you realize he's a priest. He smiles warmly, says "Hello," and continues on his way.

Each Stress Personality has had a unique experience with the priest on the country road. Each has seen him differently and has reacted in a particular way. Yet there is one common thread. Each reaction increased the stress in your mind and body.

Stress Personalities are parts of the Self. They do not represent the sum total of your personality. Just as the human body is made up of many parts, the human personality also has many parts or "Selves" that have distinct characteristics and predictable behavior patterns. You may or may not be aware of them. Stress Personalities are not WHO you are, but WHAT you do. Frequently, they are the result of stressful learning conditions in early life. From these early experiences Faulty Perceptions of the world develop. Stress behaviors are based on your belief that these Faulty Perceptions help you survive in the world. Faulty Perceptions are carried on into adulthood and form the motivation for stress behavior.

These behaviors emerge through the actions of the Stress Personalities. Stress Personalities seem to be autonomous-they have attitudes and feelings of their own, and stick to agendas that can clash with your conscious goals. Their agendas represent habitual behavior patterns used to handle the many stress-producing situations encountered in everyday living. Different stress situations call in different Stress Personalities, and the frequency of appearance varies from person to person. For some people, these personalities are very strong and dominate their lives. For others, they emerge only at work, whereas at home they are barely noticeable. As a rule, however, Stress Personalities can pop up anytime, anyplace. The trick is to stay on top of them so they don't take command and topple the balance between your physical and mental health.

Think of a time when a part of you wanted to do one thing and a part of you, another. For example, let's say you've decided to quit smoking, and you've gone without a cigarette all week. Friday evening after dinner at a friend's house, you're offered a cigarette. As you absentmindedly take one out of the pack, you hear yourself say aloud, "I've decided to give these things up."

"Really?" says your friend, striking a match.

"Yeah," you say, exhaling a deep drag. "I don't think it's good for me to keep smoking."

"Well, you've got to die of something," laughs your friend. Then as the evening wears on, you forget about the cigarette as you smoke it with that same old familiarity.

What happened to your resolve? It fell victim to a part of you that didn't care about giving up smoking. "You can say anything you want," says that part, "but I'm going to keep smoking." That part of you was a Stress Personality (Internal Con Artist) following its own agenda, uninterested in the fact that it keeps you engaging in self-destructive behavior.

When you persist in self-destructive behavior long enough, your body suffers. Stress deals its worst blow when your behavior begins to cause health problems, interferes with your work, or disrupts your relationships. When these significant problems start, you know you have reached a Stress Point.

Each Stress Personality has its own set of Stress Points. For example, if you wake up in the middle of the night worrying to the point of persistent insomnia, you've reached one of Worrier's Stress Points.

If, after being reprimanded by the boss, you suppress the angry feelings that result, only to spend the rest of the day snarling at fellow employees, screaming at other drivers in crosstown traffic, or yelling at your children for petty rule infractions, you've reached one of Sabertooth's Stress Points. When you consistently try to juggle several projects at once, feeling pressured and anxious, you have reached one of Internal Timekeeper's Stress Points. If you feel resentful because you're continually being roped into chairing committees or taking on extra work, you have reached one of Pleaser's Stress Points.

An old saying goes, "You don't need a weatherman to tell which way the wind is blowing." If you pay attention to the signals from your mind and body, you won't need a doctor or a therapist to tell you when you are suffering from stress. Your natural drive for health is thrown out of balance when features of your personality act against your own best interests. We've heard many people in our workshops tell us exactly what they did to drive themselves to the point of collapse, but they never figured out at the time why they were tired, had frequent colds, and felt chronically depressed.

In order to help people identify the signs of stress, we have developed a Stress Continuum. At one end of this continuum are Personal Discomfort states. At the other end is Psychosomatic Illness. As Personal Discomfort increases in intensity, a progressive breakdown of health occurs and you move steadily toward Psychosomatic Illness. Here you become vulnerable to more serious stress diseases like ulcers, high blood pressure, migraine, or coronary heart disease.

Stress Continuum

Personal Discomfort ———→ *Psychosomatic Illness*
anxiety → *chronic fatigue* → *hypertension* → *heart disease*

Stress induced illness occurs because your perceptions of the world create high stress behaviors. This affects your choice of a life style which can undermine your health. For example, many people become addicted to their jobs and never take the time to exercise, relax or vacation.

Helen, a project coordinator for a computer company describes how her devotion to her work nearly killed her.

"I hadn't taken a vacation in five years because I felt I was indispensable to my company. My doctor told me I had to bring down my stress level or I'd get sick, but I ignored her. Then I had a heart attack at work. I was still at my desk trying to work when the ambulance came. I got a vacation alright, but it was in the hospital."

When you pour all of your energy into a job, working long hours under extreme pressure, ignoring personal discomfort clues like fatigue and exhaustion and tension headaches, sooner or later you will have to face the music. You will be moving along the Stress Continuum, and the lyrics will tell you that the way you're living is making you sick or dissatisfied with the quality of your life.

It is well known medically that life-styles in which stress behavior patterns play an important part can destroy health, decrease productivity and cause burnout. Many participants of our workshops report either having burned out on a former job or edging close to it on their present one. The bibliography refers you to medical and psychological literature describing specific personality patterns and their relationship to disease.

When people experience high stress levels over prolonged periods of time they are more vulnerable to disease of all kinds. Since the First Edition was published there has been a dramatic increase in the number of diseases of the immune system reported worldwide. Many of these diseases are exacerbated by high stress levels. Learning how to handle stress means taking a new look at your behavior and taking responsibility for your own well-being.

Many researchers of stress-induced health problems have looked to the environment for answers in controlling stress. The thought is that if the environment can be controlled, so can stress. But a stress-free environment is neither possible nor even desirable. We believe that each of us has the capacity to control our own health. The Stress Personalities model will help you identify your most dangerous stress behavior patterns. Understanding why you feel hurt, depressed, or afraid will help you deal with stress instead of being its victim.

This book is organized into chapters that show you how specific Stress Personalities affect you in a variety of settings: as friend, lover or spouse, boss or employee. Then the focus shifts to the effect of each specific Stress Personality on health. The health information comes from the hundreds of health questionnaires that have been filled out by our workshop participants as well as from literature on psychosomatic disease and verbal reports from participants of our programs.

At the end of each chapter is a section showing you how to change the self-defeating behaviors of your Stress Personality into productive, stress-reducing behaviors.

Written as a Game Plan with Faulty Perceptions, Handicaps, Results, New Perceptions, First Moves, Pitfalls, and Countermoves, it was designed to show you how Stress Personalities operate, how persistent they can be in trying to sabotage your efforts to control them, and what you can do about it.

Once aware of the Faulty Perception that motivates a stress behavior, you will be able to figure out the Handicap, or logical progression of behaviors that follows. The result of this Handicap will tell you how that behavior causes you stress. Next you identify a New Perception which is a new way to look at a problem, issue or conflict. It provides another perspective free of the Stress Personality's influence. Your First Move is to introduce a stress-reducing behavior. It is vital that you watch for the Pitfalls in your program for change. Your Stress Personality will be using every trick in the book to maintain the stressful status quo, and you could fall back into the same old patterns. Your Countermove will be especially designed to outmaneuver your Stress Personality and help you maintain low stress behaviors.

We have listed Faulty Perceptions for each Stress Personality on the Game Plan pages. They are not inclusive. You undoubtedly will have Faulty Perceptions and Handicaps unique to you and your life situation, but we provide a model that you can follow in working out your own solutions.

Definitions for use in the Game Plan:

**FAULTY
PERCEPTION:** A belief system of your Stress Personality which causes you to engage in stress behavior.

HANDICAP: A deeply ingrained stress behavior pattern that puts you at an automatic disadvantage in the game of life by rendering you vulnerable to the ravages of excessive stress.

RESULT: This is the specific damage or malfunction caused by the Handicap, its effect on you in relationships, your general functioning, and your health.

NEW
PERCEPTION: A new and different way to frame a stress
                       situation. It often comes suddenly like an
                       insight or "ah ha" experience. It provides
                       you with another perspective free of the
                       Stress Personality's influence.

FIRST MOVE: A program of steps you can take to alter
                       or extinguish the stress behavior of your
                       handicap.

PITFALLS: Traps disguised as old, familiar, and com-
                       fortable behaviors that are obstacles placed
                       in your path to change by your Stress
                       Personality. You must be aware of these
                       Pitfalls because your Stress Personality
                       will resist change.

COUNTERMOVE: A maneuver to use in avoiding the Pitfall.
                       It is a helpful suggestion for reinforcing
                       the steps you have begun in the First
                       Move and making sure they are carried
                       out.

The Game Plan In Action

To learn how to use the Game Plan, follow Fred and his
frenetic Internal Timekeeper from chaos to order. Let's look at a
typical situation he gets involved in.

Fred is a harried Quality Control manager. He describes
how daily crisis thwarts his heroic efforts to conquer his "To Do"
list.

"I write a 'To Do' list adding items from the list of the
previous day. Because my normal day is determined by crisis
rather than planning, I never get to the items on the list. I keep

the list handy to remind myself of all the things I'm not getting to. When someone interrupts me with the inevitable crisis, I cut their explanations short with a curt, 'Just give me the punch line.' My hope is that they will go away so I can get back to my list."

The first step for Fred is to figure out what Faulty Perception is driving his Internal Timekeeper.

FAULTY PERCEPTION:	"If I keep a long 'To Do' list on my desk, then the tasks will get done."
HANDICAP:	Fred gets anxious every time he looks at the "To Do" list. This anxiety stimulates him into more activity, such as; adding more tasks to his evergrowing list.
RESULT:	He is always functioning at a crisis level which impairs his ability to prioritize and finish what he starts. His curt responses to colleagues estrange them and preclude any help he might get.
NEW PERCEPTION:	"I'm using lists to motivate and organize myself but instead they tyrannize me and make me less efficient."
FIRST MOVE:	Fred has to prioritize only key items on a short list he can finish.
PITFALL:	His Internal Timekeeper will insist that everything is a top priority, therefore nothing can be dropped from the list.
COUNTERMOVE:	He has to adhere to the true definition of priority, which is, to establish time, order

and precedence. His Countermove is to complete at least one, preferably the first item on his list, before he goes to another.

When using the Game Plan, think of a typical situation that causes you stress, what behaviors you use and what Stress Personality is involved. Then figure out the Faulty Perception that Stress Personality is operating from. Ask yourself how that handicaps you and the result. Then you're ready for a New Perception and a First Move. One tip; a New Behavior is sometimes the opposite of what you're doing now. For Fred, his stress will diminish and his efficiency will improve when he learns to narrow and focus on his list instead of expanding it. You have to remember that Stress Personalities are familiar comfortable habits which will resist change. Your Countermoves need to include steps that will help you avoid the Pitfall.

Getting out of the habit

Stress Personalities are habitual behaviors. These parts of ourselves like to keep repeating the same behaviors over and over in response to stressful situations. Since you never get rid of Stress Personalities your objective is to get them to work with instead of against you. This requires retraining. For example, to retrain your Pleaser you have to discourage the "automatic yes." You do this by telling your Pleaser, "We need to think before we respond and decide if we can or want to fulfill the request. Then respond to others with delaying techniques such as; "Let me check my calendar and get back to you." Another retraining step is to say something like, "I can do that for you, but not until next week." This way you are controlling the interchange and not reacting automatically with your Pleaser.

At the end of each chapter is a list of suggested New Behaviors for each Stress Personality. Practice these techniques to retrain your Stress Personalities and bring them into balance.

The final chapter describes Guided Dialoguing. We developed this technique from Gestalt therapy. It's an effective way to communicate directly with your Stress Personality and often the most powerful tool used in our workshops. We highly recommend that you try it.

Another resource for helping you gain balance is dialoguing with your Better Judgement-the part of you that can talk back to the Stress Personalities. We like to think of it as your "better half." All of us have it, but too often we ignore it. Recognize your Better Judgement; learn how to become more in tune with this part of your self and how it can contribute to stress reduction.

You may meet parts of your self in this book that you only dimly suspected were there, or parts that come as a complete surprise to you. Meeting and dealing with your inner selves puts you in control of them and in charge of your life.

I. INTERNAL TIMEKEEPER
No Time to Say Hello, Goodbye, I'm Late!

*Y*OU glance at the clock. Ten minutes until you have to leave for work. Just enough time to take the clothes out of the dryer. As you're taking them out, you hear a familiar voice saying, "Why don't you just fold them while they're warm so they won't wrinkle. It'll save time later." "Good idea," you agree. You glance at the clock again. Two minutes to go. As you open the closet door to put the clothes away, you're horrified at the sight. Internal Timekeeper nudges you with a quick elbow to the conscience and says, "This closet is a mess. It'll only take you a minute to straighten it out." Ten minutes later you tear yourself away in a frenzy. Now you really have to hurry or you'll be late for work. Your daily war with the clock has begun.

Every stoplight becomes an enemy sabotaging your progress to the office. "Let's take the shortcut," the voice suggests. You speed along the side streets through the old railroad yard to cross the tracks. The minute you start to congratulate yourself on saving ten minutes, you look up at the crossing to see the engine of what seems like a mile-long freight train blocking the tracks. As you impatiently clench the steering wheel, your anger at yourself builds up and you mutter, "Damn! Another day and I'm late again."

Who was that familiar voice? It was Internal Timekeeper. Internal Timekeeper is the Stress Personality that is always concerned with time but has no time sense. Internal Timekeeper always misjudges how long a given task will take and constantly puts you behind schedule. It will convince you that the busier you are, the more you're getting done, even as you get more and more frazzled. Internal Timekeeper believes that every self-imposed task is absolutely necessary, and it is blind to the impossibility of finishing every task on your ever-growing list. You inevitably end up running late and feel continually hassled.

It is easy to spot people whose lives are ruled by their Internal Timekeepers. Think about that friend who finishes your sentences for you, or that fellow worker who drinks a cup of coffee, smokes a cigarette, reads the paper, and carries on a "now-you-see-it, now-you-don't" conversation all at the same time; or the busy boss who rushes your speech along with, "Uh huh, go on," while he glances back and forth from his watch to the window and then back to you, hearing about a third of what you've said. These behaviors usually are inherited from an Internal Timekeeper-dominated family.

If you're a "chip off the old block," it's a good idea to figure out from which block you've been chipped. To understand better how the seeds of this Stress Personality are planted, drop in with us on a hypothetical family governed by Internal Timekeeper behavior and observe the interactions around the dinner table.

Sitting around the table are Mom, Dad, older sister Ann, and our Internal Timekeeper seedling, Billy. The first thing you notice is how difficult it is to get a word in edgeways. Everyone is trying to talk at once. Ann is telling Dad what the teacher said about her creative writing ability. She stops to take a breath and Mom cuts in with "Oh, by the way, that reminds me, Henry. . ." Mom is off and running in her own direction. Ann's enthusiasm evaporates as once again she finds herself cut off from sharing what's important to her. Her tendency to clam up has earned her the family reputation of "the quiet one." Billy, on the other hand, is Ann's opposite. He never shuts up. He has learned the technique of holding his parents' attention by talking as fast as he can. He barely pauses between sentences or subject changes, getting to the point in a hurry and always telling the most important part first. Billy is fast, but not always coherent, as he darts from subject to subject, rarely completing a thought or sentence.

Billy is having problems at school. His teacher says he doesn't listen to instructions and seldom finishes his homework. Mom and Dad can't figure out why, especially because he's so bright. The real problem is that the communication pattern Billy uses to get his parents' attention doesn't work in the outside world.

As we follow Billy into adulthood, we begin to see the consequences of Internal Timekeeper behavior. He has developed the habit of interrupting the flow of his own ideas, actions, and thoughts. He uses little discrimination or discipline to follow a thought through to a conclusion and chases haphazardly after every new idea that presents itself. This kind of scattered thinking keeps him from taking concerted action. He is frequently overwhelmed by his half-finished projects and unconnected ideas.

He is interrupting his own children now, finishing their sentences for them, cutting off their ideas. As his children attempt to communicate with him, he feels pulled and torn because he wants to hear what they have to say, but is pressured and anxious about his lack of time.

Clearly, Internal Timekeeper behavior has been passed down to a second generation. As Billy grows older, he begins to realize that his children no longer try to confide in him. He has seen the world as a rat race for so long that he has never slowed down long enough to find out what the race is all about, whom he's running from, or where he's running to. Now it looks as if he's really too late.

Internal Timekeeper is one of the most prevalent Stress Personalities at our workshops. It seems that the axioms "Idle hands are the devil's playground," "If you want something done, give it to a busy person," or "Do something, even if it turns out to be wrong," were drilled into many peoples' early consciousnesses. These principles have become the foundation for the belief that being busy is absolutely vital, no matter what the situation. You begin to acquire the Faulty Perception that your self-worth and value as a human being are dependent on how much work you do.

Here's a case. "My dad raised me with the belief that you should accomplish as much as you can every day," reported Charles, a forest ranger. "This means my weekends are often busy extensions of the work week, only it's the house, yard, and garage that get my attention. On Saturday morning I make a list of everything I have to do. Dad always said, 'If you don't have everything done by noon you aren't accomplishing anything.' So I get started and something goes wrong right away to upset my timetable and pretty soon I'm way behind. I start working faster and something else goes wrong and I get irritated. Then I begin to feel guilty and like a failure. By noon I'm a nervous wreck. I've dreaded Saturdays for years."

Charles' Internal Timekeeper has put him in a bind. His self-imposed deadline of noon locks him in a stress-filled torture chamber.

Although there is no inherent danger in hard work, when it becomes a habit born of anxiety, fear of failure, or of a compelling need to stay busy in order to feel secure, you have become Internal Timekeeper's slave. The misguided counsel of Internal Timekeeper is particularly tenacious because it is often endorsed by such influential institutions as family, school, and church. Charles really believes that his value as a human being is based on how well he keeps his nose to the grindstone. He invites Internal Timekeeper to help goad him into constant busyness and never-ending work, but when Internal Timekeeper reaches the Stress Point, it will inevitably cause problems. Some will be minor, some major, others potentially fatal.

Assessing Your Internal Timekeeper Behavior

Assess your own Internal Timekeeper behavior by answering the questions below. Answer them honestly, choosing one of the five responses and placing the corresponding number in the box opposite each question. Add up your score and place the total along the Stress Behavior scale. Pay special attention to those questions on which you scored a 6 or 8. If your total score is 48 or greater, you've been engaging in enough Internal Timekeeper behavior to be significantly disruptive to your life.

(Almost always=8)   (Frequently=6)   (Sometimes=4)
(Occasionally=2)   (Never=0)

1. ( )   Do you have difficulty seeing things through to completion?
2. ( )   Do you have trouble concentrating on one issue at a time?
3. ( )   Do you juggle several projects simultaneously?
4. ( )   Are you preoccupied with time schedules, yet do you often run late?
5. ( )   Do you feel anxious, guilty, or frustrated when you're not busy?
6. ( )   Do you make lists of things to do and feel guilty about those you never get to?
7. ( )   Is the amount of work you do and the speed with which you get it done more important than how creative you are?
8. ( )   Do friends and family expect you to arrive late?
9. ( )   When out to dinner with a friend, are you preoccupied with other things you have to do?
10. ( )   Is "time for yourself" the last item on your list?
11. ( )   Are you unable to engage in meaningful conversations because of internal distractions?

12. ( )   Does your life lack intimacy because you don't take the
             time to cultivate friendships?

       ( )   TOTAL

---

0   48   96

INTERNAL TIMEKEEPER FRIEND

If Internal Timekeeper tags along when you're with friends, chances are they'll feel as though they were following the March Hare on the way to the Mad Hatter's tea party. Although you may not speak in riddles or dip dormouses in teapots, when Internal Timekeeper takes over, your behavior will be just as inexplicable. You will always be scurrying off somewhere, leaving your friends with the exasperating task of piecing together your unfinished thoughts and guessing your probable whereabouts. You'll be too busy to notice their concern until one day you'll find, like Alice, they've disappeared out of your life.

Internal Timekeeper's ambivalence about the importance of relationships will frustrate and disappoint both you and your friends. You will vacillate, setting up dates and then cancelling at the last minute when Internal Timekeeper decides you don't have enough time this week. You may set up another date, but this process will continually repeat itself until your friends get tired of the disappointment and the inconvenience of constantly rearranging their schedules for you. Soon you've lost your credibility. The next time you call, your friend will suggest, "Why don't you just call me sometime when you have a free moment. I think it's best that we don't plan anything judging from past experiences." Of course, Internal Timekeeper will never allow you a free minute, so another friendship is lost.

Jake, a police officer, told us how Internal Timekeeper interferes with his relationships.

"Every time my friends and I make plans to go fishing in the mountains, I start to think why I can't do it this weekend. I have to work a rock concert for the extra money or I have to study for the sergeant's exam. Inevitably I end up cancelling. Do you realize I've been trying to get to the mountains for the last three months? Until I took this workshop, I thought it was just the nature of police work, but now I know my Internal Timekeeper is the culprit."

Recognizing this process and being determined to show up for scheduled dates with your friends is a starter, but you need to do more to ensure an improvement in the quality of your relationships. A lunch date should be a relaxing break in your day and a chance to get in touch with a friend. Unfortunately, if your Internal Timekeeper joins you, lunch will be an annoying interruption in an overcrowded day.

With Internal Timekeeper you will work up to the last possible second, dash to your car, and race across town to get to the restaurant. You'll end up ten minutes late (which is fine with Internal Timekeeper, who considers ten minutes within the range of respectability), rushing to your table, out of breath, and apologizing. Your stomach is upset, and you feel anxious and disturbed. You start to rush your friend's speech by saying, "Uh huh, uh huh," and finishing her sentences for her. Finally she stops talking, in exasperation, and you apologize. "I'm sorry," you say. "I'm a bit rattled today, but it really is good to see you again. Tell me about your new job." She begins to tell you, but you find yourself distracted by Internal Timekeeper who is reminding you not to be late to your one o'clock appointment. As you realize you're going to be late, a familiar feeling hits. You have to be in two places at once. Interrupting your friend in the middle of her story you blurt out, "I'm so sorry, but I've got to get back to the office. I wish we could have had more time." Your friend doesn't hide her disappointment, and you feel guilty. As you grab the lunch bill to make up for having to hurry off, you feel another surge of angry irritation—you left your money in the car. Now you really won't make your appointment. You try to turn your attention back to your friend, who is saying good-bye, but your internal distractions are obvious. When you part company, you're both relieved that the luncheon ordeal is over.

Experiences like this one do not enrich friendships. They hinder them. The next time your friend calls someone for lunch, she may choose someone who makes her feel more at ease and with whom she can converse in a more meaningful way.

Don't fall prey to Internal Timekeeper's suggestion that if seeing one friend is good, then seeing many is better. A favorite ploy is to take care of all your friendship obligations in one fell swoop. You'll throw one big party a year, inviting everyone you know, and then desperately try to spend five minutes with each guest, catching up on the last twelve months. Spending lots of money, having lots of laughs, and seeing lots of people all at once doesn't really save lots of time. It is no substitute for a number of small get-togethers. If you want to renew old friendships or foster new ones, you simply must put in the time.

You may have your social calendar completely booked, but the question you must ask yourself is, "Whom out of all these people can I really count on?" In the hustle and bustle of your work-filled day, you probably don't take time to think seriously about your flock of superficial relationships. When your energy eventually fails, you'll cancel plans, too tired to go out. Home alone you have to face yourself, your fatigue, and the loneliness that slowly creeps in to fill the empty spaces usually reserved for activity. You realize not only that you haven't been together with real friends in months, but that you can't even think of a friend to call on an evening like this.

Friendships take nurturing, and nurturing takes time. If you wait for extra time to materialize to keep up real friendships, you will wait forever as long as Internal Timekeeper has a strong hold on your appointment book.

INTERNAL TIMEKEEPER MATE

Are you one of those people who immediately attracts everyone around you because you're so full of life and energy? You may appear to be an unending reservoir of activity. Even low-key people are attracted, eager to share your life in the fast lane. What they don't know, however, is that if they try to keep up with your schedule, they're in for a turbulent ride.

Internal Timekeeper interferes with your love life in a variety of insidious ways. You'll be convinced that you're too busy to date, much less get involved in a serious relationship. And should you find time to spend with someone you care about, Internal Timekeeper's schedule is so chock-full of activities that you may well wear out your partner. When your lover suggests less frenetic activities such as an evening at the symphony or a class in meditation, you'll cringe from a deep-seated fear of sitting still, being bored, or wasting time.

If you're lucky to silence Internal Timekeeper long enough to get acquainted with someone and settle into a relationship, you may still have a rocky road ahead. A long-term relationship with you is one thing; a long-term relationship with Internal Timekeeper is another. It becomes tiresome, annoying, and frustrating for your lover to keep asking to be put on your agenda, only to be met with Internal Timekeeper's usual response, "Not now, I'm busy."

Does this scenario sound familiar? You and your mate finally do get away for that long overdue weekend. You're on the way to a secluded mountain cabin. You arrive, put your snow gear away and settle in to recapture those feelings that brought you together in the first place. Your lover is putting pillows in front of the fire, and there you are, pacing back and forth like a caged panther trying to decide whether you should: (a) chop some more wood, (b) get out the toboggan and try the hill, or (c) drive to the slopes to check the powder. Your mate sighs and reminds you what you both had in mind — a quiet evening in front of the fire, a bottle of wine, and a dinner by candlelight.

"After all," your lover points out, "how long has it been since we've been alone? We could just hole up here all weekend and do nothing if we want to." Even though you are madly in love with this person, the thought of doing nothing will immediately put Internal Timekeeper into a panic. "Nothing" is a word that conjures up to Internal Timekeeper endless minutes strung together, unplanned, and possibly wasted. Since Internal Timekeeper believes that survival depends on being busy, it follows that "going with the flow" will be a threat to your very existence. This time needed to cultivate a good relationship will be very stressful if you're caught between your lover's wishes and Internal Timekeeper's anxieties.

If you're typical, Internal Timekeeper had you bring along several projects to work on during this romantic two-day interlude. As your lover contemplates the fire, you're wondering aloud, "Would you mind if I took a look at some of this work? I mean, since we aren't doing anything anyway." The shocked look on your lover's face prepares you for the protest.

"But we are doing something we're spending time together!"

Unless you take the reins from Internal Timekeeper, your weekend plans will be doomed. Internal Timekeeper will crawl into bed with you and your lover. Your lovemaking will be connected and alive as long as you are concentrating, but when Internal Timekeeper captures your attention, reminding you of things to do or bringing up problems for you to solve, your mind will wander and the flame will start to flicker. The more distracted you become, the cooler your lover is going to feel.

In one of our workshops, Allen described this process perfectly:

"Sarah and I reached a crisis point in our relationship about five or six months ago. She finally got angry one night when my attention wandered during the middle of our lovemaking. She pushed me away and demanded, 'Where are you now?' I was taken back. 'What do you mean,' I said. 'I can tell when you are not with me. You seem mechanical. It's eerie having sex with a robot, Allen. For God's sake, where do you go? What is the matter?' Well, this shook me. She was right. I was studying for the bar exam, which I had failed last time. I was uptight, distracted, working, fixing the house, and I would go to bed at night with my head buzzing like a telephone wire. Internal Timekeeper wouldn't let me indulge myself in lovemaking when there were more pressing issues at hand. It took Sarah's getting fed up to make me take another look at my priorities."

Sex is not exempt from the debilitating effects of stress. When you are experiencing high levels of stress, interest in sex declines. You will either feel that there just isn't enough time, or you'll be so worn out by the end of the day that you'll collapse the moment your head hits the pillow. If you are able to engage in sex with Internal Timekeeper around, it will prevent you and your partner from sharing the total experience.

Try to talk to your lover about Internal Timekeeper and how it comes to bed with you. Tell your partner what happens, how you get distracted, and where your mind wanders. It is very common for the mate of an Internal Timekeeper-driven person to feel unloved, unattractive, or un-you-name-it. Such a conclusion is not unreasonable when interest evaporates in the heat of passion. To maintain the relationship, it is vital to tell your partner what is going on. This communication can also help unleash some of the things on your mind so that you can be more committed to the lovemaking.

It may be hard at first to share your intimate feelings, whether about lovemaking or anything else, since Internal Timekeeper believes feelings are unproductive. Staying busy keeps feelings from bothering you — in the short run.

Even worse is when Internal Timekeeper prevents you from listening to your lover's feelings. The following exchange between George and Martha illustrates the alienation Internal Timekeeper can cause. George has asked for a raise and his boss has turned him down. George and Martha sit at the kitchen table to discuss

George's feelings:

"So how do you feel?" she asks, lighting a cigarette.

"I feel terrible. I have been with the company a long time. I told . . ."

"Excuse me, George," Martha interrupts. "I'll just be a minute. I have to run and get my cancelled checks so I can balance my checkbook while we are talking." Martha returns and begins to lay her checks out in piles on the table. "Anyway, so you felt terrible huh?"

"Yeah," says George. "I got mad, and I told them they were a cheap outfit."

"Oh, that reminds me, I've got to show you that new outfit I bought for the tennis club dinner dance . . . So go on."

George continues. "Well, I told them if they think that they can take me to the cleaners on this deal . . ."

"CLEANERS!" exclaims Martha. "Oh my God, I forgot to pick up my suit for tomorrow's meeting. I'd better give them a call and tell them that I'll be right over."

By this time George has given up on the conversation. He feels annoyed with his wife, who cannot sit still long enough to listen. He withdraws. Martha goes on, oblivious to the fact that Internal Timekeeper has completely taken over and is manipulating the conversation in order to avoid feelings.

One of Internal Timekeeper's tricks is to change the subject to avoid dealing with the real issues like what step George should take next or why Martha may be nervous that George will quit his job. Internal Timekeeper has so much energy that it takes little or no effort to continually sweep things under the carpet. However, we can predict that the time will come when the relationship will suffer and Martha will lament to George, "Why don't you ever talk to me anymore?" This is a question she should ask her Internal Timekeeper.

A relationship requires attention and time willingly given. Internal Timekeeper treats communication superficially and creates the stress of a relationship devoid of intimacy. You stay so busy that the interchange between you and your mate becomes limited to the exchange of information: "Oh, there you are. Have you seen our income tax forms?" Although this information is necessary to run an organized household, it must not become your only mode of communication.

The intimate part of a relationship requires communication at a deeper level. It is characterized by talking about feelings and exploring each other's fantasies. It needs to be unhurried and often unplanned in order to unfold and develop. When people have to condense and hurry what they have to say, they will not use these moments to share what is closest to their souls. Be aware that it is Internal Timekeeper that robs you of this closeness, and that an intimate relationship is incompatible with Internal Timekeeper behavior patterns.

INTERNAL TIMEKEEPER BOSS

If you are a boss with a dominant Internal Timekeeper, you probably tell your employees, "My door is always open." Your door may be open, but let them try to find you. Internal Timekeeper bosses are typically very busy, but rarely available, and they are very frustrating to work for. "My boss is everywhere but where I need him/her," is the typical employee complaint.

Internal Timekeeper pressures your employees by demanding everything be done yesterday. Internal Timekeeper pressures you so that you appear to be too busy to be disturbed, thus defeating your role as manager. When you are available for conference, your employees feel they must rush to get everything into the time slot allotted them.

Laura, an executive assistant, explains her dilemma working for an Internal Timekeeper boss:

"I hate to go into the boss's office for a meeting. He never has his phone calls held, and as soon as we start getting into something, he answers his phone. Twenty minutes later he hangs up and can't remember where we left off or what we were talking about. I know he is a busy man, so I try to hurry through with what I have to report to him. I almost always get back to my desk with unanswered questions, but once I remember them, he's either tied up or gone."

Internal Timekeeper bosses have difficulty finding the time to confer with their employees. Hence, the whole department suffers from a lack of guidance. When Internal Timekeeper behavior prevents you from being there to offer support to those with whom you work, office morale starts to break down. Decisions are delayed. Employees experience frustration or resentment at having to stop what they are doing and wait long hours to have one question answered.

As head of the office, it is important that you use good judgement as to what can reasonably get done in a day's work. Internal Timekeeper will always pile on more work than any human being can handle healthily.

Ada, an R.N. supervisor, explains how her Internal Timekeeper affects her attitude and job performance:

"I work long hours and take work home just trying to keep up with my endless lists of waiting jobs. I start to feel pressured, tense, anxious, resentful, and sometimes angry with those around me. A headache may develop or I may feel extremely fatigued and unable to continue with whatever I happen to be doing. I guess that's a sign that Internal Timekeeper is taking over."

Since stress is a given in most work settings, it is important that you, as head of the office, do not escalate the stress already inherent in the environment. You have to set priorities and realistic goals, both for you and your employees. Keeping Internal Timekeeper under control will ensure that your expectations are reasonable. Ada had to learn the hard way:

"I expect my staff to work as hard as I do, even though it isn't realistic. I resent seeing my key assistants leaving on time, particularly when I know that some of them are just as far behind in their work as I am. I can't seem to stop setting the same sky-high standards for them that I do for myself."

Ada is still learning that Internal Timekeeper can't run the office efficiently. She is still unable to distinguish the quantity of time worked from the quality. It is a myth, and a widespread one, that putting in a sixty-hour work week means you will be more successful than those who don't.

Look at how much of your workday is spent in an unnecessary flurry of activity. Much valuable time is spent trying to make sense out of the trail of loose ends Internal Timekeeper has strung behind. All Internal Timekeeper cares about is how busy you are. Whether or not you reach your goals is inconsequential. You'll end up frustrated because invariably the results achieved will not be worth the amount of extra time you give.

Tim works for a boss with an Internal Timekeeper: "My boss is a workhorse. Because he works so hard, rest periods for employees are given grudgingly. It seems vacation time always comes when the boss is swamped with work, and he makes you feel like a rat deserting a sinking ship for leaving on such a frivolous thing as vacation. I work hard, and I need this time to rejuvenate, to spend more time with friends and family. Though I don't spend much time thinking about work, I always come back with fresh ideas. Unfortunately, my boss is too busy to notice."

With Internal Timekeeper you may not only want your employees to cut their vacations short, but you may also encourage them to take shortcuts in their work. This practice is dangerous to the high-quality standards that distinguish leaders. When Internal Timekeeper makes it difficult to pay attention to details, you hear yourself saying to your employees, "Forget the details, the secretary will take care of them later. You'd better get to work on that next project. I'd like it finished by tomorrow." You're falling victim to the classic haste-makes-waste syndrome. You deprive your employees of the satisfaction of seeing a project through to completion and you offer a sloppy model. Internal Timekeeper makes life a war and work the battlefield, demolishing satisfaction and contentment along the way. Your work needs to be free of the desperate nature that Internal Timekeeper brings to it. Only then can there be gratifying rewards.

Internal Timekeeper thrives in the work arena since, traditionally, people have believed there is a causal relationship between looking busy and success. Our society believes that to resist Internal Timekeeper is to court failure. With such strong societal pressure, it is little wonder that one hesitates to risk a behavioral change and chooses instead to risk the unpleasant health hazards associated with Internal Timekeeper.

Don't let Internal Timekeeper rob you of your vacation. Vacation is an important time for the mind and body to unwind, and for you to indulge yourself in some activities that are not work-related. It is also important to relax and clear your mind during a regular workday, even if just to take a few deep breaths or read a chapter in a novel during a brief break. Without any outside activities, not only do you become less interesting, but your creative channels become blocked so that you begin to lose the innovative ideas and clear thinking that characterize an effective administrator.

Success is possible — in fact it can flourish — without Internal Timekeeper. Here's an example from our own experience:

Some time ago, we met with the president of a large publishing corporation in his plush, paneled office. He greeted us warmly, apologized for the five-minute delay, and seated us comfortably. He asked his secretary to hold his phone calls and then directed his full attention to our presentation. Throughout our appointment we were struck by his calm, even manner. He listened attentively, never veered from the subject, and was completely engaged in our material. When we were finished, he offered some intelligent suggestions and good leads. He gave us time to think of additional questions and, as we were leaving, he introduced us to his secretary and asked her to make some phone calls on our behalf. He thanked us for coming and ushered us out promising to get back to us with some information we had requested. Less than one week later, we received a hand-written letter from him with the information in detail.

This man was extraordinarily successful without any discernible Internal Timekeeper behavior. We believe his freedom from Internal Timekeeper's stress helped him make it to the top. So if you think you are successful because of Internal Timekeeper's guidance, look again. You may be successful despite it.

INTERNAL TIMEKEEPER EMPLOYEE

When your boss gives you a deadline, do you always seem to need Federal Express to get the job done? With Internal Timekeeper at your side, you're unable to prioritize and each new task on your list increases your frenzy. You end up working at a crisis-preparedness level all the time. Every project is treated like a rush job because Internal Timekeeper distorts the relative importance of its various facets.

With so many projects vying for your attention, you leave the ones you've started incomplete until the last possible moment. Then, when the project can no longer be delayed, Internal Timekeeper has you drop everything to finish. The only problem is that with Internal Timekeeper, everything is a priority, with the most pressing issue pushing its way forward in the guise of another emergency. You'll always wind up with your finger in the dike trying to stave off disaster. Deadlines will haunt you and become major sources of stress in your life.

Dave, an insurance salesman, explains how he has difficulties with deadlines:

"Deadlines overwhelm me to the point that I'm unable to concentrate. My brain actually stops working. This always happens, so in anticipation, I set artificial deadlines. For example, if I have a report to prepare for Friday, I set a deadline for Wednesday evening. Then I work like crazy to meet the new self-imposed deadline. If I can't meet the Friday schedule by Wednesday, I suffer the same feelings of panic I do when I'm late for the Friday deadline. I get headaches, clench my jaws, and am generally miserable during these times."

The pressure of deadlines is inevitable, but Internal Time-keeper will create added pressure under the illusion of saving you time. Creating an artificial deadline in order to provide yourself with "extra" time for more activities is an example of the Internal Timekeeper's Faulty Perception; i.e., "The busier you are the better off you'll be." If you think about it, there really is no "extra" time. There is just time. How you view time will determine how much stress you'll suffer.

A deadline is just a benchmark of your progress. When you panic because you are running behind, ask yourself, "Behind what?" If it is a self-imposed deadline, remember who set it. If someone else set it, it represents an agreement or contract which may be negotiable. Be careful when you set deadlines. Don't volunteer to cook a gourmet dinner for twelve the same week your year-end financial reports are due. Internal Timekeeper will try to convince you that you can work under a deadline while conducting business as usual. You can't. When you are working under a deadline, don't take on any new tasks until your work is completed.

One of life's most satisfying experiences is to be completely absorbed in an activity, whether completing a year-long business project or varnishing a sailboat. Whatever you do, you'll need to direct your full attention to the project, creating new perspectives and solutions. Internal Timekeeper is a hindrance because it can break your concentration with internal and external distractions. As the quality of your work slips, you feel stress because you're working at cross-purposes with your desire to do the job well. If you regard concentrated time as a luxury that isn't necessary to your job performance, your enjoyment of the job for its own sake is gone. All that's left is the momentary and dull satisfaction of task-completion. In most large organizations, this attitude guarantees you will be passed over for promotions. Harry, a middle-management supervisor, sets a sad example:

"I don't understand it," says Harry. "I train these younger fellows, teach them everything I know, and a few years later they pass right by me. I do a lot for this company. I even got high blood pressure in the bargain. I'm not appreciated for all the work I do." Harry has never paid a lot of attention to the quality of his work. Quantity was his goal. "I get the job done my way and it's been good enough for twenty-four years," he says. The company may appreciate Harry's devotion to hard work. Many organizations rely on such spear carriers, but they rarely move them into the higher echelons of management. Harry is experiencing dissatisfaction, resentment, and a gnawing sense of inadequacy based on his suspicion that the company doesn't really value him. Now he's in his fifties and suffering from hypertension. He is beginning to feel the effects of a chronic, debilitating condition. The sad part is that it could have been avoided. Had he focused years ago on what he was doing and why, not just how much he was doing, he could have seen the difference between himself and those being promoted. Questions like, "How did those people who never worked as hard as I do get promoted?" "What are they doing that I am not?" or "What are they not doing that I doggedly insist on doing?" can provide the answers.

Quantity cannot replace quality, so don't let Internal Timekeeper detract from the quality of your work. You may be fast, but when you constantly give in to Internal Timekeeper's interruptions, you can't be as effective. Your work will be late as often as on time, and most likely it will be sent back to you for time-consuming corrections.

Your colleagues, who end up sharing your workload, will resent you with good reason. As you read this next example, note how Cal's attempt to be two places at once puts Nancy on the spot and affects others around him adversely.

Cal's colleagues have just settled in for the monthly staff conference. As the meeting gets under way, Cal still hasn't arrived. His colleague, Nancy, looks around the room frantically trying to locate him since she is the first speaker and Cal has her notes. At last he dashes in the door, just in the nick of time. After her obviously nervous, disjointed presentation, Nancy glares at Cal, who smiles back feebly and shrugs his shoulders in an I-couldn't-help-it gesture. Next thing we know, Cal slips out the door because Internal Timekeeper has just reminded him that he is due at another meeting.

Controlling Internal Timekeeper isn't easy. At first you will feel the loss of a long-time companion. Just remember, Internal Timekeeper was only a companion, not a friend. You may want to start by learning to control just one aspect of Internal Timekeeper. Soon you'll find your efforts mushrooming.

As you gain more and more control over Internal Timekeeper, you'll notice subtle changes in the quality of your time. Internal Timekeeper speeds you through life so fast that you miss a lot along the way. As you slow down, you see more.

The immediate benefits include relief from pressure, freedom from redoing things, and a real reduction in the number of hours needed to get your work done. Why? Internal Timekeeper has quit interrupting you. You will gain the satisfaction of seeing something through from start to finish. The time you spend with coworkers will also be more enriching because it will be less distracted. You may even find time to share something personal about yourself.

This new way of looking at life is possible once you decide you want to change the Internal Timekeeper behavior that's been driving you. Next, you must practice calming Internal Timekeeper and stilling its passion for activity. It can be done. After one of our workshops and months of concentrated effort spent learning to silence Internal Timekeeper, Leslie wrote us, "You wouldn't believe the new me. I barely recognize myself without Internal Timekeeper running my life. I'm a new person."

Like all the Stress Personalities, Internal Timekeeper diverts your energy and attention toward unproductive action and away from your Better Judgement. Only when you learn to take control back from this part of yourself can you replace it with more productive behavior.

INTERNAL TIMEKEEPER AND HEALTH

Drivers who tailgate, pass on curves or double yellow lines, speeding along oblivious to the danger they are creating, have Internal Timekeeper behind the wheel. With Internal Timekeeper in the driver's seat, you're living recklessly. Most people with Internal Timekeeper behavior don't slow down until they develop some serious illness. It often comes as a complete surprise when they learn they have high blood pressure or heart disease even when there is a family history of such disorders.

Edna, a teacher who attended one of our workshops, realized that high blood pressure and heart disease ran in her family, as did Internal Timekeeper behavior and stress. She suffered from high blood pressure, and her father and grandfather, models of Internal Timekeeper behavior, had died of heart disease.

How can you fight heredity? Watch for the signals. We call them Stress Points, the indicators on the barometer that show the toll a Stress Personality is taking on your health. You don't have to wait until you're laid low by a coronary to catch on.

Common indications that Internal Timekeeper is interfering with your day-to-day life, in other words, that you've reached the Stress Point, include: loss of concentration, inability to complete tasks, and an increase in time spent away from home, mate, and family. Internal Timekeeper's places insatiable demands on your time. You may be firmly convinced that your nightly exhaustion and daily fatigue are the price you have to pay for success.

You don't reach the Stress Point all of a sudden. There are predictable clues. Do you remember the Stress Continuum described on page xxv? At the Personal Discomfort end of the Stress Continuum you'll be feeling the minor discomforts of Internal Timekeeper's daily pressure such as chronic anxiety, frequent feelings of being overwhelmed, scattered concentration, pressured thought or speech, and periodic cycles of high energy followed by collapse into exhaustion. If Internal Timekeeper is persistent and left unchecked, you'll be pushed along the Stress Continuum.

There is a driven quality to Internal Timekeeper behavior that keeps your body working overtime year after year. This treadmill effect can literally wear you out and push you to the brink of physiological disaster. Paul's experience vividly demonstrates how this can happen. Paul was referred to our workshop by his doctor, who told him he would have to quit his job because of extreme high blood pressure. A slim, wiry man in his early fifties, Paul spoke in a slow, concise manner without any apparent signs of severe stress. He reported, however, that he was experiencing fatigue, sleep disturbances, and loss of energy along with his hypertension. His doctor told him he was headed for a coronary unless he slowed down.

"For years and years," Paul said, "I always had three or four jobs. I'd come home just bushed every evening. But give me fifteen minutes, I'd eat something and be right back up and going again. I learned a method to help me. When I was tired, I'd rev myself up imagining I was going to run a race or get into a fight. I'd feel a surge of energy and I'd force myself out again, forgetting all about being tired. I'd be geared up again and my muscles would always respond. Then I wouldn't wear out again until about midnight, when I'd come home and fall into bed exhausted."

Paul's Internal Timekeeper drove him so relentlessly that he had learned to psyche himself up like a football player preparing for the Super Bowl. In so doing, he had developed a method of stimulating his body into maintaining an accelerated stress level. The image of the race or fight set off a chain of physical responses: increased adrenalin flow, hormone release into his bloodstream, and heartbeat acceleration leading to a rise in blood pressure and a surge of blood flow to his arms and legs. His body was preparing for emergency action. In this case, the chronic emergencies were the added demands of his extra jobs. After putting himself through this cycle several times a day, month after month, Paul became addicted to his own adrenalin and the energy "hit" it gave him. The jolt supercharged his cardiovascular system countless times year after year, keeping his body in a continuous state of high stress. In order to meet the demands and obligations of his life, Paul had made a pact with the devil, and the role of Lucifer was played by

Internal Timekeeper. Paul's experience is a good example of the long-term physiological effects of Internal Timekeeper stress behavior. When he was young and strong he tapped into his seemingly boundless stores of energy on a daily basis, but by systematically ignoring his nightly exhaustion, he turned his life over to Internal Timekeeper. Gradually he moved along the Continuum. From the Personal Discomfort end, characterized by his being "bushed" every night, he eventually moved into the danger zone with high blood pressure at the Psychosomatic Illness end of the Stress Continuum. Hopefully Paul can stop there, because as serious as high blood pressure is, it's only a precursor of even more debilitating disease.

INTERNAL TIMEKEEPER GAME PLAN

FAULTY
PERCEPTION: Survival and self-esteem are based on the amount of work you do. Therefore, the busier you are, the better off you'll be.

HANDICAP: You do not manage your time efficiently.

RESULT: You try to crowd too many things into a given amount of time and you schedule your time so tightly that unexpected demands throw you off schedule. This increases your feelings of frenzy, frustration, and urgency. Being constantly busy means you won't have time to be focused, concentrated and effective.

NEW
PERCEPTION: Being constantly busy means you won't have time to be focused, concentrated and effective.

FIRST MOVE: Build into your schedule a time period
                   that will enable you to meet unexpected
                   demands. When the same demands in-
                   terrupt you day after day, they are not
                   unexpected and must be planned for. Cut
                   your daily activity list by one-fourth.

PITFALL: Internal Timekeeper will try to get you to
                   use up any "extra" time because it is waste-
                   ful not to make use of every second. You
                   will try to work faster, and in so doing you
                   will lessen your efficiency.

COUNTERMOVE: Prioritize your time and duties each morn-
                   ing. List the important things in order.
                   Set a time in the day when you no longer
                   take on new tasks in order to finish those
                   you've started.

FAULTY
PERCEPTION: **"Once I get everything done, dear, I'll
                   have time for you."**

HANDICAP: You are too busy for love.

RESULT: Internal Timekeeper will bring distrac-
                   tions to bed with you. Your sex life will be
                   affected by your wandering thoughts and
                   constant reminders of things to do. When
                   Internal Timekeeper's voice goes on, ar-
                   dor turns off.

NEW
PERECPTION: When Internal Timekeeper is in charge
                   of setting a time for lovemaking, "later"
                   never comes.

FIRST MOVE: Encourage your mate to tell you when you seem distracted. Let your mate know Internal Timekeeper is vying for your attention. Enlist your mate in a cooperative effort to help you focus your attention on lovemaking.

PITFALL: Internal Timekeeper will suggest you set a time schedule or a time limit on your lovemaking.

COUNTERMOVE: Tell Internal Timekeeper you are setting aside an evening for intimacy when the time is right. Give yourself a chance. Make a production of it if necessary. You will need concentration because you are competing with a very persistent part of you.

Take yourself through this Game Plan by writing down one Handicap caused by your Internal Timekeeper. What is the Result? Determine what your First Move will be. Acknowledge and list a Pitfall you might encounter when you put your First Move into practice. Then figure out a Countermove designed to outmaneuver your Internal Timekeeper.

**FAULTY
PERCEPTION:**

HANDICAP:

RESULT:

NEW
PERCEPTION:

FIRST MOVE:

PITFALL:

COUNTERMOVE:

Any problems that occur while implementing your Game Plan might be a subject for a dialoguing session with your Internal Timekeeper. If so, you now have a specific problem to deal with and to focus on.

NEW BEHAVIORS TO RETRAIN INTERNAL TIMEKEEPER

What to do . . . *Slow Down*

- Finish what you start.

- Stop thinking about all the things you have to do.

- Recognize you have limits and space work accordingly.

- Focus on the quality of life, not the quantity of tasks accomplished.

- Accept interruptions as a normal part of the work day and plan for them.

- Cut your daily "To Do" list to one third of its length.

- Save fifteen minutes a day for unplanned time and use it for yourself.

- Take breaks and stop for lunch.

2. PLEASER

When I Say Yes, I Feel Used

*Y*OU'VE just settled down on the couch with a sandwich, a glass of milk, and a new novel that you've been dying to read. The kids have gone to a birthday party and you have two hours of peace and quiet. The time is a long-deserved luxury. Just as you finish the second page, the doorbell rings. "Oh no," you mutter to yourself, "what now? Well, I'm just not going to answer it." Just then you hear an internal voice. It's your Pleaser saying, "Maybe it's someone who needs your help." "Oh, shoot," you say, throwing the book on the couch as you storm to the front door. Quickly donning your Pleaser mask, you open the door and exclaim brightly, "Oh, hi," to your neighbor Howard, whose face lights up at seeing you.

"Thank heavens you're here, Jenny. The shades were drawn, and I was sure no one was home. Listen, I need a favor."

"Again?" you reply.

"Hey, Jenny, don't think I wasn't grateful last time. You were the only one in the neighborhood who would feed my attack dog while I was on vacation."

"That's OK," you reply, managing a smile. "The scar on my hand has almost faded."

Howard continues, "Well, anyway, my car is being repaired and I have to pick it up by four o'clock. Can I have a lift?"

You hesitate, shifting your weight from one foot to the other as you try to think of an excuse. "Uh — why don't you ask Courtney up the street? She just bought a little sports car, and I'm sure she'd be glad to take you."

"Nope, can't. She meditates every day between three o'clock and four o'clock."

"Well, you see," you reply, beginning to feel the anxiety churn in your stomach, "I was just starting to read a new novel, and . . ."

"Oh good, then you weren't doing anything anyway," says Howard. "I'll just get Angel and be back in a jiffy."

"You're bringing your dog?"

"I have to drop her off at the vet on the way," Howard reassures. "Don't worry. I promise to watch her so she doesn't chew up your back seat."

"She won't bite me again, will she?" you ask.

"Not unless you panic," smiles Howard. "See you in a minute. Thanks again, Jenny, you're a real sport."

If you've been in a situation like this more times than you'd like to admit, you probably have a Pleaser.

Pleaser is the part of you that stops you from standing up for yourself. It is the nonassertive part of your personality. When Pleaser is around, the word "no" is exempt from your vocabulary. "You can't say no without insulting people," coaches Pleaser. So when you try to assert yourself, you feel so guilty you back down. You end up going through life as a one-person Red Cross agency — always doing favors, but never asking for them, even when you need help. You continue to roll out the red carpet for others and then feel resentment when they walk on you.

It's Pleaser who traps you into prolonged conversation with your grocery clerk while your friend is double-parked in five o'clock traffic. Pleaser is afraid of hurting his feelings by saying, "I have to get going." When your waiting friend looks angry, Pleaser suggests buying her an expensive bottle of champagne, even if it means your account will be overdrawn. Pleaser wants you to be liked, even at your own expense.

At the office Pleaser talks you into letting a colleague use your computer because hers is down and because of it you miss your deadline. And Pleaser obligates you to pay the lunch bill even if you were the one asked out as the guest. If you lend a book to a friend, Pleaser will have you drop by and pick it up yourself rather than ask your friend to return it. Pleaser makes commitments for you without considering the responsibility or all the other things you have to do. Suddenly you realize you're always doing favors, and finally ask yourself, "Why do everyone else's wishes come before my own?"

Pleaser has you convinced that unless you are pleasing others all of the time, no one will like you. "Don't upset the apple cart" is Pleaser's motto. Soon you become a "yes-person" always nodding in agreement with others. "Yes, I feel that way too. I know just what you mean. Isn't that the truth, though?" Before you know it, the other person has run out of ideas and the conversation is exhausted. With Pleaser, you never voice your opinion or open up a new conversation for fear of being rejected. You are so busy trying to second-guess the needs of others that you end up becoming a reflection of them instead of just being yourself.

People with deeply ingrained Pleasers have been practicing pleasing since childhood. "Tell me what kind of person you want me to be when I grow up, and I'll be it," is the little Pleaser's plea. "A brilliant student — I'll study and become valedictorian! The lawyer you always wanted to be — I'll go to law school. An athlete — I'll be a football star. A pretty little girl — I'll be feminine. Oh, you wanted a boy — I'll be a tomboy. Just tell me what kind of child you want me to be and I'll be it!"

Pleaser got the message early on that if you were good and didn't cause any trouble your parents would love you. In fact, the less you bothered them, the better you were. It probably seemed that if you just disappeared you'd be terrific. But that thought was sent scurrying into the depths of your subconscious, too painful to accept. Since you couldn't literally disappear, you tried to cause as few problems as possible in exchange for love. Love and security quickly were associated with not "making waves." Here's a typical example:

Young Ron comes in from a party at one in the morning, an hour later than he had promised. His father is sitting in the chair looking very cold and stern. "You're late!" he challenges. "Give me the car keys. You are grounded for a week." For the next few days Ron is on his best behavior. While Dad offers only cool hellos and good-byes, Ron brings him the paper and his slippers, laughs at his jokes, and watches television with him, until gradually things warm up and get back to normal. It doesn't take long for Ron to realize, however, that he had to earn his way back into Dad's good graces. Not until he proved himself the model child would he feel loved again. Many children have had experiences like this with their parents at one time or another, but when it happens continually, Pleaser gets a strong foothold and is tough to shake. No matter what the particular circumstances were, those who relied on Pleaser as a survival behavior in childhood learned to be good and to put others' needs before their own in order to earn love.

If Pleaser helped you as a child, you may still feel you need this part of yourself to survive in the adult world. This is a fallacy. People's expectations of you are not the same as those of your parents, and your life is no longer dependent on how others view you. Your dependency will only make you feel angry at yourself and those you try to please. When you start pleasing yourself first, you'll begin taking responsibility for your life and your actions.

A Pleaser Faulty Perception is that unless everyone loves you, you will not survive. You'll feel just as threatened if a coworker at the office snarls at you as you do after a lovers' quarrel or a fight with your best friend. If it were up to Pleaser, your life would be lived only for others. Your well-being wouldn't be a consideration at all. This becomes a highly stressful position to maintain. Pleaser makes you feel helpless to change an unpleasant situation, and you feel endlessly victimized by forces "beyond your control." Here are some typical examples taken from the stories of our workshop participants to illustrate the victim-of-circumstance dilemma to which Pleasers seem especially vulnerable:

"I'm always the one who gets the extra work. Everyone knows I won't say no, so they take advantage of me. I'm almost always busy but it doesn't seem to stop anyone from giving me more work."

"At home, when my family won't cooperate with me, I get so upset that I get angry and start crying."

"I keep taking on more than I can handle, and I keep getting farther behind. Others get complimented for being caught up and efficient. You know attention often goes to the complainers."

"I feel angry at work all of the time. What I can't figure out is if I'm mad at my boss because I can't defend myself, or if I'm angry at myself for not speaking up."

Those using Pleaser almost always express an underlying resentment because they can't say no, allowing others to take advantage of them. This smothered anger induces stress. Whenever you betray yourself by putting others first, another part of yourself feels angry. This anger is directed toward the people you think are making you do all these things. Your first lesson to learn is that only you are making you do them.

It's really Pleaser who makes you feel resentful, not extraneous situations or individuals. There is a difference between giving freely and being driven to please by the threat of feeling guilty if you don't. The difference is whether or not you feel resentment when you give. Assess your Pleaser behavior by answering the following questions. The remainder of the chapter will help you recognize Pleaser's subtleties and how to deal with them.

Assessing Your Pleaser Behavior

Answer honestly, choosing one of the five responses and placing the corresponding number in the box opposite each question. Add up the score and place the total along the stress behavior scale. Pay special attention to those questions on which you score a 6 or 8. If your total score is 48 or greater, you've been engaging in enough Pleaser behavior to be significantly disruptive to your life.

(Almost always=8) (Frequently=6) (Sometimes=4)
(Occasionally=2) (Never=0)

1. ( ) Do you have a work overload because you can't say no?
2. ( ) Do you make commitments to clients that your organization can't keep?
3. ( ) Do you serve on committees because they can't get anyone else?
4. ( ) Do staff members take advantage of you?
5. ( ) Is it hard for you to confront an irresponsible coworker or employee?
6. ( ) Do you find things you once did as a favor are now expected of you?
7. ( ) Do you feel guilty after you've said "NO"?
8. ( ) Do you feel it is an insult to friends if you say no to their requests?
9. ( ) Are you so busy saying yes to everyone else that you have no time for your family or friends?
10. ( ) Do you feel responsible for protecting the feelings of those you care about?
11. ( ) When you are not in agreement with others, are you afraid to say so?
12. ( ) Do you often volunteer the services of your mate?

( ) TOTAL

0   48   96

PLEASER FRIEND

Do people think that you're "just too good to be true?" With Pleaser, you might be. Most people wouldn't dream of putting out for others the way you do. Under your Pleaser's influence, you can easily feel like Florence Nightingale and the world's doormat rolled into one. Since Pleaser sets no limits on your volunteer services, you'll continually be relied upon and expected to do the impossible.

Intimate sharing relationships come second to playing nurse, psychiatrist, chauffeur, cook, and entertainer. And Pleaser never allows these courtesies to be returned. Difficulty being on the receiving end of a relationship stifles friendships even more than does the lack of time. If Pleaser is a significant force in your life, you probably feel vulnerable or uncomfortable receiving attention and love since you're so used to putting others first. You probably don't even know how to ask for what you want from a relationship. You may feel guilty and uneasy about asking for things or stating a minority opinion. Yet denying yourself honest needs puts distance between friends and adds stress to relationships.

Here's an example:

Joan and her Pleaser have just seen a movie with a friend. As they leave the theater, Laura, Joan's friend, asks, "So what did you think of the film?"

"Well — I — uh, thought it was interesting," Joan hedges.

"I didn't like it. It was too pedantic." Laura's opinion is clear.

Pleaser immediately makes Joan feel anxious for having a differing opinion, so she quickly agrees with Laura even though she's not sure what pedantic means.

"It had no breadth, no daring, no verve. In short, it was a bore," continues Laura.

"You're right," Pleaser is now in command of Joan.

"On the other hand," Laura says, "the photography was excellent."

"Yes, it was, especially the sunset scenes," Joan offers hesitantly.

"Really? You liked the sunsets? I thought they were trite."
Joan is threatened again. "Actually," offers Laura, philosophically,
"it wasn't a bad film."

"You're right, it wasn't," agrees Joan.

"Nope," confirms Laura, "it wasn't bad, it was awful."

Looking at Laura, Joan laughs and agrees, "It sure was."

At this point Laura suggests getting something to eat. Joan
thinks that's a great idea.

"What would you like to have?" Joan asks.

"Suggest something." Laura has put the ball back in Joan's
court. Nervously she suggests a hot fudge sundae.

"I don't like ice cream. It's not good for me."

Once again Joan is thrown and Pleaser takes over. "You're
right. I don't really like ice cream either. What do you suggest?"

By now Laura is wondering if Joan has an opinion on anything. Joan is exhausted after bobbing up and down like a puppet
with Pleaser in control of the strings. Pleaser has so obliterated
Joan's thoughts and feelings in order to accommodate Laura's that
her uniqueness as a human being has been buried. Laura has no
idea who Joan really is.

Pleaser is afraid that once people get to know you, they won't
like you. This attitude makes intimate relationships become one-
dimensional, lacking the depth and honesty crucial to good friendships. Think about it. People have to know who you are before
they can feel close. If you can't tell your friends what you're feeling
or thinking, you need to re-evaluate the quality of your relationship. Contrary to Pleaser's beliefs, it's not speaking out, it's the
withholding of your true feelings and the suppressing of your needs
and desires that create stress in relationships. One of our workshop
participants sums up the interference Pleaser causes in relationships:

"It looks as if Pleaser has been my dominant Stress Person-
ality all my life. I always have difficulty expressing my views when
I am with another person. I begin to feel angry and depressed when
I don't speak up. I'm afraid of telling people how I really feel, afraid

they will confront me and I'll ruin the relationship. Now I realize that these relationships are shallow, and I don't think a shallow relationship is really worth protecting any more. Nobody knows me — they just know my Pleaser."

Pleaser does worse things than keep your friends at a distance. Pleaser makes your sincerity questionable. People may distrust you or think you are manipulating them with your good deeds. When you behave like a chameleon, changing your opinion to suit the occasion, need, or friend, nobody knows who's behind Pleaser's mask. You don't seem honest when you appear to be telling people just what they want to hear.

Trust is as basic an issue in friendships as it is in a solid marriage. And if you make promises you can't keep or treat everyone as your best buddy, your trustworthiness will come into question. Since Pleaser is notorious for saying one thing and then thinking or doing another, you may volunteer your services and then back out at the last minute.

Dependable Pleasers have a different problem: resentment. Marjorie, a forty-year-old housewife, tells her story:

Every year for three years her best friend asked her to chair the Cub Scout Blue and Gold Dinner. Every year she gritted her teeth, smiled, and did it. This year she could not bear to do it again, although she'd already said yes. She called her husband to tell him how furious she was at her friend for asking a fourth time. Hadn't she already gone way beyond the call of duty? He suggested she tell her friend how she was feeling. But with Pleaser she couldn't handle a direct confrontation. Consequently, while she carried out the dinner arrangements, she was crabby with her family, didn't feel like going to work, and began to feel her ulcer acting up. But not once did she consider telling her friend she wouldn't chair the dinner. To her that would have been an insult to her friend. She saw no choice but to take on the responsibility.

Pleaser traps you into a no-win position. Unless you learn to see more than one option, you'll always feel as if there's no way out. Marjorie had several choices available to her had she stopped listening to Pleaser and tuned into Better Judgement. One choice was to level with her friend by saying, "I really don't want to chair the dinner this year. I hate to tell you this because I'm afraid it will hurt your feelings, and our friendship means a lot to me. How do you feel about my saying no?" If she had initiated this honest exchange, chances are they would eventually feel closer than they had before. Another choice Marjorie had was to help her friend think of someone else for the position, volunteering her own services as back-up person or consultant.

Always look for the many solutions that really do exist for any problem. This will help you escape Pleaser's entrapment.

Contrary to your Pleaser's belief, it is not essential that you like everyone and that everyone likes you. It just isn't realistic. Some people won't like you for reasons as uncontrollable as the fact that you remind them of their former mother-in-law, ex-husband, or the salesperson who cheated them out of $500. People can be capricious and whimsical about first impressions, and there is little you can do to alter them. Pleaser seems to be challenged by those people who don't like you. Avoid this losing challenge and quit trying to create artificial chats with such people or trying other useless ploys. You'll invariably turn people off even faster when you look as if you're lobbying for the Congeniality Award.

Start to spend more energy on people who genuinely interest you and show signs of reciprocation. Don't encourage a friendship unless you feel you will get some satisfaction from it. If you have no intention of seeing someone again, don't say, "Let's get together next week. I'll call you." You might have to bite your tongue at first, but you'll feel better once you start spending your time as you decide. And you won't disappoint people by backing down from obligations you can't live up to.

No matter who you're around, be yourself. Otherwise, the effort to relate will be exhausting. If you find yourself seeking the refuge of solitude too frequently because you just can't stand being around people, you'd better find out why. You may be continually putting your best facade forward, so afraid to let down that you are free to be yourself only when you're alone. Being on stage twelve hours a day is too much work even for an actor. Take lessons from friends who are getting what they want out of life. Being "good" or "nice" doesn't ensure rewards, despite what Pleaser tells you. When you assert yourself and actively seek out both whom and what you want, your chances of getting them multiply. Asserting yourself this way isn't selfish or aggressive. It's healthy. Develop relationships with assertive people and learn from them. Keep Pleaser out of these relationships. Instead of Pleaser being so concerned about pleasing others, get Pleaser to start pleasing you.

PLEASER MATE

How many "perfect couples" — the ones who never fought — can you think of who are now divorced? Everybody is shocked when they break up. Friends blindly console the hurt party saying things like, "She's going to have to go to great lengths to find a guy as sweet as you. When she comes to her senses, she'll be sorry." If you have a Pleaser and find yourself in a similar situation, chances are you're puzzled over your mate's seemingly irrational actions.

When Pleaser enters into your intimate relationships, your mate will feel inexplicably frustrated by your reactions. Pleaser interprets discussions as fights, associates anger with hatred, and disagreement with open warfare. Pleaser's fear of conflict creates distance between you and your mate. Any hint of unrest or unhappiness in the relationship will be squelched by Pleaser. "Life's too short to cause a fuss," Pleaser advises. "Avoid unpleasant situations or smooth them over as quickly as possible."

Look what happens when Pleaser is approached by a concerned mate.

"I feel that you've been distant lately. I notice it especially in our sex life. Are you feeling OK? Is there anything wrong?"

"Of course not. Everything's fine with me," is Pleaser's cheerful reply.

"Well, it's not fine with me. You haven't wanted to make love for a week, and last night when you turned away from me, I felt hurt and angry."

Pleaser immediately feels uncomfortable. "Let's not fight. I've just been a little tired. That's all. We'll make love tonight, and things will be back to normal. Don't worry." This is a less than satisfactory response, but if the conversation is pursued, Pleaser will feel pushed into a corner and start looking for the nearest available exit. "Let's talk about something else instead of starting an argument," is Pleaser's solution.

Pleaser tries to play Cupid after a lovers' quarrel by bending over backwards to fulfill your mate's needs. Pleaser won't stop for you to realize that maybe your cooling off toward your partner is a signal that something in your relationship is awry. No matter how large or small the gripe, don't let Pleaser prevent you from uncovering your reason for withdrawing. Any irritation or upset can turn you off. A comment made at a party, a disagreement over vacation destinations, a problem with the kids, a poor investment, or the fact that you're angry with your spouse for putting on weight may cause trouble. Whatever it is, serious or mundane, you must communicate these thoughts before Pleaser takes the words right out of your mouth.

When you let go of Pleaser, sometimes just venting angry feelings will clear the air. "Hey, I am feeling a little resentful that since I've begun to work you still expect me to cook every night. Would you be willing to cook every other night?" Sometimes it will take a while and require in-depth discussions to get to the core issues, but the point is, get them out so they don't fester. Next time you get into one of these difficult situations tell Pleaser, "No, I am not going to gloss this over. I'm going to resolve it." Just sticking it out once will help the communication that Pleaser blocked. The more honest you are the first time, the easier it will be the next. If you're involved in a long-term relationship, you have the freedom to be yourself without worrying that the other person will walk out on you for one harsh word. That makes it easier to practice sharing your innermost thoughts with your loved one.

Don't believe Pleaser's Faulty Perception that ignoring your problems makes them go away. A woman in one of our workshops saw the futility of this philosophy when she explained a typical evening with her husband. "Anytime my husband and I were about to have an argument, I'd run out to the driveway and hide in our van. Every time it happened I really believed that this time when I came back things would be back on an even keel. They never were."

Pleaser can use far more sophisticated and subtle techniques to shut off a loved one's attempts at dealing with troublesome issues. A hurt look, a change in the topic of conversation, or maybe even a joke can work. Pleaser may fake conversation while cleverly avoiding responsibility. For example, you hear yourself say, "OK, what do you want to talk about?" Mate replies, "Well, sometimes I feel as if I don't know you. I'm sure there are times you get angry with me, but you never say so." You counter, "You know, honey, I don't feel that's my problem, but if it is a problem for you, maybe I can help you with it." Pleaser has adroitly maneuvered your mate into a defensive position.

It's tough for Pleaser to deal with anger. This often results in subtle suggestions that your mate act out or express anger for you. For example, if you are mad at your neighbor, you'll get your mate to go talk to him for you. This way you don't have to take responsibility for your anger, and in your neighbor's eyes you'll always come out smelling like a rose. If your self-image is heavily dependent upon others seeing you as a "nice guy" or such a "sweet person," you will avoid tarnishing this image by avoiding any display of anger.

Trying to live up to a nice-person image will also affect your relationship with your children. Under Pleaser's influence, many parents step in to save their children from painful learning experiences. They bail their kids out of trouble, cover for them, and excuse their behavior when it's out of line. One parent will often resort to such behavior without the spouse's knowledge. Protecting your children from a spouse's anger is detrimental in the long run because it robs them of meaningful interchange. When one Pleaser parent acts as mediator, the other parent and child never have to exchange words because Pleaser parent does it for them. Common examples are, "Your father wants you home this weekend" or "your mother feels you've been inconsiderate lately." Not only are cross-relationships blocked within the family, but the Pleaser parent experiences high stress levels because he or she is always in the middle.

Nola's example is typical of what happens to a Pleaser mother when she lets her son take advantage of her:

"My husband is unhappy with me for not standing up to our son whom he thinks irresponsible. Yesterday something happened that was typical of the problems I feel cause stress in our family. I had tried to get all of us together for a nice dinner and I ended up eating alone. When I came home from work, I told my son Jack I was making his favorite meal — corned beef and cabbage. He said he was in a hurry and couldn't wait — could I make him something else? I did, even though my husband kept mumbling, 'We're not in the restaurant business.' When Jack came downstairs, he was ready to grab a sandwich and leave. It made me mad because I had gone to all of this extra trouble and he didn't even say thank you. So I started to tell him, 'I do things for you as an expression of love, and you don't show me any expression of anything. You gripe about washing my car, you don't do anything around the house without being asked twenty times, and you never say please or thank you.' Just then, my husband walked into the kitchen. Jack quickly said he had to go and left. I started to complain to my husband, and of course, he agreed with me. He reminded me that the garbage can was still sitting in the middle of the floor where it had been put this morning for Jack to empty. But then, almost inexplicably, Pleaser came in and immediately took Jack's defense. 'Well, I think all boys his age are that way. I'm sure he doesn't mean it, and he did make his bed this morning. Don't be so hard on him, dear.' With that, my husband got so infuriated that he stormed out of the room and I was left alone with the corned beef and cabbage."

It is aggravating for your mate to watch you get manipulated by others, especially your own kids. On the one hand, your spouse feels bad that you are suffering, but on the other hand feels anger and disrespect for your inability to handle the situation. If you feel uncomfortable using firm discipline, just remember that children need limits just as much as you need to learn to set them. Children, like adults, will walk all over you and come to take for granted the favors you do for them. In order to avoid resenting your children, you'll need to subdue Pleaser.

Because Pleaser will do anything to keep the peace, you'll not only have children who take advantage of you, but a spouse as well. Many people with strong Pleasers marry a Sabertooth mate who knows Pleaser will accept anger without so much as a peep of resistance. A Sabertooth spouse will humiliate you, but Pleaser will seldom want you to stand up to him or her. There is always some compelling reason why Pleaser feels trapped. "I stay with her for the sake of the children," is one. "My husband says if I don't like the way he's treating me I can leave," is another common excuse. Others are afraid to question harsh treatment for fear of making it worse. Consider Freida's plight:

"When my husband comes home from work in a bad mood, he will start a fight over any little thing. His food isn't hot enough or I've said the wrong thing. He'll jump on me right at the table in front of the children. I just try to smooth things over and keep from antagonizing him further. But he gets abusive with the children, as well. It seems the nicer I am, the ornerier he gets. Finally, one day last month, I blew up at him. I shocked myself. I was so furious I lost control. He was shocked, too. He thought I'd gone crazy. Maybe I had — but I just couldn't take it anymore! So what did he do? He started pouting and wouldn't talk to me for days. Finally, I felt so guilty I begged for his forgiveness, but he still wouldn't talk to me until he was good and ready. Now I'm meeker than ever. I guess he's got some kind of a hold on me." Somebody has a hold on Freida, but it isn't her husband. It is her Pleaser.

If Pleaser dominates your life and you have a Sabertooth mate who uses verbal or physical abuse, the first problem you need to deal with is your fear of what might happen should you decide to stand up for yourself. You can't fight fire with fire. Calmly and firmly let your mate know that such manipulative behavior is no longer OK with you.

If your mate is violent, ask yourself why you are willing to live with someone who beats you up. Don't you think you're good enough to find someone else? Are you afraid you won't be able to take care of yourself? Maybe you subconsciously enjoy feeling like a suffering saint. Or maybe fear of experiencing embarrassment when other people learn about your problems makes you keep the lid on everything and suffer year after year.

Since Pleaser tries to get love and caring from others to fill your lack of love for yourself, your need for outside affection is insatiable. The bitter irony is that an abusive mate with uncontrollable behavior will challenge you to be pleasing and accommodating. Yet you can never be nice enough.

Nobody will respect you if you don't respect yourself, and Pleaser doesn't foster self-respect. All those people who you think see you as a saint for enduring the hardships of life probably feel more pity for you than admiration. Fortunately, most mates are not abusive. They are willing to help if you'll let them. Ask your spouse for help. That way you'll have two people watching for Pleaser's appearances.

Ask your spouse to point out any signs of Pleaser. One technique is to have your mate keep asking you, "Is that Pleaser, or are you agreeing with me because you think I'm right?" Then sit down and talk it out, making sure you share the way Pleaser makes you feel. If you start to resent or feel used about something, discuss it. You can always change your mind. If you decide to disagree with something to which you had previously agreed, tell your mate and ask for support. You may even want to roleplay the situation. Sharing your vulnerable or dependent feelings can enhance the intimacy between you. If you're feeling like a failure say so. "You know, sometimes I feel so incapable of taking care of myself that I feel helpless. How do you see me? How do you think I can change?" Talk, talk, talk, with your mate. We can't encourage open communication enough. It doesn't need to be threatening. It's good practice, and it's free. It's far less costly than suffering with silent dignity while pent-up resentment eats an ulcerous hole in your stomach. It takes more courage to admit feelings of weakness and sadness than it does to kid yourself that you can handle anything all by yourself. If you free yourself of Pleaser, communication with your mate will improve by leaps and bounds and your love will keep growing.

PLEASER BOSS

If you're using your Pleaser to manager or supervisor, you're in trouble. Pleaser is the antithesis of boss. Pleaser is the part of you who can't say no, who won't ask for anything, and who will avoid confrontation at all costs. As boss, you have to give orders, reprimand employees who may be shirking responsibilities, and lead a team toward a common goal. You must say no, ask for things, and confront people even when it's difficult. If you don't, your job success will be squashed by Pleaser, and you'll experience a lot of stress. Your employees will recognize your shortcomings and your self-esteem will be threatened.

Let's look at an example in which Pleaser double-crosses you. As a manager, it's your responsibility to represent your employees' opinions in meetings with top management. One day your employees come to you with a new idea they're very excited about. You agree with the idea but you're not sure the big boss will. Pleaser would rather die than present the idea to him. If you don't present the idea, you'll have a lot of disgruntled employees on your hands. If you do present it, and the big boss doesn't like it, chances are you'll back away, say that you thought it was a stupid idea anyway, and lose his respect for wasting his time on a half-baked idea. You lose either way, unless you leave Pleaser behind.

It's your responsibility to set limits for your employees. This means taking a stand and seeing it through to completion without backing down, even if it means being unpopular. Pleaser will fight you on this because Pleaser can't see that confrontation can be positive behavior. You have to sit on Pleaser to take back your position of authority. Tell Pleaser that an effective boss lets employees know both when they are doing a good job and when they are not.

It's Pleaser who is taking over when an employee, suspecting you're irritated at his habitual tardiness, asks, "Are you mad at me because I've been late so often?" and you say with a smile, "Oh, of course not. I realize you've been having some problems." You really wanted to say, "Yes," but Pleaser stepped in. You back off and add, "But, uh, some of the other people are complaining that they have to pick up your workload, so maybe you ought to watch it a little." The message your employee receives from your approving nod and indirect answer is that the tardiness really doesn't bother you. Then one day when you've had it up to your ears and your employee breezes in forty-five minutes late, you hit the ceiling and threaten to fire him if he is ever again even one minute late. He ends up feeling confused, frustrated, and angry with you.

As a boss, it's your responsibility to offer honest appraisals of your employees. When you hold back, they sense it and feel uneasy, and you are doing nothing to advance their careers. So when Pleaser tempts you not to make a scene, not to confront your employees with their shortcomings, realize that you're being dishonest with them. It's just not fair to let an employee think he's doing a wonderful job — right up until the day you fire him.

Bob, a young dentist, tells how Pleaser created miserable personnel problems for him when he failed to set limits. Bob was experiencing stress because his office staff didn't seem to respect him. One assistant came in late about three times a week, as capriciously as if her comings and goings were ruled by the position of the planets in her horoscope. Her most recent excuse was difficult even for Bob's Pleaser to accept. When she showed up two hours late, Bob asked, "Where have you been? I've been answering the phones, making appointments, and taking care of patients. Norma is out sick and I've been frantic — you didn't even call in." Bob felt she looked at him as if he were a bothersome disturbance in her busy day.

"I had to take my poodle to be clipped this morning. You know how hard it is to get an appointment. I couldn't do it at lunch because that's when I'm having my hair cut." Bob was appalled, but felt powerless. This was just a typical example of the way his staff abused him.

Bob's staff had little concern for his authority because he never exercised any. When we started to look at remedies, we asked him if he ever sat down with his employees and developed a set of rules for them to follow. In typical Pleaser fashion he replied, "Well, yes, kind of, but I was outvoted." Apparently he tried to install a time clock to resolve the lateness problem, but his staff complained bitterly. In an attempt to pacify them, he tried to convince them it was for their own benefit, but they still didn't buy it. Pleaser then suggested a democratic vote. His staff cast their ballots unanimously to remove the time clock, and the next day it was taken out.

How could Bob let his employees behave like that and still maintain a successful business? With a great deal of stress. During guided dialoguing, Bob came to grips with Pleaser. He learned that this inability to set rules stemmed from Pleaser's feelings that if Bob were just a good guy, reasonable, pleasant and easy to work for, things would take care of themselves. But that approach wasn't working. He went back to the office, became more direct with his staff, and required that they follow his rules. He found the results astonishing. He had never seen before how he had caused his own problems by putting Pleaser in charge.

Allison, a supervising nurse, found that by recognizing Pleaser, she could regain her seat of power. After learning about her own interaction with Pleaser, she wrote us about how her change in behavior paid off. "After mulling over the information about Pleaser and Better Judgement that I learned in your workshop, I finally got the nerve to confront one of the women on my staff who I felt had not been doing an adequate job for some time. I put Pleaser on the shelf and faced her straight on with my evaluation of her work performance. It ended up producing excellent results. This woman, whom I had been scared to death to approach, put her arms around me and thanked me for being honest, and said she would do better from now on. She's kept her promise, and needless to say, I feel better, too"

Jim, district manager of a financial services organization, was able to trace the gross inefficiencies in one branch office to a Pleaser office manager named Tom. At first Jim didn't have a clue as to where all the stress problems — which were interfering with even the most routine office procedures — were coming from. We were called in as sleuths after he was given the ultimatum, "Clean up your act within three months, or heads will roll!"

A workshop involving the entire office seemed in order. We found an office staffed by employees barely meeting minimum performance standards, not knowing or caring what a colleague was doing, and many threatening to quit. To us, it seemed like the writhing scramble of potato bugs when a rock is lifted.

Apparently, promotions had been made on the basis of seniority alone. Tom had not only little managerial experience, but an unrelenting Pleaser. Stories about him unfolded quickly. One woman complained that he couldn't make policy decisions, and those that he did make he didn't back. Yet when she was elected chairperson of a committee on which they both sat, Tom wouldn't allow her to make decisions without consulting him first. She felt that the only reason he denied her the autonomy she needed was that he was afraid she would make a mistake and then senior management would blame him. Since Pleaser tagged along in his role as boss, Tom was trying to do everything himself in order to avoid any kind of disapproval from the top.

Other people complained that their hands were tied, and they felt there was no way out of their situation. They felt that their opinions weren't really heard even when they voiced them clearly and rationally. A what's-the-use attitude was plaguing the staff. This frame of mind was at the core of their inability to solve even minor problems. They had stopped using imagination, creativity, and problem-solving skills.

One woman who called herself an "old-timer" seemed to get to the heart of the problem. "As I see it," she said, "Tom is afraid of senior management. We tell him what's going on, make suggestions, and when he takes our ideas to his boss, a real bully type, Tom just backs down and acquiesces. In essence, he is what you call a 'yes man.' As a result, this place is going to pot."

Believe it or not, Tom was present during all these discussions, though he did miss the "old-timer's" confidential analysis. Amazingly enough, he didn't seem to recognize that the thinly-veiled anger that pervaded the whole discussion was directed toward him. He wore a perpetual smile, never said a word, squirmed a lot, but seemed to be thinking, "I have no idea what these people are talking about. It certainly can't involve me." After the Pleaser problem was diagnosed, Tom was confronted. The staff agreed to stand firm and insist on being heard, but they also agreed to support Tom in overcoming his Pleaser. Tom recognized he had the choice of staying with Pleaser or keeping his job. With the problem so clearly identified, Tom was now able to take action.

How can you avoid Pleaser's pitfalls when you're the boss? First, learn to recognize Pleaser. Suppose you find yourself in this situation. An overwhelmed employee comes into your office in hopes that you will rescue her or excuse her from her unfinished work. Pleaser pops up and you hear yourself say, "Oh dear, I had no idea you were so overburdened. I'll take over some of your workload myself since the others are already swamped." Although it's your responsibility to make sure that the job gets done, it's not your responsibility to do it all yourself.

There are many creative and productive ways to approach this situation without Pleaser. The most suitable course of action is to listen to the employee, acknowledge her frustration, and then take a look at the problem. Is there really too much work for this person? If not, where is she bogging down? Could she benefit from additional training? Is there anyone else with whom it might be helpful for her to talk? Are there personal problems involved? Whatever your diagnosis, move this subordinate through the appropriate channels so she can get the help she needs. Be understanding, but make it clear that once you have helped by giving direction, you expect her to deal with the problem from now on. Of course, if the truth is that your employees have more work than they can possibly handle, it's up to you to see that an additional staff member is hired. Your employees will look to you for guidance and decisions. When you offer both, office morale and productivity will improve.

One word of caution: don't get involved in the personal problems of your staff. Pleaser could book you for the day listening to war stories of an unhappy marriage or someone's concern about his teenager's drug problem. Unless you're a counselor, it is your staff's responsibility to find solutions to personal problems. Don't let Pleaser put you in the role of office confessor.

Instead, as boss, you must make it clear that you will only listen to problems that pertain directly to work. Make suggestions for finding professional help, but don't try to be that help. You've got another job to do. Pay special attention to this advice when an employee has a drinking problem. Many Pleaser bosses are particularly vulnerable to this employee and tend to foster a dependency. With Pleaser you will want to help this person by covering for him or excusing hangover-induced absenteeism. As this employee relies on and confides in you, you may even feel important and powerful — a very appealing position for Pleaser who seldom gets to enjoy this feeling. Such a relationship is cataclysmic for both parties. You will be doing your job only when you refer the employee to a professional counselor.

As long as Pleaser goes to work with you, it's practically

impossible to be a good team player, let alone a leader. If your goals are to join or advance in management, Pleaser has to stay behind.

PLEASER EMPLOYEE

Harley looks at his watch. It's half-past four. "Just a half hour and I'll be on vacation for a month," he says to himself, already tingling with excitement just thinking about the Caribbean beaches. His work is caught up and he's ready to go. Just then, his boss walks in with a menacing looking load of papers tucked under his arm.

"Harley, I hate to do this to you, but these reports have to be out by Monday and there's nobody to do them but you."

Harley looks at the pile of papers and feels sick to his stomach. "Gee, I don't see how I can get to these today. I'm leaving on vacation at five o'clock."

"Harley, I really hate to do this to you. You deserve a vacation. But what else can I do? Everyone else has left for the weekend."

"But my vacation . . ."

"Look, I promise I'll never do this to you again. You've got my word if you just pull through for me this time." Harley finally agrees. "I know I've said this to you before, but I'll say it again. You're a real saint, did you know that, Harley?" The effusive praise doesn't help Harley's mounting headache.

As he leaves, his boss glances at his watch and says to himself, "Good, now I can make my six o'clock tennis date." He says to Harley, "See ya. Have a terrific vacation when you do go." Looking up from behind the new pile of papers, Harley smiles pathetically and picks up the phone to postpone his airline reservations.

At work, Pleaser keeps you overworked, overwrought, and underpaid. Your desk becomes the "drop site" for everyone's unfinished business because you can't say no. No matter how hard you try, when you take on the work of others you'll end up disappointing most of the people most of the time. You'll have the best intention of getting to all the extra work, but you don't always get to it. With three or four other jobs waiting in line ahead, it's not surprising. Before you take on any extra work, make sure that your own work is finished. Promise just one thing at a time. Sit on your hands before volunteering to take on more projects so that Pleaser doesn't make commitments that you can't keep.

People with strong Pleasers often experience high levels of stress from the guilt feelings associated with failing to deliver what they promised. When failure to deliver becomes a habit, you're beginning to jeopardize your job. Your work will be viewed as incompetent and unreliable, and you'll never get promoted.

Norma's Pleaser put her in that kind of predicament:

"When I saw someone who was behind, I used to ask if he needed help. I was caught up on my work at the time so it wasn't stressful, but pretty soon word got around that I was a "friend of the needy" and the whole floor started coming to me. Of course Pleaser couldn't turn them down, so I ended up working overtime and still fell behind. The straw that broke my Pleaser's back was when one day at a staff meeting the boss congratulated several of the staff members, whom I consistently helped get caught up, on how efficient they had been, and implied all the rest of us had better shape up."

It is common for employees with Pleasers to take on more work without taking a stand. Instead they work overtime to mask the fact that their productivity is slipping. What can you do, for example, if the boss comes in at five o'clock and you've already committed your time to someone else? Ask the boss to help you solve this problem. After all, this is what he/she is paid to do. Tell him/her that you have a problem. "I promised a coworker that I would get her work out by five o'clock, and if I take on your work, I won't be able to finish in time. Do you have any suggestions?" What Pleaser doesn't realize is that the most important thing to the boss is that the job gets done. Who does it is not nearly as important. As soon as you let go of Pleaser's belief that you are indispensable, you will be amazed at how quickly you and your boss come up with a solution. It is not necessary for you to carry the weight of the office on your shoulders, especially when you are not getting paid for it.

Speaking of money, when was the last time you asked for a raise? You may gripe about your salary to other employees, or feel seething resentment, but you need to confront the person holding the purse strings. You can't expect a raise beyond the normal cost-of-living increase unless you ask for it, even though your boss may recognize how hard you work. It's not necessarily that your boss doesn't think you deserve more money. If he/she is under budgetary pressure and thinks you're happy with your current salary, why would he/she offer more? Asking is no guarantee that you'll get what you want, but if you think about successful people, you'll find that their success was based on both working and asking for what they wanted.

Most employers like to hear what their employees have to say. Ironic as it may seem, assertive challenges are especially appreciated. We know a woman who works at a major bank in San Francisco in a managerial position. One afternoon she attended a meeting introducing a new executive vice president of the bank. She was impressed by the man's intellect and progressive ideas, and decided she wanted to work for him. Two days later, she made an appointment to see him so that she could introduce herself to him and give feedback on his presentation. He was very impressed by her assertive step and commented that she was the first person to come in to discuss his material. Three months later he assigned her a position in his department.

Another executive, this one from a worldwide computer organization, told us, "I can recognize people with Pleasers in our firm as soon as I go overboard on an issue at one of our weekly meetings. The most assertive employees challenge me, but the Pleasers will allow me to jam my dogma right down their throats. I wish they would just speak up." The sad truth is that most employers think that if you don't say anything, then you don't have anything to say.

Pleasers, even in the lowest ranks of a corporation, can exert powerfully negative influences. One sales manager told us that his organization was having problems with telephone operators whose job it was to notify clients of delivery dates for equipment they'd ordered. He discovered, after talking with us, that those operators who had Pleasers tended to be the ones who were unable to handle insistent customers. They would make promises about delivery dates that were impossible to meet, upsetting customers and putting unnecessary stress on the working unit. In trying to please, these operators created turmoil for everyone.

Pleaser may keep you from speaking out on the job because of unfounded fears that your job security is threatened. This attitude keeps you under constant stress. You need to venture opinions when necessary or your loyalty, responsibility, and reliability will have little impact. Although there are plenty of people in the work force, there are only a handful who are top-notch. Most employers will bend over backwards to keep good performers. So chances are you can afford to take a few risks and grow by doing so. Here is an unusual example told to us at lunch one day by an attorney in Seattle.

"I just hired a new private secretary, and she won't do what I tell her. She's the kind who gives orders but won't take them. Just to give you an idea of what she's like, one of my clients told me my letters were going out with the salutation, "Dear Gentleperson." I don't care if she is a liberated woman. My clients have conservative attitudes and so do I. I told her she had no right taking this liberty without my permission, and from now on my letters would say, "Dear Gentlemen." Well, she simply refused to see it my way and even had the gall to bring up other issues that were not satisfactory to her.

The attorney's wife, who was also sitting with us at the table, said, "I'd just fire her."

The attorney responded, "That's just my point. I can't. The fact of the matter is she's too good to fire. She's the best secretary I've ever had. I'm just going to have to get used to her." This secretary obviously does not have a Pleaser. It is important to note that she has confidence in her ability to stand up for her beliefs.

Even more important, her boss respects her competence to do the job right. With Pleaser you run the risk of paying so much attention to being liked that your performance is overshadowed. It is not a personal issue between this attorney and his secretary. He is not threatened by a subordinate challenging him, and she is not intimidated by his authority into compromising her professionalism. If you, as an employee, can leave Pleaser out of the office, your work life will be far less stressful.

PLEASER AND HEALTH

Do nice guys finish last, or do the meek inherit the earth? Does the squeaky wheel get the grease, or should you turn the other cheek? These questions will confront your Pleaser daily. For some people, these conundrums might be nothing more than an intellectual exercise. For Pleaser, they represent a source of stress.

Pleaser will put you in the very difficult position of trying to survive in the world without openly expressing basic needs such as the need to be acknowledged as a force in the world, the need to express strong emotions (anger, fear, and anxiety), and the need to be loved and accepted. Pleaser looks to others to supply these needs instead of looking within. Even if you can keep up the facade of being content with your life, you can't lie to your body about your inner turmoil. Pleaser carries a heavy burden of guilt, resentment, and depression which wears you down and limits your effectiveness. Pleaser puts you under stress by trying to keep the real you hidden from the world. This can be a deadly game.

Pleaser usually raises havoc with your stomach. Many participants of our programs link stomach problems to their predominance of Pleaser behavior. Personal discomfort states commonly reported are feelings of guilt, resentment, helplessness, and hopelessness. It's important that you pay attention to the way you feel since feelings are good indicators of how close you are to the Stress Point.

You have reached Pleaser's Stress Point when you experience

resentment after saying yes to others, when you have a legitimate complaint but are afraid to express it, when you feel helpless to get what you want, when you put the needs of others before your own because you feel guilty, or when you repeatedly feel like a victim of circumstance, powerless to change an unpleasant situation. If you can learn to recognize your Stress Points, you can deal directly with some of Pleaser's less serious stress ailments before you end up with a full-blown stress induced disease.

Barry, an advertising account executive, ignored his Stress Points. He was the perfect model of an ulcer-prone personality: ambitious, eager to please, afraid to confront authority, and fearful of expressing his needs. He withheld his anger and chose instead to live with a chronic knot in his stomach from all his resentment.

Barry had worked for an advertising agency for seven years. He was a good employee and was promised a promotion to account supervisor, the goal toward which all his labor had been directed. Two months after the promotion was first mentioned, there was still no sign of it. His boss said nothing and Barry couldn't bring himself to confront him with the issue. He was afraid to annoy him and lose his chances altogether. He complained to friends and coworkers, felt depressed and disappointed. When he was with his boss he tried to hide his anger, but he still hoped. Finally, he couldn't stand it any longer. He decided his new job would never materialize. He gave two weeks' notice and quit without any explanation.

Even after his decision, Barry fumed and boiled inside at his failure. The pain in his stomach grew worse and began to interfere with his home life and interrupt his sleep. When he couldn't tolerate the pain any longer, he went to his physician, who diagnosed a duodenal ulcer. Given the standard treatment of bland diet, antacids, Probanthine, and Valium, Barry felt somehow vindicated by his sickness. Now he was a bona fide victim of stress.

Barry's example is typical of what happens to ulcer victims. The setting and situation may be different, but through it all, Pleaser will be swallowing the frustration and anger causing intolerable stress. Your body can take only so much before it starts turning on you.

Pleaser keeps you hungry for love, hungry for recognition, or hungry to express your own autonomy. This hunger creates resentment that literally gnaws at your stomach, imitating physical hunger. Your unconscious tells your brain that you're hungry, your brain relays the signal to your stomach, and your stomach starts digesting. But it digests itself instead of food. You will literally be eaten up with stress, joining millions of Americans who suffer from ulcers.

When you are unable to assert your rights in order to attain what you feel is your fair share of life, feelings of despair, futility, and hopelessness will plague you. Over time, such feelings can cause physical harm. Psychologically, they can wound. Researchers have found that cancer patients who experience feelings of hopelessness or powerlessness, have a much poorer prognosis than do those who are able to mobilize themselves to resist the disease. Although you may not be suffering from ulcers or cancer, if you are suffering daily bouts with Pleaser, you may be making yourself vulnerable to those diseases that require you to fight, to mobilize your immune system, and assert yourself against the disease.

Whether you are suffering serious illness or are simply disturbed by your inability to stand up and be counted, you really can change. Many people with Pleasers despair at ever being different, especially when family and friends reinforce Pleaser behavior. One woman we met had taken assertiveness training three times, but has been unable to apply it. She told us:

"Oh, the techniques may be fine, but I've never been able to use them. One evening I tried being assertive with my husband and he told me to 'knock that crap off,' and I never tried it again." Clearly, Pleaser was behind her inability to try again. If Pleaser stands in the way of your getting what you want, acknowledge this part of your personality and start to dialogue with it before your health and well-being are seriously affected.

PLEASER GAME PLAN

FAULTY PERCEPTION:	**If you set limits on the amount of work you take on, others will not consider you a team player and you could get fired.**
HANDICAP:	You have difficulty saying "No."
RESULT:	People will take advantage of you at work, and things you once did as a favor will now be expected of you.
NEW PERCEPTION:	People who control their work flow, get more done.
FIRST MOVE:	Get some guidance and direction from your supervisor. Always let others know exactly what your limits are and tell them you will be changing your Pleaser attitudes.
PITFALL:	Pleaser will flail you with guilt for standing up for yourself with anxious reminders that you depend on others for approval and love.
COUNTERMOVE:	Begin saying "NO" to at least one request made on your time per week. Instead of letting someone dump extra work on you that you know you can't complete, negotiate on the spot with him. Make the decision a joint problem; don't take it on as your's exclusively.

FAULTY PERCEPTION:	People love you for what you do for them.
HANDICAP:	You let your children take advantage of you.
RESULT:	Your children will assume you like doing all the dirty work. "Ask Mom, she loves to do laundry." You will start to resent helping your family and lose track of what you do out of love and what you do out of duty.
NEW PERCEPTION:	Getting your children to do their share, teaches them responsibility.
FIRST MOVE:	Sit down with your family and redefine the household rules. Start assigning everyone some household chores you previously did. Begin saying "No" to your kids.
PITFALL:	Pleaser will tell you that you're failing as a parent. You will be tempted to regard yourself as indispensable, and your children will resist giving up their privileges to use you as a short-order cook, chauffeur, and housemaid.
COUNTERMOVE:	Institute talk sessions with your family in which everyone can express feelings about the changes. Let go of the idea that kids should want to pick up their rooms, etc. Set limits on yourself and stop doing ev-

erything for your children. Teach them responsibility by requiring they assume responsibility.

Take yourself through this Game Plan by writing down the Faulty Perception and one Handicap caused by your Pleaser. What is the Result? Identify a New Perception for this situation. Determine what your First Move will be. Acknowledge and list a Pitfall you might encounter when you put your First Move into practice. Then figure out a Countermove designed to outmaneuver your Pleaser.

**FAULTY
PERCEPTION:**

HANDICAP:
RESULT:

NEW PERCEPTION:

FIRST MOVE:

PITFALL:

COUNTERMOVE:

Any problems that occur while implementing your Game Plan might be a subject for a dialoguing session with you Pleaser. If so, you now have a specific problem to deal with and focus on.

NEW BEHAVIORS TO RETRAIN PLEASER

What to do . . . *Speak Up*

- Be persistent.

- Let people know what you're thinking, don't expect them to guess.

- Stand up for yourself.

- Be direct.

- Do one thing for yourself each week.

- Confront conflicts early on.

- Express your feelings when others upset you or when you disagree.

- Ask for what you want.

3. SABERTOOTH
Mad at the World

$\mathcal{H}$AVE you ever sat in your car, daydreaming, while waiting for the light to change when suddenly, just as it changes, you are jarred out of your fantasy by the blaring of a horn? The driver of the car behind you is shaking his fist and yelling obscenities. You've just encountered Sabertooth. Sabertooth is like a steaming teakettle with no spout.

With Sabertooth in charge, you'll find it difficult to express anger directly, so it seeps out indirectly, disguised in arguments, sarcastic observations, or caustic statements. Like a volcano, when you let Sabertooth erupt, there's no limit to the damage it can do. Anger and how to deal with it is a key factor in all interpersonal relationships. Teachers want to know how to handle angry kids. Housewives want to find out what to do with irate husbands. Nurses cork their wrath at doctors. Secretaries describe the guerrilla tactics they use on their bosses. Police officers want to know how to keep from exploding when having to present themselves to a hostile public. Getting in touch with Sabertooth is a key to understanding anger.

If you experience free-floating hostility, feel chronically crabby, are irritable and prone to explosive outbursts of rage, you are probably under the influence of Sabertooth. Sometimes you can't even pinpoint the particular person or situation that upset you. "I just feel mad at the world," is a frequent Sabertooth statement. With Sabertooth you'll stalk around all day feeling irritated and carrying a chip on your shoulder. Yet chances are you'll deny your angry feelings if someone confronts you with them. "What do you mean angry!" you say in a bristling tone. "I'M NOT ANGRY!!" Instead of dealing with your anger in a healthy manner, you will either suppress it or blow your top.

Sabertooth often shows up when you're playing recreational sports for "relaxation." A Saturday afternoon tennis match or basketball game with friends can take on the aura of a street fight if you let Sabertooth play with you. We observed an unforgettable Sabertooth display one sunny spring morning while driving past a golf course. A lone golfer had just teed off. The ball made the unfortunate mistake of landing in a water trap. The golfer was infuriated. He dumped the clubs out of his bag in white hot anger and started smashing them against a tree. Under Sabertooth's control, this man was displacing his anger on the most convenient target, the tree.

Unfortunately, children often become Sabertooth's victims. When you've suppressed your anger all day, all week, or all month and can no longer contain it, home seems the safest place to vent it. One man told us he felt so angry one afternoon that when he drove home and saw his kids' bikes lying in the driveway, he drove over them, smashing the bikes to pieces. In every workshop we conduct, young mothers talk about their explosive outbursts toward their small children and the feeling of shame and embarrassment that accompanies such episodes. Sabertooth outbursts are frequently followed by remorse and guilt, especially when those who get the backlash of your Sabertooth temper are innocent victims. If you're wondering whether or not Sabertooth expresses your anger, just ask yourself if you feel bad afterward. If it was a Sabertooth outburst, you will. Because of this guilt, you will try even harder to keep the lid on your temper, adding to the stress caused by this personality.

Sabertooth behavior is easy to identify in others. In its more obvious forms it can be seen in the person who fumes while waiting in lines. Cynicism is another of Sabertooth's characteristics. Think of someone who constantly belittles those in government, fellow workers, associates, and even friends. In its subtler forms, Sabertooth stress behavior shows up as extreme jealousy, in hostile competitiveness, moodiness, or pouting.

Sabertooth is also a protective behavior. It's the part of ourselves that feels responsible for seeing that others don't take advantage of us. It emerges if you let your Pleaser handle things too often. "Ok, that's enough," seethes Sabertooth. "No more letting people screw us over." The result is often an explosive outburst which catches someone by complete surprise.

Sabertooth can make you unpredictable. People complain that one minute you display a pleasant disposition and the next, you bite their head off. This Stress Personality will keep you on a seesaw of unpredictability that can easily cause you to lose friends and influence people negatively.

The signs of Sabertooth behavior are unmistakable. Let's look now at how this behavior develops from childhood. How and why do we cut our Saberteeth?

"Mom was what you'd call 'Hell on Wheels,' " Jane starts out, remembering her family's experience with a Sabertooth mother. "You really had to tiptoe around the house." Sabertooth family life is usually characterized by a lot of tension. Our research shows that many people who develop a Sabertooth grew up with a mother or father who had a dominant Sabertooth personality. A child raised in this kind of atmosphere learns at an early age that anger is a powerful weapon that can be used to manipulate people. Angry interchanges between family members cause fear that someone might get hurt. If the family is under the thumb of a dictator who rules with an iron hand, the child learns that one wrong move and he'll "get it." You'd think that after growing up under these conditions, one would want to live differently as an adult. Unfortunately, this behavior follows you into adulthood until you learn to recognize and change it.

Sabertooth behavior develops in children who want but can't express anger at home because their parents believe anger is synonymous with aggression, and they don't allow it. Thus, anger or resistance from children is suppressed or "corrected." Children are admonished with "don't talk back to me" or "take that scowl off your face and go to your room." Even though children may have legitimate grounds for being upset with a parent, they are conditioned to hold anger in check or suffer the unpleasant consequences of adult power over them. Lost is the appropriate channel for the child to express anger in order to form an intimate growth communication between parent and child. The child's angry feelings need an outlet, which is found in fighting with schoolmates or acts of vandalism. The issue is further complicated when a Sabertooth parent uses violence as a disciplinary measure to punish the child's physical aggression. Here is an example:

In this household, Dad is moody, unpredictable, and given to outbursts of rage. He doesn't like his job much, but he feels he can't get anything else. He is often cross with co-workers, complains most of the time about his job, and makes sarcastic comments about his boss's abilities, but not directly to the boss, of course. He goes to work unhappy every day. His irritation builds up so that by the end of the day he is in a very unpleasant mood. Mom likes to keep the household quiet and smooth so that Dad will not get upset when he comes home. At dinner, the children are tense. Dad is just waiting for one of them to get out of line. Sammy and his brother Tim are restless. One kicks the other accidentally under the table. Retaliation inevitably occurs and a glass of milk spills on the table. Dad's Sabertooth fuse has been lit. He explodes at the boys, who are trying to blame the accident on each other. As his fury grows, he orders them to their room with accompanying whacks. Once in their room, the boys take their frustration out on each other while they listen to Dad yell at Mom, who is unsuccessfully trying to pacify him. Even though this scenario is played out over and over, Dad doesn't understand why the neighbors and teachers complain about the boys' behavior. They stand stiff and docile as he addresses them in his drill sergeant manner. He threatens them with punishment if they don't come right home from school, if they get poor grades, or if they talk back to him. But when the boys are out of his jurisdiction, they get into frequent fights, break other children's toys, or the neighbor's windows. What Dad never figured out was that the boys were expressing their anger at him, and using his own techniques. Bullying, causing trouble in school, or mistreating animals are common childhood Sabertooth behaviors. Others include pouting, dragging the feet when asked to do chores, or constantly picking on other siblings. The common thread is an indirect expression of anger in ways that the child finds acceptable or possible.

There are a variety of ways children can express Sabertooth anger, and many reasons why they do. It might be done as an attention-getting effort so that a seemingly disinterested parent will take notice. One young man described how he handled his jealousy over his mother's boyfriends:

"I would always be ignored when they came over, so I would throw tantrums, steal their hubcaps, or start fires in the backyard. There were no limits on what I would do to get attention." He later pointed out that both his mother and her boyfriends tended to focus on his misdeeds rather than looking behind the behavior for the cause.

Some parents encourage Sabertooth behavior, especially with boys. An example is the father who encourages his son to fight "to make a man out of him." One young man described how he and his brother were made to fight out their disagreements with fists while their dad stood by silently approving.

However, children can be taught about anger in a healthy

way. Curt's story is a good example of this. "My son and I were home alone one weekend while my wife was away at a conference. One day when I felt particularly rushed, I gave him some money to go buy us hamburgers and milkshakes. He began putting his shoes on and, like most nine-year-olds, he was dawdling with his head somewhere in the clouds while tying his shoes. I became impatient at his snail's pace, and I grabbed the money out of his hand and went to get the hamburgers myself. When I got outside, I began to have second thoughts. I had violated his autonomy and displayed a behavior I didn't like. I went back into the house and apologized, returning the money to him. He wrinkled up the bills, and with tears streaming down his cheeks, threw the money back at me, saying, "Keep your money!" At that moment I realized the importance of this encounter. I never would have dared do such a thing to my father. My initial reaction was that kids shouldn't do this and that he should be punished. But I hesitated, realizing that his anger was in response to my behavior. So I said to him, "I'm willing to listen to your anger, but it is not OK for you to throw the money at me." We sat and talked about our feelings and about anger in a way we never had before. It was one of the most moving experiences of my life, and it certainly drew us closer." Curt had been able to interrupt a behavior pattern that he learned in his own family; i.e., don't talk back to Dad and vent anger in such a way. In doing so he provided his son with a completely new view of anger and how to express it. Instead of being a Sabertooth model for his son, he set a precedent of honesty and caring that provided a model of strength and tenderness.

A basic Sabertooth Faulty Perception is that the world is hostile. In order to survive you must maintain a position as adversary, always on guard against the manipulations of others. Believing this, you develop an attitude of fear without admitting to the fear directly. You desire intimacy and closeness but are threatened by them. No one, especially those with some authority over you, ever knows where you really stand. This is a high stress position to maintain, and the energy it takes to hold these feelings back is exhausting. The fear or inability to express anger directly accumulates like water behind a dam. Because Sabertooth tells you that expressing anger clearly and openly will leave you vulnerable to retaliation, you store the accumulated anger and the accompanying stress until the next break in the dam, which can come with the slightest provocation.

Sabertooth may seem the most difficult to control of all the Stress Personalities. Ironically, however, compared to Pleaser, Sabertooth is much easier to change. Others support and reinforce changes in Sabertooth behavior but are rarely upset or put off by the effects of Pleaser. Sabertooth is a protective behavior, normal to all of us. Once, and not that long ago in our evolutionary history, we could get rid of aggression by fighting like Sabertooth Tigers. But today we must find more acceptable ways to channel these feelings, without biting off the head of anyone who looks about ready to infringe on our rights or take advantage of us. The first step is to learn that anger is as natural an emotion as hunger, love, or joy. It is not a deadly sin to be suppressed and hidden away. But those using Sabertooth as a primary way to deal with their anger need to find ways to disconnect from their rage. It cannot be locked up indefinitely without causing you stress. After you take your Sabertooth Assessment, you will have a clearer idea of how strongly this Stress Personality affects you.

Assessing Your Sabertooth Behavior

Assess your own Sabertooth behavior. Answer honestly, choosing one of the four responses and placing the corresponding number in the box opposite each question. Add up the score and place the total along the Stress Behavior scale. Pay attention to those questions on which you scored a 6 or 8. If your total score is 48 or greater, you are engaging in Sabertooth behavior to the extent that it will be significantly disruptive to your life.

(Almost always=8)   (Frequently=6)   (Sometimes=4)

(Occasionally=2) (Never=0)

1. ( )   How often do you get into arguments with coworkers?
2. ( )   How often do you hold grudges?
3. ( )   Are you fearful of being manipulated by management or fellow employees?
4. ( )   When working on groups or committees, do you become uncooperative and disinterested when you don't get your way?
5. ( )   Do you clam up, pout or "freeze-out" people when you're angry?
6. ( )   Do you lose your temper when those you supervise or work with challenge your directives?
7. ( )   When playing recreational sports, do you fly off the handle if you do not play your best?
8. ( )   How often do you experience angry impatience with your children?
9. ( )   Are you concerned about losing control of your temper?
10. ( )   Is sarcasm a common mode of expression for you?
11. ( )   When driving your car, how often do you get angry at other drivers?
12. ( )   Do you think that to show warm or tender feelings is a sign of weakness?

    ( )   TOTAL

0	48	96

SABERTOOTH FRIEND

Sabertooth has trouble distinguishing between friend and foe, and will make you suspicious of even your best friends. Sabertooth requires that friends pass a loyalty test. This means they better support you no matter what. If a friend fails that test Sabertooth will encourage you to "forgive but never forget." This attitude can get you in trouble. An outburst toward a friend who cares about you can be very stressful for both you and the friend. You may find yourself apologizing and if you're lucky and it's not too late, the friendship can be saved.

If you're wondering why you have any friends at all, the answer is easy. Your friends know you under more than one circumstance and like the person you are when Sabertooth isn't around. In fact, they'd like to know you better, but Sabertooth interferes by putting other people on the defensive.

Even an old friend can be exasperated by Sabertooth's confounding style. John has planned to attend a reunion picnic of some old friends. Secretly, he's been looking forward to the occasion all week, but he's kept it to himself since Sabertooth keeps reminding him that it's silly to get nostalgic over old friends. When the day arrives, he starts thinking about the people who are going to be there, and a sense of excitement develops. When he arrives, the frivolity has already begun and the group is as lively as it was in college. After the hugs and kisses, John sits down and opens a beer. An old friend, Sheila, sits down next to him.

"Hi, John, it's so good to see you. I was hoping you'd be here."

"Yeah, same here," John replies. "How was your vacation?"

"Oh, Gary and I had a fantastic time in Hawaii."

"So, the old hippy finally broke down and took you there, huh?"

"John, let's not start that again. Gary is a respectable CPA. Growing a beard does not make him a hippy."

"OK, OK, don't get sore. So, did you do anything interesting?"

"Yes, instead of staying at hotels, we decided to camp in the state park on the Kona coast. It was beautiful, and we saw things we never would have otherwise."

"I bet you did. Did you know that state park is crawling with hippies? They live in the jungle like animals with no clothes and no sewage facilities. Now if a man wants to live in the jungle like an animal, that's his business. But the people of Hawaii are fed up with it and I DON'T BLAME THEM! FURTHERMORE . . . "

"John, what are you mad at?"

"I'm not mad."

"Are you mad at me?"

"Of course not. What are you trying to do? Start an argument?"

"No, no, I don't want to do that. Anyway we had a terrific time and it was very economical."

"It may have been very economical, but it wasn't very smart."

"What do you mean?"

"That park in which you stayed is in a jungle that is full of poisonous snakes. Didn't you know that?"

"Oh, that's not true. We checked that out before we left and the ranger confirmed it. There are no poisonous snakes in Hawaii."

"Well, that ranger is an idiot. That area is full of poisonous snakes."

"John, there was even a sign that read 'NO POISONOUS SNAKES.' "

"Are you kidding? What's the matter with you, Sheila? Do you think a snake is going to read a sign?"

"John, I don't want to discuss this any further," says Sheila, losing her aplomb. "THERE ARE NO POISONOUS SNAKES IN HAWAII!"

"Hey hey, take it easy," John tries to calm her. "Say, did you know you've got a temper? You'd better watch that."

By this time, everyone at the picnic table is on edge. They couldn't avoid hearing the conversation. Even the people at the next table have been disquieted. A couple of people laugh nervously. "Hey," he tries again, "what's everybody so quiet about?

Sheila and I were just having a little fun. Weren't we, Sheila? We understand each other, don't we?" Sheila nods numbly. Emotionally, Sheila feels as if she's been picked up and thrown down to the ground. John's Sabertooth has taken a sharp nip out of her hide and she wants to get away from him. He's obviously alienated everyone else as well.

When you let Sabertooth take over, your friends may feel batted around like a Ping-Pong ball. One minute you want to get close, and the next, you're too close for comfort. Out comes Sabertooth, and your friends are left wondering what went wrong. Why did John react like that to Sheila? Maybe it was the kiss she gave him before she sat down. Maybe it was the warmth she exuded. In any event, Sabertooth was threatened. Nothing makes Sabertooth back away like too much affection.

This "come close-stay away" syndrome is characteristic of the Sabertooth Stress Personality. You may want deep relationships more than anything, but Sabertooth fears manipulation. So off-color stories or subtle put-downs become a replacement for the affection you're afraid to demonstrate. Don't let Sabertooth fool you into believing that jokes and sarcasm are good substitutes for intimacy. Most people, while they may laugh or throw a barb back in your direction, do not feel nourished by such exchanges. In fact, your friends will start to feel on guard when you're around. Since they never know when they will be the brunt of one of your jokes, to protect themselves they will presume everything you say is a joke, and you'll never be taken seriously, even when you want to be.

Once friends make excuses for you like "Don't pay attention to Philip. He's just a lot of hot air," or "You'll just have to take her with a grain of salt," you can be fairly sure Sabertooth is running your social life. Don't be fooled by someone who laughs or plays along with you either. He may have a Pleaser and be covering up his feelings. Others may be afraid to come right out and say "I didn't like that," for fear of igniting your Sabertooth. Look at your intentions if you want to see if Sabertooth is dominating your actions. If your only goal is to entertain and be humorous, Sabertooth is not in the picture, but if your impulse is to sting, win, or create an undercurrent of rancor, Sabertooth is doing the talking. Ask yourself what it is about the person or situation that is disturbing you. Why do you feel the need to cut your friends to the quick under the guise of humor? Discover your ulterior motives and then deal with them straightforwardly. Direct your feelings to the real targets. Although you may want closeness, Sabertooth mistrusts intimacy and you'll have to face that issue or be without real friends.

People may want to see you, but they don't want to see Sabertooth. Friends will hesitate to ask you over with people who don't already know you because they're worried how your Sabertooth will react. Trying to set you up with a partner for a dinner party is not an easy task. The planning stages might go something like this:

"Let's see, who would be a good match for Maureen? Not Laurence, he's too sensitive. He'd take her too seriously. Certainly not Paul. They'd be swinging at each other somewhere between the salmon and the chocolate mousse. Maybe Jack, he's so good-natured. If she flared up, it probably wouldn't bother him." So you might end up with quiet Jack and spend another evening with someone who won't speak up to you. Your Sabertooth won't be threatened, but you'll end up bored.

If you're at the other end of a relationship, trying to maintain a friendship with someone dominated by Sabertooth can be a stressful experience. Larry shared an experience with us that he had with Ralph, an old friend. Larry was going through some serious life changes. His marriage had broken up, he was in a new job, and he had moved to another city. Feeling uprooted and anxious, he went to Ralph for some support and kind words. But Ralph's Sabertooth got in the way. This is how Larry reported feeling:

"Maybe I've changed, but Ralph's behavior has become more and more difficult for me to tolerate. We've always related to each other with bantering and teasing, but I believed there was more. I always considered us more like brothers. I thought he was one in whom I could confide when there was a problem. I was wrong. All I got was cynicism and sarcasm. That sort of friendly antagonism doesn't interest me anymore, especially when I am feeling low. I don't know whether or not to tell him about how uncomfortable I feel when I'm around him."

Larry was experiencing a familiar dilemma. How do you handle a Sabertooth friend? Should he tell Ralph how ill at ease he felt and face further bellicose behavior or just let the friendship go? Since he wanted to keep the friendship, he decided to confront Ralph with his feelings.

"My worst fears came true. Ralph got very nasty and accused me of trying to analyze him like some "cheap" psychologist. He didn't see anything wrong with his behavior despite my protests that I wasn't judging him. That provoked him even more. 'Judge me? Who the hell are you to judge?' he shouted. Finally, he informed me that he was satisfied with himself, and if I didn't like it, I could go to hell. It was a very disturbing meeting. I feel sad about it. It looks as if an old friendship has gone down the drain."

In defending himself so vigorously, Ralph displayed one of the obstacles in dealing with Sabertooth behavior. Although Sabertooth's intent is to protect you from some perceived threat, it often isn't clear what that threat is. Good friends are the ones to discuss your Sabertooth behavior with. Tell them what makes you angry and how. Maybe they will even have some suggestions. Bring up the subject of anger when you are feeling calm and relaxed. Discuss ways to express anger with each other and then try them out. Help your friends by explaining that you need them to react with assertiveness and firmness when Sabertooth rears its head toward them.

Ask them to tell you that your behavior is not all right with them, and to tell you with conviction. Sabertooth's bark is usually much worse than its bite. Furthermore, it is a distancing behavior, and if you and your friends recognize it as such, it is much easier to deal with.

Sabertooth behavior can be overcome with persistence and a willingness to take a serious look at yourself. First of all, if you learn to express anger at the moment of provocation by simply saying, "I feel angry," you will begin to de-fang Sabertooth. This approach works especially well with friends who are willing to help you. You need to stop seeing the world as an adversary, and you should allow friends to tell you when your behavior bothers them. Remember, and tell your Sabertooth this: "Friends are vital. We all need enriching friendships, and they can be an important factor in reducing stress levels." Don't let Sabertooth get in the way of these important links in your life.

SABERTOOTH MATE

A recent Dear Abby letter was written by a woman who signed her name, "End of my Rope." In the letter she wanted to know what to do about her husband, who constantly beat her and mistreated the children. She told Abby how she would threaten to leave him, but each time he would tearfully beg her forgiveness, promising never to lay a finger on her again. Of course, the promise was short-lived and he was back to his fiercely jealous, hot-tempered, and violent self within a week.

"End of my Rope" was married to a man with a dangerously out-of-control Sabertooth. While this behavior is totally unacceptable in primary relationships, many lesser forms of Sabertooth abuse are common. Belittling your mate in front of friends and apologizing in private is one example of this type of abuse. Walking out in the heat of anger and leaving the spouse frantic and concerned is another. By definition, a loved one is someone you'll let into your inner circle. You are presumably willing to risk being vulnerable with this person because you value him or her enough to take a chance. The fear of being manipulated or taken advantage of by loved ones is greater since there is an important commitment involved. Sabertooth is threatened by such a commitment, so this Stress Personality sits just outside of consciousness waiting for you to get hurt or disappointed. Then out it comes — fangs bared and snarling, daring your mate to get closer. Your partner may become very confused and disheartened, interpreting your Sabertooth's messages as, "You don't love me. You just couldn't treat me this way if you did."

"End of my Rope's" husband is a good example of how Sabertooth is just one part of the self. His remorse and tearful expressions of regret are probably genuine. "End of my Rope" forgives him because she sees another contrite feature of her husband's personality. However, Sabertooth is just too powerful, so he's soon back terrorizing the one he loves.

Because Sabertooth behavior involves a fear of being hurt, it frequently appears as ambivalence. This was clear in Dave and Carol's relationship. They had been going together for three years and were to be married soon. Dave took the initiative to make wedding plans and set the date, but his Sabertooth kept interfering. Whenever Dave and Carol sat down to talk about the issue, Sabertooth found a way to inflame the subject. Deep down, Dave's Sabertooth was afraid of being trapped in a relationship he couldn't handle. When Carol talked about their future together, Dave began to feel annoyed.

"We ought to have children when we're young," reasoned Carol. "That way we'll be able to keep up with them."

Dave balked. "Lets not rush into this. We'll have to save money for a few years, which means we'll both have to work. I don't want to get stuck supporting you and kids before I'm ready." Dave felt irritation building up. Sabertooth was afraid that Carol would be too dependent on him. The phrase "getting stuck" was the tip-off.

Carol was hurt that he would consider supporting their family as being "stuck."

"Well, of course, I'll do my part," she replied, but you said you wanted to have children."

"I do, I do," Dave countered, getting a little more irked. "It's just that you want to rush into things. How do I know I can keep my job? What if I get transferred? Children are an enormous responsibility. You never seem to consider that."

Carol realized that Dave was getting upset, so she changed the subject. "I think we ought to buy a house as soon as we can afford it."

"I don't know," replied Dave, "that takes a lot of money. Who do you think will be responsible for making all the payments if we've got kids?" Dave was feeling edgy now. Sabertooth was telling him that he was crazy to get committed.

"What if we get a divorce? You know what will happen — women always get everything. She'll get the house, the car — she could really take you to the cleaners."

"A house is a good investment," said Carol.

"For whom?" asked Dave, his voice rising. "For you maybe, but what if things don't work out? What then?" Why do you have such a negative attitude?"

"I'm not negative," shouted Dave. "Just because I want to be practical doesn't mean I'm negative, for God's sake." Carol wondered aloud if he still loved her.

"Of course I do," retorted Dave hotly. "I wouldn't be talking about these things if I didn't, would I?"

"Why are you bristling so?" asked Carol.

"I'm not bristling," he said heatedly. "It's just that you are always accusing me of being thin-skinned and I am sick of it."

Carol retreated, feeling cut off and a little shaken at the intensity of the outburst.

Now Dave felt remorse. "I'm sorry. I do love you but I just think we ought to be more cautious."

Carol began to doubt the idea of marriage. Would he always be like this?

Sensing her concern, Dave made a peace offering. "Let's talk about this tomorrow when we've both cooled down."

Carol felt a familiar sense of confusion. "What do you mean 'both' cool down? I wasn't the one hot under the collar!"

Dave felt another surge of anger. His Sabertooth wanted to accuse her of starting another argument, but he struggled to hold the feeling back. His pulse was throbbing and his heart began to ache. A wave of sadness passed through him and he thought to himself, "There I go again, screwing things up." Aloud he said, "I promise we'll discuss this tomorrow when we both — when I feel better."

Carol agreed, but some of her glow was gone. The warm and tender evening had ended tense and distant. "Maybe he's right," she thought to herself. "Maybe this marriage is a bad idea." Once again Dave's Sabertooth personality had succeeded in creating the distance that seemed necessary for his protection.

Sabertooth can be really hard on your love life. It deprives you and your loved one of the tender feelings you'd like to share and puts your heart in a tug-of-war. You feel ambivalent and confused when you have strong feelings for someone but can't express them. Contrary to what Sabertooth believes, you can't experience love in its totality without revealing yourself. The next time you are aware of holding back what you're really thinking, try talking about what you're feeling instead. This is not a position of weakness, but one of strength. And it will really make a difference in your relationship. If Sabertooth plagues your love life, you're used to biting your tongue to stop from saying things you'll later regret. For example, you can get in trouble by accusing your mate of flirting. But if you admit that you have jealous feelings, you are promoting intimacy. Accusations produce defensive reactions. Acknowledging feelings opens yourself and allows your mate to offer concern, warmth and sympathy. Once you let down Sabertooth's protective armour, you might even be willing to share something you never would have shared before. You'll soon learn that this "top secret" data isn't as threatening or embarrassing as it seemed. If Sabertooth doubts the wisdom of this, ask if there could possibly be anything more threatening or embarrassing than your dramatic outbursts that are the result of trying to suppress these feelings. That should keep Sabertooth quiet for a while.

Anger in a relationship ought to be expressed as naturally as pleasure, but the anger must be expressed appropriately so that fights produce growth, not just stress. Any honest communication, even of anger, can cement the bonds of intimacy between two people. Disagreement and resolution are normal and need only disrupt harmony temporarily unless one party has a strong Sabertooth personality. Then, an ordinary skirmish can turn into a civil war. When both partners resort to Sabertooth behavior to deal with a crisis, stress reaches critical levels.

Let's say you have had a disagreement with your husband. Perhaps you feel he is being unreasonable, and you are irritated by what he's done. Instead of letting him know, you withhold the irritation. In predictable Sabertooth fashion you begin to feel like retaliating. Maybe Sabertooth is telling you, "See? You can't trust him. He's selfish and spoiled." You become distant and aloof. Your mate picks up your vibrations, and his Sabertooth advises him that if you are going to pout, you should be ignored. "Don't reinforce her childish behavior." Before long, the atmosphere between the two of you is tense.

Nevertheless, you decide to go to a party in the hope that it will lift both your spirits. Once there, you quickly move off and mingle with others. It seems nice to converse with someone who isn't mad at you. After a couple of drinks you start to relax and it's easier to talk. Alcohol not only lowers inhibitions, but it also has a way of letting Sabertooth out of its cage. When you look around for your spouse and notice him talking to a pretty stranger, he seems to be enjoying himself a little too much. Your anger wells to the point of rage. Your unresolved disagreement is leading you into a potentially ugly scene. You march over to him and in a strained voice say, "I want to talk to you."

"What about?"

"Alone," you growl. "I want to talk to you alone."

The other woman, quickly getting the picture, begins to edge away. Your husband, whose inhibitions have also been lowered by a few drinks, becomes irritated. "I'll talk to you later," he says, turning back to the pretty stranger, who is really uncomfortable by now and looking for a way to escape. At this point, a number of Sabertooth possibilities emerge: (1) you could grab your husband by the arm and drag him out of the party, (2) you could start screaming at each other, (3) you could turn away coldly, vowing never to speak to him again, (4) you could leave him with the pretty stranger and dedicate the rest of the party to finding someone for yourself, (5) you could get really drunk, or (6) you could ignore him until you get home and then really let him have it.

These options, of course, are guaranteed to increase the stress level that is already percolating. Had you resolved the original issue, you'd never have reached this point. Solving problems before they turn into major battles means negotiating without Sabertooth. In the long run, you can protect yourself much better by expressing your concerns, anger, or fears from a nondefensive position. Sabertooth wants to protect you from getting hurt, but doesn't do a very good job. You wind up emotionally battered in the end.

Sabertooth thinks that losing a fight is intolerable, but in truth nothing can erode a love relationship faster than this belief. When you and your mate tangle, Sabertooth's presence means no holds are barred. This Stress Personality is a dirty fighter who doesn't hesitate to hit below the belt, and when your feelings are hurt, Sabertooth will go to any extreme to get back at the one who hurt you. Once damage is done from this position it is not easy to repair. Sabertooth may accuse your partner of unfounded infidelity and threaten to kick him out and take the children away. Name-calling or even violence may result. When Sabertooth throws the lance, the wound is deep and doesn't heal quickly. Even when all seems patched up, a rift may remain that can take months to close.

You can tell if your fights are growth-producing or growth-stunting by the way you feel afterward. When you are straightforward with your anger, refrain from name-calling, and deal with your feelings about what occurred, you will feel closer, relieved at having said what was on your mind. If you use Sabertooth to fight your battles, you will probably experience guilt for having lost control, as well as pain and sadness. Sabertooth will also try to convince you that it is OK to take out your angry, aggressive feelings on your partner. "After all," says Sabertooth, "you know your mate loves you and won't leave."

One man told us, "I don't know if this is right or not, but I relieve my stress by yelling at my wife. She really gets it when I have a bad day." Another man reported, "I don't dare show the slightest anger with my wife or she blows up."

When you take out your anger inappropriately, you rob yourself of the soothing, caring, and supportive actions your mate could give you that would lower your stress level and bring you closer together. It is highly unlikely that you will be folded in loving arms, reassured, or given a back rub in return for abusive treatment. You must give each other the freedom to express angry feelings healthily and openly.

Encourage your partner to help you by setting some ground rules as to how you'll discuss volatile issues and express anger. For your part, don't squelch your spouse's opinion or let him/her live in fear. To counter Sabertooth, you'll need help. Many years ago, we heard a psychologist answer a woman's call on a radio talk show. She had said that her husband made fun of her in front of friends. She had asked him repeatedly not to do it because it hurt her feelings and humiliated her, but he persisted. She wondered what she could do to stop it. When the psychologist asked her if she really wanted to get rid of this behavior in her husband, she replied without hesitation, "Yes."

"All right," said the psychologist, "here's what you do. Tell your husband that the next time he makes a joke at your expense in front of friends, you are going to comment on it right when it happens by saying, 'Fred, I told you it embarrasses me when you make jokes about me and I don't like it.' If he does it again, remind him again and say it in front of everyone. Then tell him that the next time he does it you are going to comment on it and get up and walk out." She hesitated. He asked her again, "Do you really want your husband to stop that behavior?" At that point she said she would do it. We couldn't agree more with this advice.

In dealing with Sabertooth behavior in a loved one, be firm, direct, and make yourself unmistakably clear. It is important not to hide your feelings when Sabertooth outbursts hurt them. It is also important to be consistent in expressing your position, beliefs, and anger. Remember, there is another facet of your spouse's personality that is not Sabertooth. Encourage, support, and cultivate those positive, tender, and more healthy traits. It will help manage Sabertooth behavior.

SABERTOOTH BOSS

"I don't have ulcers, I give them." That's the motto of the Sabertooth boss. In nearly every seminar we give for managers, we hear this. It is usually accompanied by a defiant smile as if the unspoken addendum were, "So what are you going to do about it?" The statement is as inaccurate as it is revealing. People don't get ulcers from someone else; they give them to themselves. What is unsettling about this remark is that the speaker clearly has a strong Sabertooth and relishes the fact. A boss taken over by Sabertooth rules rather than supervises. Although Sabertooth behavior can be an effective way to intimidate and thus control employees, the work environment will not be a pleasant place to spend eight hours.

"I spent eighteen tortuous months working for a supervisor with an out-of-control Sabertooth," relates Herb, a federal employee. "He could be warm and friendly one day and a growling beast the next. He was rigid and very controlling. He was also very mediocre, though he worked longer hours than the rest of us, a fact he broadcast loud and often. He liked to intimidate the staff and frequently threatened to fire one or more of us. Someone was always getting written up or verbally assaulted. Then he would turn around and be pleasant to the person he had reamed out and act as if he were doing you a favor by saying, 'I threw the reprimand in the wastebasket. Just see to it that I don't have to write you up another one.' Fortunately for my sanity, I was transferred out of there."

Herb's description fits any number of situations that exist in a work setting dominated by a Sabertooth boss. Sabertooth believes that in order to keep employees in line, one must always keep them in a state of fear. "If they see a chink in your armor," says Sabertooth, "you're finished." This belief makes it next to impossible to change your mind or admit a mistake. You feel you don't have the option to say, "Look, I've made a hasty decision and I'd like to reconsider." This prevents you from being flexible in dealing with employees. Should a subordinate ask to try a new approach on a project, your automatic answer will be "No" if Sabertooth has anything to say about it. Later you may even change your mind when you've thought it over without Saber-tooth, but your employee's confidence will be shakier the second time he approaches you. Because Sabertooth is so concerned that you and only you be the source of power, you will have trouble delegating responsibility for fear it may erode your authority. The picture is pretty clear: things will be done your way or not at all.

An underlying current of volatility pervades Sabertooth's office. Since no one knows what will happen next, the tension in the department is constant, affecting everyone's job performance and creativity. Since you, as a Sabertooth boss, are easily exasper-ated when asked to repeat directives or give an explanation, uncer-tainty and fear of eliciting your anger can inhibit the employee who requires some gentle, persistent help and guidance. If the employee does muster the courage to ask a question and then doesn't understand the answer, chances are he'll say, "Oh yeah, I get it. Sure, sure, this is simple. Yes, well OK, I think I'll be going now," just to avoid lighting your fuse. The employee beats a hasty retreat, afraid to admit to not learning anything from your expla-nation. You may even sense this, but what can you do? You've got other duties. So you shake your head and wonder why it's so hard to get decent help these days, only vaguely aware of the tightness in your chest. The worst possible encounter is between boss and employee, both of whom are Sabertooth-dominated. Nothing triggers Sabertooth behavior more than another Sabertooth. The friction may be subtle, because the subordinate will probably have enough sense not to challenge the boss directly, but the Sabertooth behavior will come out in abrasiveness, seething resentment, or endless arguments. The Sabertooth employee usually loses the battle and goes underground, letting anyone who's interested know what a disagreeable, rigid, rotten boss he has. If you are a party to a situation like this, deal with this employee directly without letting his gripes hook your Sabertooth. Don't take the problem personally or get defensive. Just get to the root and resolve it. Once people start talking behind your back, office morale breaks down and you start losing the respect of your employees. Stop this domino effect by dealing with issues directly.

As obvious as it seems, many bosses forget that it is difficult for employees to admire someone who is continually losing his cool. While bosses are expected to get angry when there is appropriate cause, it must be done in a constructive manner. If you find that production has slipped, schedules aren't being met, or the sales quotas have dropped, sit down with your staff and talk about it. Ask why job responsibilities aren't getting fulfilled, and get an answer. Offer a new course of action from your Better Judgement, and make it clear, without raising your voice, that you want it followed.

Be aware of those high stress situations that cause your Sabertooth to surface. Very often it may come in response to a situation in which you feel you have little control.

Larry is a unit supervisor of a mobile health team. His responsibilities include managing a multidisciplinary staff of health professionals who travel to remote regions of the state, often for days at a time. There are built-in stresses in his job. Staff shortages are common, and people don't like leaving home for extended periods. They are often overworked, and many times their work is undermined because of inadequate follow-up care. When the atmosphere gets tense, Larry's Sabertooth erupts — usually when he can least afford the interference.

"I become unpredictable, especially when I am traveling. Sometimes the staff is intimidated when I pound the table and raise my voice. I know I can be hard to live with. Yet at other times, I'm easygoing. I really do like everyone on the team. It's just that when things get tense, I don't handle the situation as well as I'd like to, and too often I blow a fuse when I need to be calm and collected. As a result, I've made some big mistakes."

Larry's Sabertooth adds unnecessary stress to an already stressful situation. Sabertooth behavior can cause delays and confusion when your leadership falters. Larry discovered that when his control of a situation was threatened, his Sabertooth was recharged. This need to control others is a very common Sabertooth trait, and, ironically, sometimes this very need is what makes you lose control of yourself. Sabertooth clouds your Better Judgement, sometimes with blind rage, and then you lose your ability to exercise judicious control.

The power struggle with Sabertooth is frequently the hardest to contend with, especially when you are in a position of authority. Sabertooth believes that in order to administrate, you must dominate. You must win at all costs. No one can win all the time; certain situations require compromise. Healthy competition can't be encouraged when Sabertooth boss discourages competition in order to guarantee that he always looks good. What's important is not how you look at any given time, but how your decisions benefit the organization and its personnel. As an administrator, your first responsibilities are to get things done as efficiently as possible and to support the people who work for you. Try to work with your employees both as individuals and as a team.

A costly side effect of Sabertooth behavior in the boss's chair is absenteeism. When the stress level in the office is elevated, employees will be more vulnerable to real and imagined illnesses and start finding reasons to stay away from work. If the office is infected with the boss's hard-nosed competitive nature, there's bound to be some employees snarling at one another. If you want to reduce absenteeism, you have to reduce office stress. Look at your anger and frustration level. Are you a Sabertooth on the job and a pussycat at home? If so, you need to evaluate why you're unhappy in the role of boss. Maybe you don't want to be a boss, or perhaps you feel overwhelmed and would like to ask for help but feel afraid to do so. If you can reduce the intensity you bring to your role as boss, the stress level of the office will be reduced. If you need advice or help, ask for it. Take more people into your confidence, not fewer. Stop mistrusting people because they're potential competitors. You'll only foster their mistrust of you, and you will be perpetuating a vicious circle.

Learn to let go of some of the controls you have on your work force. Delegate more authority so you learn to trust others. When the Sabertooth atmosphere diminishes, production goes up and stress symptoms go down.

SABERTOOTH EMPLOYEE

If you bring Sabertooth to work with you, your popularity among coworkers diminishes fast. Maybe unresolved problems at home are the real reason you're unhappy at work, but the touchiness you display there can rub off on those you work with. Perhaps Sabertooth has convinced you that since coworkers are not as important as your family and loved ones, you can take out your frustration, from whatever source, on them. Everyone you work with will soon become a potential adversary. You'll gain a reputation as uncooperative. In group meetings or conferences, you'll withdraw your attention and energy, look bored, or make sarcastic comments. No one will like to be around you.

If you have a job that deals directly with the public, the consequences of your Sabertooth behavior can be serious. Henry, who was in charge of customer complaints for a utility company, described how his Sabertooth behavior caused him problems on the job:

"There are days when I just can't stand listening to those complaints. My blood begins to boil by midmorning, and as soon as someone insults me or the company, I see red. At my best I control myself, even though I'm shaking with anger. At my worst, I blow my top and the customer complains to management. It never used to be this bad, but since I've had family problems, oh boy."

Henry's first step is to deal with the problems at home or separate them clearly in his mind from his work. Succeeding in this will enable Henry to listen to customer complaints without taking them personally. Complainers may just want to let off steam or express their indignation at the organization. Henry needs to lend a sympathetic ear and let the organization take the rap. "But what," he asked, "about those people who are more interested in stirring up a fuss than they are in resolving their complaint?" Treat them politely but assertively. For example, say, "I know, Mrs. Paulsen, how lousy you must feel about getting overcharged. We will reimburse you as soon as possible." If it's a customer demanding some action that is impossible at the moment, be polite and tell him or her you'll get to it when you can. It is important not to let Sabertooth escalate the tension level between you and the customer. If you're in the customer complaints business, you have to expect complaints. A prize chef, around food all the time, doesn't have to be fat, and a complaint manager doesn't have to be miserable.

With Sabertooth, you may feel trapped by your job. That's because of the alienation and the resultant insecurity Sabertooth creates. While you may hate your job, you may be afraid to quit and that makes you even more unhappy.

Tom, a 33-year-old businessman discovered why he had been so edgy with clients. After his marriage, Tom joined his father-in-law's firm and was given a very responsible position. He seethed inside, however, because his father-in-law wouldn't give him any autonomy. At the same time, he was afraid to tell him how he felt.

"What can I say? I owe everything to Art. Not just because I married his daughter. Art has taught me a lot, but he's so stifling. He wants to know everything I'm doing, why, how, etc., etc. He's not very flexible either. Every day I feel that free-floating hostility you folks talk about. I snap at my secretary, the kids, and just about everybody. Lately, I've been turned off to Ellen sexually. I think I resent her closeness to her dad, but I'm afraid to speak out. What if I blow it and scream at him? That would be disastrous."

If Tom had repressed these feelings much longer, the results would indeed have been disastrous. But Tom chose to talk to his Sabertooth instead. During the dialogue, Tom found out not only that he wasn't happy working for his father-in-law, but that he was afraid to tell Ellen. He was afraid she would neither understand nor support his desire to go out on his own. Finally, he decided to tell her rather than live with the constant pressure. Much to his amazement, his wife was supportive and suggested they both talk to her dad. They had such a productive meeting that Art decided to retire and leave the business to Tom and Ellen.

"Art discovered he was worried too much of the time about the business and was afraid to let go of it," said Tom. "All of my worst fears turned out to be groundless."

If you're a budding entrepreneur, it is vital that you leave Sabertooth out of business dealings. Starting your own business is no easy matter, but if you have a Sabertooth, you can easily view routine setbacks as some sort of "conspiracy" against you. If you are entering a field with a lot of other competitors, be prepared. Sabertooth will try to focus angry energy on the "unfair" competition. Re-channel this energy to stir your creativity and come up with new and different ideas, angles, or products.

Here are clues to identify your Sabertooth behavior at work. If you go to any lengths to get your way, Sabertooth is around. If you overreact to inconsequential issues or are continually uncooperative although you rationalize or deny it, that's Sabertooth. Shifting blame for a project's shortcomings to others is another way in which you alienate fellow workers and cause added stress. You may feel you work harder than anyone else but aren't being rewarded for it, or maybe you feel others are taking advantage of your efforts by sloughing off. These are all signals of Sabertooth behavior. Sabertooth will be quick to blame others for your problems. You find yourself in a double bind because when you abdicate control over the solution of problems, you lose control over your own destiny, the very thing your Sabertooth fears most. You may miss opportunities and fail to advance because you feel paralyzed, unable to act within a system you distrust. "I can't transfer to that department because the supervisor has it in for me." "If I speak out to my boss, my name will be mud in this company, and I'll never get promoted." These are examples of nonproductive Sabertooth blame-shifting tactics.

Don't let Sabertooth shorten your career or make your work life miserable. Focus realistically on what is possible and stop looking at what isn't. It doesn't have to be a dog-eat-dog world unless you insist on clinging to that view.

SABERTOOTH AND HEALTH

Anger is such a loaded emotion that keeping the lid on it requires a lot of energy. There are countless numbers of people walking around like human time bombs. The inability to express anger in a clear, straightforward manner is a leading contributor to a host of emotional and physical, as well as job related, problems.

Not all anger originates from Sabertooth. We all get angry at times, cool off, and then go about our business. Such behavior usually doesn't create a health hazard, but it creates powerful reactions inside your body. Next time you get really angry, pay attention to your body. Your heartbeat increases, your jaws clench, your temples throb, and your muscles tighten. These reactions were originally meant as biological signals to help you ward off danger and survive. But in our civilized society, few of us encounter danger that requires such extreme responses. Yet, anger still triggers these primal reactions. When you use Sabertooth, you will experience these reactions more often than do most people. A traffic jam or your children's behavior can set you off. Sabertooth's response will keep your body in a constant state of high excitation and stress. Contrary to popular belief, getting your anger "out" may not be healthy. If it builds like nuclear fission, you stay angry, hold grudges and plot revenge it can be hazardous to your health. You need to recognize that when this happens, you've reached the Stress Point. You feel irritable from the moment you wake up until you fall into a restless sleep; you feel flashes of hatred and carry grudges like loaded guns; you explode into angry outbursts over trivial provocations and plunge afterward into remorseful despair; you live with constant muscle tension and daily headaches from struggling to stay in control; or you have frequent accidents because of a rash of impulsive behavior. Your physician won't discover these symptoms in a routine medical exam. You need to recognize them and take control before your body becomes Sabertooth's victim.

At the Personal Discomfort end of the Stress Continuum, Sabertooth causes chronic irritability, anxiety, explosive temper outbursts, remorse, hostility, and resentment. Your body is in a constant state of Red Alert, as if you were encountering daily physical threats. Since you cannot combat the sources of your anger with physical force, all your repressed emotion pours back into your body, pushing you closer to the Psychosomatic Illness end of the Stress Continuum.

The chronic nature of Sabertooth presents you with daily reminders of the storm inside you. A principal physical complaint identified with Sabertooth is headaches. One third are of the migraine variety. Migraine is a cardiovascular disorder caused by a period of constriction, followed by dilation of the carotid artery that supplies blood to the brain. It can be a disabling illness and is most prevalent in people who display the Sabertooth characteristics of rigidity, poor judgement, explosive hostility, and a tendency to view relationships with pessimism and suspicion. When your attempts to establish intimate, fulfilling relationships are thwarted by Sabertooth, and you react by pulling back, pouting, and then denying the negative feelings with a cool "Nothing's wrong," you're asking for a headache. Psychologist Ken Pelletier describes this process in the migraine patient: "With patients who suffer from migraine, the initial psychological event seems to be a drawing in and withdrawing of energy from emotional involvements. That person literally ceases to let emotional expression flow out towards others and begins to contain anger. When this becomes habitual, sensations such as coolness in the extremities, clammy hands or feet are reported." (Pelletier, p. 152.) The "drawing-in" process described by Pelletier means that your body tightens up, usually without your being aware of it. This internal animosity creates tension and contributes to the constriction of the carotid artery. If you've ever experienced a migraine, you have probably noticed that it often occurs some time after the incident that provoked you. As you begin to unwind and let the pressure off, the blood starts flowing at a greater velocity. This is when carotid dilation occurs, triggering the intense pain that migraine sufferers know only too well.

Many accidents occur during Sabertooth's hostile preoccupations. This behavior can be lethal if you're driving a car. One man told us he was returning his new car to the dealer for the fourth time in one week. They still hadn't corrected a factory flaw, and he was hopping mad. "I was so busy going over in my mind what I was going to tell that crook, that I missed a four-way stop and plowed into a station wagon. My brand new lemon was totalled. I got a broken nose and lost two teeth. Fortunately the other driver was unhurt. Yeah, my Sabertooth was behind the wheel that day."

Many people let their Sabertooth personalities use the automobile as an extension of their aggression, often with ominous consequences. Sabertooth has the dubious distinction of being responsible for more broken ankles, noses, jaws, legs, and ribs than any other Stress Personality.

Another stress-related condition linked closely to Sabertooth is bruxing, or in common language, teeth grinding, a serious dental problem. Since Sabertooth's anger is not always released during the day, it shows up at night in bruxing. Maybe you are reliving that daytime nightmare when you were reprimanded in front of the entire staff. Your teeth grind back and forth as you clamp down on the angry things you wanted to say on your behalf. Bruxing isn't confined to nighttime, either. You may do it unconsciously during the day in response to something that occurred earlier.

Here is an easy way to determine how much damage your Sabertooth is doing to you. Imagine there is a little buzzer in your head timed to go off exactly when you are engaging in Sabertooth behavior. When the buzzer rings, stop and pay attention to what you are doing. Listen to the tone of your voice. Is it belligerent or sarcastic? Are your temples throbbing, or is your heart beating faster? List all of the symptoms you are experiencing. Then count how many times per day you go through these stress reactions. If it is ten times, then you've had ten imaginary brushes with death that were close enough to set off powerful physical responses designed for defending your life.

With Sabertooth every interaction is a life-and-death affair. When your body follows suit — and these physiological reactions go on for weeks, months or years — the cumulative hardship on your body can be debilitating. One simple visualization that helps defuse Sabertooth is to imagine an electric cord plugged into a socket in your chest. When you feel anger build, stop, take a deep breath and visualize yourself "unplugging" the cord. Being aware and taking active control of this volatile Stress Personality takes patience and practice. But it can save your life.

SABERTOOTH GAME PLAN

FAULTY
PERCEPTION: The world is a hostile, unfriendly place.

In order to survive you must maintain an adversary position toward life.

HANDICAP: You have difficulty expressing anger appropriately.

RESULT: You misplace your anger and direct at innocent parties like your children, spouse or clerks in stores.

NEW
PERCEPTION: Anger can be replaced by assertiveness.

FIRST MOVE: When you feel anger building, deal with the issue that triggered your anger and not the person. Clearly ask for what you want but be willing to negotiate.

PITFALL: Sabertooth will have a tendency to come out against "safe" targets that will be unwilling to retaliate.

COUNTERMOVE: When you're not angry, talk to family members about what makes you angry. Acknowledge your anger openly whenever you feel it even if it's just to yourself. When you experience or express anger, focus the feeling only on the provocation; don't generalize. Do not let anger build inside you. If you talk about it as it occurs, it will not accumulate and you will be less vulnerable to explosions.

FAULTY
PERCEPTION: If you compromise, people will take advantage of you.

HANDICAP:	You will be rigid, suspicious and unwilling to cooperate.
RESULT:	You will tend to view negotiations from a win-lose perspective.
NEW PERCEPTION:	Cooperation and compromise insures that you will get what you want more often.
FIRST MOVE:	Identify what outcome you'd like to see materialize. Is it realistic? Can you get part of what you want? Figure out what would satisfy you not what would satisfy Sabertooth.
PITFALL:	Sabertooth will focus on what you're NOT getting by compromise, and try to sabotage the process.
COUNTERMOVE:	Stay focused on your outcome which is your goal in the negotiation. Tell Sabertooth to butt-out.

Take yourself through this Game Plan by writing down a Faulty Perception and one Handicap caused by your Sabertooth. What is the Result? Identify a New Perception for this situation. Determine what your First Move will be. Acknowledge and list a Pitfall you might encounter when you put your First Move into practice. Then figure out a Countermove to outmaneuver your Sabertooth.

FAULTY PERCEPTION:

HANDICAP:

RESULT:

NEW
PERCEPTION:

FIRST MOVE:

PITFALL:

COUNTERMOVE:

Any problems that occur while implementing your Game Plan might be a subject for a dialoguing session with your Sabertooth. If so, you now have a specific problem to deal with and to focus on.

NEW BEHAVIORS TO RETRAIN SABERTOOTH

What to do . . . *Calm Down*

- Work problems through instead of reacting with anger or aggression.

- Request clarity from others when you're suspicious of their motives.

- Deal with explosive issues when you're calm, at home and at work.

- If the situation you find yourself in is untenable, walk away and don't label yourself a loser.

- Think before you act.

- After arguments with mate, go back and clear matters up when you cool off.

- Beware of holding grudges. They're hazardous to your health.

- Instead of yelling at other drivers, listen to soothing music on your radio.

4. CRITICAL JUDGE
Don't I Ever Do Anything Right?

*Y*OU'VE been sitting in a meeting. The topic is controversial and you'd like to comment. But every time you start to raise your hand, you feel your heart pounding. You feel flushed, and it seems as if an invisible weight is holding your arm down. Finally you shoot your arm up in the air. When called on you say, "This may be a stupid question, but . . ."

Who decided that was a stupid question? Critical Judge. Critical Judge is the sternest of all the Stress Personalities. It is the part of you that believes self-criticism is necessary to your survival. "Why, you wouldn't even get out of bed in the morning if it weren't for me, you lazy bum," says Critical Judge. Since flaw-finding is one of Critical Judge's prime duties, you will always be hearing what you've done wrong. Critical Judge doesn't believe in telling you what you've done right — you should already know that. What's important is to find out what you are doing wrong — so you can be perfect. Perfection is Critical Judge's standard. Anything less than perfection is failure. Not only must you be perfect, you must be perfect at any new endeavor from your first try. "If you can't play the guitar like Andre Segovia after your first lesson, don't bother," says Critical Judge.

No matter what you do, it will never be good enough. Critical Judge's verdict will always be "guilty," and you will be sentenced to feelings of hopelessness, despair, self-loathing, and depression. Critical Judge is convinced that the worse you feel about yourself, the harder you'll work at becoming a perfect human being, but it doesn't work. You can never satisfy Critical Judge. Instead, you are slowed down and paralyzed, unable to try anything new. Why make the effort when you're doomed to fail? You are especially vulnerable to Critical Judge when you are trying to make important decisions such as changing jobs, careers, or spouses. Critical Judge is so negative that you'll feel inadequate to follow through. Your risk-taking will be limited as Critical Judge tries to protect you from failure.

Many of the risks Critical Judge tries to protect you from are minor, as in this example. Imagine you're vacationing at a winter ski resort, complete with a heated outdoor swimming pool, saunas, jacuzzis, and an ice skating rink. Today you and your friend have planned to do a little ice skating. Even though you haven't skated in twenty years, you've been looking forward to it. As you approach the rink, you see that the only person on the ice is Katerina Witt's double, a graceful and accomplished figure skater. At that moment, you hear Critical Judge admonish, "You're not going out on the ice with her. You'll look like a fool." All the excitement you had been feeling evaporates and you lose the desire to skate. You call ahead to your friend, "I don't think I want to skate after all." Your friend goes on to skate anyway, and you are left to watch.

Critical Judge is like a thief robbing you of life's golden opportunities. You become an unhappy spectator. Under Critical Judge's influence you'll lack self-confidence and find it hard to trust yourself. "Oh no, I couldn't go backpacking; I'm too clumsy." "I could never change jobs, who'd hire me?" There is always a negative undertone to anything out of the routine.

Self put-downs are tip-offs to Critical Judge's presence: "I'm certainly not the best-qualified to give this speech, but I'll tell you as much as I know — which isn't much." Speakers with Critical Judges are easy to identify. They're the ones whose voices quaver as they speak or whose hands shake while writing on the blackboard.

The audience has its Critical Judges too. They usually sit in the back of the room and look the speaker up and down. "Would you look at that man's suit and tie? He must have dressed in the dark." "Doesn't that woman have a lisp? You'd think she would have had it perfected if she's in the speaking profession." Critical Judges are the first to detect flaws, no matter how inconsequential. "This is a darling restaurant, but they really cut corners by using cheap fixtures." Critical Judge has an uncanny knack for putting a damper on any occasion. It is always hard to enjoy the positive aspects of life when you are always sniffing out the negative.

Critical Judge can be subtle or blatant. No part of your life will be exempt from its harsh appraisal unless you put your foot down. The way to start is to understand where Critical Judge came from and how it gained such a stronghold over you.

As a child, if you felt you weren't getting enough love, you might have thought you weren't doing enough for your parents or doing things the "right" way. Perhaps they always pointed out your faults, and since, in your mind, your parents were perfect, you concluded it was your fault. Enter Critical Judge. When you asked, "Am I perfect enough yet? Am I doing everything right? I improved all of my grades from B's to A's. I am getting recognition from others as to how pretty, smart, and talented I am." Critical Judge countered, "But are you being loved in the way that makes you feel safe and secure?"

"Well, no . . ."

"Then you are not perfect enough."

"OK, then, tell me what's wrong with me."

"Well, to begin with, you can't draw, you'll never be an

athlete like Dad, and Mom thinks you're ugly because your hair's too curly."

Soon you found yourself listening attentively to Critical Judge, working diligently on correcting each flaw, no matter how small. Maybe you ironed your hair, modeled yourself after every famous painter, or played every sport, even though you hated athletics. Depending on how successful this behavior was with your parents, you bought Critical Judge behavior for life.

The roots of Critical Judge behavior can be seen readily in school-aged children. Barbara, a school nurse, told us, "I am very much aware of this Critical Judge demon. I hear examples of it every day when youngsters say, 'I can't take this, I am quitting, I hate this school, I hate my teacher, I hate the other kids.' I see this in the seventh and eighth graders' repeated visits to the Health Room. They want to escape this class, this teacher, or that subject. Their attitudes come from home."

Nancy, a fifth-grader, is a good example. Her teacher, Mrs. Baker, is concerned about Nancy's inability to learn math. Even with hours of tutoring after school, Nancy's test grades haven't improved.

At a conference with Nancy's mother, Mrs. Baker says, "One of the things I hear most from Nancy is, 'I just can't do math.' I notice she often makes derogatory remarks about herself like 'I'm a dunce' or 'I'm so stupid.' She really is such a bright child — I can't understand why she gets so down on herself."

Nancy's mother interrupts Mrs. Baker. "I'm not surprised she can't do math. I was never good in it myself. Now my son, he's practically a mathematical genius. No, poor Nancy, she just isn't a numbers person. I don't think she'll be able to learn it. She's just like me."

Mrs. Baker, completely frustrated, makes one more try. "Maybe we could get her another tutor. Perhaps the extra help would give her the added confidence to overcome her self-defeating attitude. Could her brother help her at home?"

"Oh, I doubt it would help much," her mother says. "Once

she gets it in her mind that she can't do something, she's as stubborn as a mule."

Here we see how the Critical Judge pattern passes from mother to daughter, and another generation falls under the tyranny of this self-imposed hanging-judge. Nancy's Stress Personality started with her mother and will follow her into adult life. By accepting her mother's criticism of her as a true and valid feature of her personality, Nancy will continue to endure the debilitating stress of this relentless, punitive part of herself. She can walk away from her mother, change schools or employers, but her self-image will be the same. Once Critical Judge has moved in, no court order will get this Stress Personality to move out. Not until Nancy recognizes that Critical Judge survival behavior is outdated, and realizes that her survival and self-esteem are no longer dependent upon the approval of others, will she be free to challenge the Faulty Perceptions of Critical Judge.

People who suffer with Critical Judge mistakenly think they must be perfect in order to be loved. In one of our workshops, we were helping a dental assistant work with her Critical Judge. She told us she was really trying to improve herself but kept "blowing it." When we asked what she meant she told us, "I'm just not perfect enough yet." When we asked her how many perfect people she knew, to our surprise she answered, "Two."

"Two!" we exclaimed in unison. "You actually know two perfect people?"

"Well, not absolutely perfect," she admitted. "I suppose they do slip up now and again, but I've never seen them."

This young woman's Critical Judge had not only convinced her that she had to live up to this phantom standard, but that others had actually achieved perfection.

Stress inevitably results when you believe you should be perfect. Since you are bound to make mistakes and fail at perfection, you leave yourself wide open to Critical Judge's criticism and scorn. If Critical Judge decides that a particular performance was not adequate, you'll see yourself as an inadequate person. Critical Judge ignores your successes and identifies you only with your failures. There are no such things as learning experiences — only losing experiences.

Many people feel they need Critical Judge in order to avoid complacency. It's not Critical Judge you need, but Better Judgement. Distinguishing between the two is crucial. Better Judgement sees what went right as well as what went wrong. Better Judgement emphasizes your strengths while you work on changing your weaknesses.

Think back to the last time you made an error. How did you feel about yourself? If you felt embarrassed, ashamed, disquieted, or helpless, you are looking through Critical Judge's eyes. If, on the other hand, you felt stimulated, interested, and full of ideas on how to improve the situation, you had Better Judgement on your side.

Assessing Your Critical Judge Behavior

Answer honestly, choosing one of the five responses and placing the corresponding number in the box opposite each question. Add up the score and place the total along the Stress Behavior scale. Pay special attention to those questions on which you scored a 6 or 8. If your total score is 48 or greater, you're engaging in Critical Judge behavior to the extent that it can be significantly disruptive to your life.

(Almost always=8) (Frequently=6) (Sometimes=4)
(Occasionally=2) (Never=0)

1. ( )   Are you easily discouraged when trying to learn a new task or skill?

2. ( )   When you get an evaluation, do you disregard the positive and concentrate only on the negative?

3. ( )   Do you feel the best way to motivate those you supervise or work with is to focus on what they did

wrong?

4. ( ) Are you fearful of taking tests or committing your ideas to paper?

5. ( ) Do you feel the need to defend yourself when your work is scrutinized?

6. ( ) Do you think critical thoughts about others?

7. ( ) Do you blame yourself when a relationship doesn't work out?

8. ( ) Are you reluctant to take risks or try something new because you lack self-confidence?

9. ( ) Do you use judgement words on yourself like "I'm silly", "stupid", or "dumb for doing this or that"?

11. ( ) Do you have trouble accepting compliments?

12. ( ) How often do you hear yourself say, "I can't," "It's too hard," "I quit"?

    ( ) TOTAL

0   48   96

CRITICAL JUDGE FRIEND

One sure way to end up friendless is to listen to Critical Judge's opinion of the friends you have. Critical Judge isn't happy confining its activities to criticizing you. It drags every friend you have into the courtroom for the slightest infraction. It's all too easy to find fault in others, especially when you are looking for it, so beware of Critical Judge's evaluations. It may be your friend who lets her dog beg under the table when you're having dinner or your recently divorced brother-in-law, who is dating college coeds from the history class he teaches. "Imagine at his age," Critical Judge remarks scornfully. Then there's the woman next door, who is always kind and helpful to you but who has so many men coming and going you are considering selling admission tickets at her front door. The list of people and their defects goes on and on until Critical Judge decides that nobody meets your standards.

Now you have to start over with a clean slate of new friends. Of course, these friends won't live up to your expectations either, with Critical Judge setting the criteria. If you are looking for flawless friends, you may end up spending your evenings at home watching television and sharing your popcorn with Critical Judge.

Looking for perfect friends puts both you and your friends under stress. One part of you needs the intimate contact that only friends can offer, and the other pushes them aside because they're not good enough. Don't let Critical Judge tarnish the value of their companionship because of eccentricities or unconventionalities. Focus on the positive aspects of your friends and what you like about them. Friends are far too important to give up at Critical Judge's whim.

If you are under Critical Judge's influence, you need to insist on more positive thoughts and actions to replace your negative ones. It is tedious and depressing to listen to someone who is always bad-mouthing himself and others. Friends grow tired of reassuring you, especially when you deny affirmatives and refuse to accept compliments.

"Hey, you look great tonight," a friend might say.

"Oh, no I don't, I look terrible," you reply.

"No, I love your outfit. It really flatters you."

"It's too flashy. Besides, it makes me look fat."

"No," your friend says, "I think it is really slimming."

Back and forth you both will go until your friend wears out and concludes that you know best — that maybe you do look fat and flashy. The way you see yourself is eventually how others are going to perceive you. If you think positively, this can work to your advantage, but it will work in reverse if you have a Critical Judge. If you see yourself as bright, strong, attractive, and personable, others will see you in this light too. If you let Critical Judge belittle you in front of others, they'll figure you must know something they don't. They might conclude you are the awful person you think you are. Then it becomes even harder for you to build your self-esteem.

In order for friendships to deepen, you must take pleasure in your successes and be supportive of your friends' accomplishments as well. Remember that people can tell when you are genuinely glad for them, so your support needs to be honest. They can also feel when you are jealous, no matter how hard you try to conceal it. If you don't feel confident about yourself, a condition that seems to go hand in hand with Critical Judge, you will feel defeated by the good fortune of even your dearest friend. You will feel that your friend has "made it" while you lag behind. Naturally, Critical Judge forgets your past achievements and can't see what lies ahead for you. When you compare yourself unfavorably with others, you're robbing yourself of participation in their triumphs.

Let's say that your friend Cindy is telling you about a recent development in her business. A real breakthrough has occurred for her. "This job looks like the one I've had my heart set on for a long time. Finally I will have the chance to travel and test out some of my ideas. I couldn't wait to tell you about it. And, if you can believe it, it even pays well!"

"That's great, Cindy," you say, smiling stiffly at your friend, "I am so happy for you." Even as you say this you realize you are lying. You're not happy. As your friend continues enthusiastically about her plans, you feel your spirits sinking. By the time she finishes, you feel downright depressed and then you feel guilty. "What kind of a friend am I?" you ask yourself. "I actually feel hopeless and dejected because of her success."

When Critical Judge compares you with others, you will generally dwell only on your deficiencies. The fact that you and Cindy are separate individuals following your own unique paths doesn't make any difference to Critical Judge. If you start to feel depressed over the prosperity of a friend and guilty because you don't feel genuinely happy at the good news, look over your shoulder; you'll see Critical Judge. Strike back by telling Critical

Judge that what happens to someone else has nothing to do with your own successes or failures.

If something goes awry in a relationship, Critical Judge will immediately place all the blame on you. After an argument with someone, you're likely to think it's all your fault. It takes two to tangle and two to find a creative solution. When you blame yourself, you're repeating old childhood feelings: since Mom and Dad are perfect, I must be the one at fault. Once again Critical Judge compares you to others and you end up holding the short end of the stick.

Critical Judge will even blame you for things you can't control. You will feel guilty if you invite friends to a picnic and it rains. Maybe you and friends will go to a show that turns out to be awful. You'll take responsibility for the poor performance and blame yourself for not having read the reviews. If you introduce a male friend to a female friend with the good intention that they will like each other and they don't, Critical Judge will blame you for playing Cupid.

Talking behind people's backs is another habit of Critical Judge. When you feel the temptation, stay away from other people who are prone to dish the dirt. Remember how you felt the last time you ended up talking about your best friend. "What's the matter with me?" you asked yourself. "I was not going to say one word about Jeremy. I ended up telling Sally how he got fired and even agreed with her that he deserved it." There is something about Sally that encourages such talk. That something, of course, is her Critical Judge. Naturally, your Critical Judge loves to join her in scathing reviews of anybody — even those closest to you. Learn to avoid the Sallys of the world. Don't let Critical Judge tarnish the value of a friend because of eccentricities. Focus on the positive aspects. Friends are far too important to give up. Give up Critical Judge instead.

CRITICAL JUDGE MATE

You've decided to go to a cocktail party hoping to meet some new people — in particular, an interesting man. As you sit scanning the faces of the party-goers, you notice an attractive fellow. You are immediately taken by his outgoing personality, his easy congenial laugh, and the enjoyment expressed by those talking to him. The woman next to you notices your attention and offers you some information. His name is Dan and he's a journalist currently writing a travel book. Since you write as a hobby, you decide you have enough common ground to introduce yourself. Just as you're about to walk over, you hear Critical Judge say, "Don't be silly, he isn't going to be interested in your feeble attempts at writing. Anyway, he can see you. If he thinks you're interesting he'll come over. Don't throw yourself at him! What's wrong with you?"

As usual, you've let Critical Judge interfere. So instead, you walk over to someone who is sitting all alone, painfully shy, and you end up doing most of the talking. As you glance around the room, bored to tears, you see the man of your choice leave the party with someone else. You feel angry and disappointed. You've let Critical Judge pick your friends, and you're more depressed than you were before the party. Critical Judge sums things up, "You're not worthy of a relationship yet. Maybe once you lose ten pounds and get a story published, but for now you'd be lucky to find anyone to ask you out."

If you've never been able to imagine why anyone could fall in love with you — and then someone does — you're a candidate for becoming trapped into a relationship out of desperation rather than love. The most painful examples of this syndrome are battered wives. One woman told us how she and her nine-year-old son lived with a man who beat her and made threats on her life regularly. Once, in a jealous rage, he burned all her carefully collected antique furniture. When we asked why she stayed with him, she replied, "Oh, I've tried to leave him a couple of times, but I hate the thought of living without a man. Besides, I doubt I could find anyone better. I'm probably the pig he says I am. I don't see anybody knocking down my door for a date."

People who feel incomplete without a partner will endure debasing forms of humiliation just to be with someone. And Critical Judge will back up your belief that you're lucky to have anybody. After all, if your worth as a person is judged by whether you have a partner or not, somebody is better than nobody. Unless you meet someone with whom you really want to share your life, living alone would be the healthy choice, but Critical Judge interprets being alone as a sign that you have to rather then prefer to.

Critical Judge can take just the opposite tack. Rather than push you into the anyone-will-do syndrome, it may force you into the "nobody is good enough for me" trap. This happens when you are as critical of others as you are of yourself. If a prospective lover or mate fails to live up to Critical Judge's impossible standards, you will drop this person and begin the search anew. If you are looking for a partner without faults, you guarantee a no-win situation.

Try to remember that it is the unique combination of two people with all their faults and strengths that comprises a marriage. Focus on the positives while you try to bridge any gaps. Learning to balance each other can be a loving, growing experience, but keep Critical Judge away or the scale will always tilt toward the negative.

Your sex life can be ruined by Critical Judge. Critical Judge tends to depress you and, since depression is a self-absorbing activity, you won't feel much like making love. Even if you do, you won't be attractive to your mate. Depression seldom turns anybody on. Try to talk to your mate about what's bringing you down, and work to change it before it's too late and your depression becomes comfortable.

Even if you're happy in a relationship, Critical Judge can still meddle with your sex life by criticizing your lovemaking skills, and you won't get rave reviews either. The generalities this Stress Personality speaks in leave you feeling inadequate and helpless to find ways to improve.

See if this sounds familiar: "I don't think you're very good in bed," says Critical Judge. "Maybe it would help to read up on some exotic positions so you're not so boring."

When you think back on a dialogue with your lover you remember being told you were the most exciting lover ever, but Critical Judge chimes right in. "So what does that mean? Your lover's only pretending to be kind."

Before you can question Critical Judge's accusations, you begin to wonder just how much you are appreciated in bed. The next time you're in the middle of lovemaking, there's a good chance you'll start questioning your performance, changing what should be a fantastic experience into a self-conscious test of your technique.

Before you decide to take a course in Tantric Sex, remember Critical Judge often imagines problems when there aren't any. If you and your mate are enjoying your sex life now, why change it. If something is lacking, verbal communication can help maintain intimacy. Since sex is a subject that must be handled with honesty and frankness, you need feedback from each other, but keep Critical Judge out or you'll be unnecessarily threatened. You can stave off Critical Judge by direct communication since this Stress Personality thrives on innuendos, vagueness, and conjecture. If you keep discussing your fears and concerns openly, Critical Judge will find it tough to build a case against you.

This strategy is a bit more difficult when both partners live with Critical Judges. Gloom, pessimism, and hopelessness are contagious in such relationships. Before long you're both spiraling down the stairway of depression together. When one partner says, "We'll never save enough money to buy a house," the other partner feels down too, and your home takes on the joy of a city morgue. If this is the case in your relationship, try to be aware of when your mate's Critical Judge comes on duty. Protect yourself by saying, "I see your Critical Judge is strong today. I don't want it to hook mine so I'll be staying away." Although your temptation is to try to help, you're running a great risk of getting swept into the trap. What started out as "his" problem will soon become "his and hers."

It is important to work out the discrepancies in a relationship, because once you and your mate accept Critical Judge, unhealthy behavior patterns can develop. Change, even positive change, in one partner can threaten the other. For example, if your wife is overweight and talking about a diet, you may find you're not very supportive without understanding why you're not. What may be blocking your support is your fear that she'll look so svelte and sexy she'll leave you for someone more attractive. Critical Judge is telling you that the only reason she's hung around you this long is because nobody else would have her. One woman told us that she had resisted going to sex therapy with her husband for years and she couldn't figure out why. She'd used the excuse of "being embarrassed," although she suffered from her husband's impotence. After some soul-searching, she discovered that Critical Judge warned her that if he improved, women would be flocking after him and he'd lose interest in her overnight.

When you commit to a long-term relationship, you create a new entity —"us". In order for the bond to be fulfilling, you need to work together for your common happiness. Critical Judge will handicap the partnership by continually making you feel deficient with respect to your partner. You'll never give your fullest, because you will believe you haven't the fullest to give.

Many relationships grow apart over the years until divorce or separation becomes inevitable. Critical Judge can expedite this process by resisting the changes that occur naturally over a lifetime. If one partner is afraid to pursue a different career, hobby, political view, or anything new or challenging because of the fear of failure, the other will become bored. At the same time,

Critical Judge's hold becomes stronger over the change-resistant partner, who is really dissatisfied with himself or herself. The process is insidious. Becoming aware of this Stress Personality will help put the reins back in your hands. Then it's up to you to decide what you want to do with them.

CRITICAL JUDGE BOSS

A manager's or supervisor's job is stressful enough without Critical Judge. If Critical Judge helps you manage, your standards will be unrealistically high and your employees will always be on the hot seat. No matter how hard they drive themselves, they'll never get an ounce of credit from your Critical Judge and neither will you. Critical Judge will tell you that since your staff isn't living up to your expectations, you're not doing your job. With Critical Judge's insatiable demands for perfection, you'll never feel the satisfaction of a job well done.

If you can't satisfy Critical Judge, what makes you think your employees can? Martha, an account supervisor, came to terms with this problem.

"I tend to be a perfectionist. I drive myself crazy trying to live up to my own standards, and I expect my staff to meet these same standards. In my last evaluation, my boss pointed out to me that I tend to expect more from people than they can deliver. I always thought that was a virtue and would provide an incentive for them to work harder. He said he thought I was too rough on them, and told me to think it over. The next day I ran into Joan, another account supervisor. We started to talk, and out of the blue, she asked me how my 'uptight' staff was holding up. I couldn't believe it. I had no idea they were uptight. She told me later that my employees complained to her staff about how rigid and lackluster their jobs had become. At the same time they were worrying about getting fired; something they inferred from my lack of feedback.

"At first I was hurt, but later I decided Joan was right. The funny part is that I think my staff is really top-notch. I guess that's what happens when you let Critical Judge set standards in the office."

As boss you need to maintain a delicate balance between the discipline needed for productivity and the flexibility needed for office morale. This juggling act requires finesse and objectivity. If Critical Judge takes control, your employees will either tune you out, feel slighted, insulted, or scared to death. You need to be able to tell employees when the job they're doing is inadequate in a non-threatening, constructive way, but you should also be able to compliment them and reinforce their successes. A poor sales presentation will be handled by a Critical Judge boss by pointing out errors in such a way as to be discouraging. "Well, what happened to you this morning? Didn't you learn anything from that training course?" The boss who does not use Critical Judge tactics can help the employee analyze what went wrong and what else might be tried next time. "Remember, keep your presentation to the point and focus on the benefits. If you need any help, come in and see me." The latter approach promotes the self-confidence of your staff.

Don't forget the effect Critical Judge can have on your colleagues. If you're always the one to point out the potential pitfalls of a new idea, you'll be shut out of brainstorming and planning sessions. Raising questions can be productive, but Critical Judge offers no solutions. You'll be pessimistic about getting new projects off the ground, and the damper you put on others enthusiasm may put out the fire of creativity. Since taking a risk could mean failure, Critical Judge will try to get you to minimize your risks by turning down new ventures.

Imagine you're in charge of an office that is expanding to include two more departments. You've looked forward to this challenge for a long time. You've gone over the reorganization in your mind and feel confident you can handle the new responsibility, but now that your new job is about to become a reality, Critical Judge moves in to undermine your self-confidence.

"I can't wait to tackle my new job. I've waited a long time for this promotion."

Critical Judge steps in. "What makes you think you can handle this new job? You didn't do all that hot a job on the old one."

"What do you mean? I came up with that new accounting system, didn't I?"

"There wasn't anything unique about that. Besides, that doesn't mean you can handle a creative job like this. Let's face it. You are not exactly Mr. Original Thinker."

You're whipped by now, and you reply forlornly, "I wish I'd never accepted this assignment. I was lucky to have my old job."

At that Critical Judge applies the coup de grace. "You know, you should have thought of that earlier. Now you don't have any choice and you're bound to make a fool of yourself. You should at least be smart enough to recognize your own limits."

It will be hard not to feel depressed after a session like this with Critical Judge. Critical Judge has the knack of bursting your bubble at the slightest provocation. You'll know that it's Critical Judge, not Better Judgement, when any positive thought you have takes the form of an unconvincing rebuttal. Demeaning yourself for things that Critical Judge dredges up from the past is totally unproductive. All you do is block the creative channels that could lead to a brighter future. Had the boss in the previous example spent time on how best to merge the departments, everyone would have been ahead.

Be careful, too, that Critical Judge doesn't stand in the way of your learning from others. Imagine yourself meeting with your boss following your presentation of next year's marketing plan. He is raving about your recommendations but has some pertinent suggestions to add. If you let Critical Judge do the listening, you'll feel defeated at not having thought of the same things yourself.

"Why didn't you think of that?" interrogates Critical Judge. "How could you have been so negligent?"

In this example someone is able to take your good ideas and

expand on them, but you can't comprehend this because Critical Judge expects you to know everything. If you can begin to see that suggestions and modifications could never be made without your initial ideas to spark them, you will feel better, and seeing things rationally will help your overall job performance.

As a boss, you need a garden of ideas if your staff is to maintain a high level of performance. Your ability to facilitate, activate, and produce will be stagnated if Critical Judge continually creates doubt, uncertainty, and erosion of your confidence. You really don't have to be perfect or know everything there is to know, so don't burden yourself with such expectations. If you want to be a successful boss, you need to retire Critical Judge from your internal organization.

CRITICAL JUDGE EMPLOYEE

You're on the way to the boss's office for your annual review. Walking down the hall, you hear the nagging voice of Critical Judge warning you that the review won't be good. By the time you get to her office, you feel apprehensive and moderately depressed. After the standard greetings, she begins to explain the various points on your evaluation.

"Well, your overall performance looks good. Your projects are thorough and your sales are up from last year. You get along well with others and — oh yes, I wanted to speak to you about your report writing. You know, many employees are having trouble with the new system we've instituted. They're still using some of the old methods and so are you. Take a look at our new Report Manual so you can incorporate the changes in your reports and you'll be OK. Now, let's see — your sales plan for next year looks good and those classes you're taking are commendable. All in all, I'd say this was a very positive evaluation. I'm going to recommend a grade increase for you." The boss smiles and asks, "Any questions?"

"No," you reply quickly and scurry out feeling second rate.

You pass a colleague who asks, "How did your review go?" "Terribly," you reply. "I can't write good reports." You hurry away feeling dejected as the voice of Critical Judge hounds you. "Why didn't you read the manual, stupid? You're lazy and incompetent." On and on goes Critical Judge. All the positive things she said went in one ear and out the other. You've let Critical Judge evaluate your performance, and of course you've come up wanting.

As long as Critical Judge scrutinizes your job performance, you'll experience unnecessary suffering on the job. Any criticism from a superior will throw you, since Critical Judge gives those in authority exaggerated credibility. Your self-esteem is apt to be linked to their opinion of you. For example, you may bounce up with elation when the boss compliments you for one thing, but come down with a thud when he suggests an area for improvement. Constantly commuting between peaks and valleys is stressful. When your self-esteem is nourished entirely from the outside, you are setting yourself up for misery. Remember, work represents only one part of your life, and your performance there — good or bad — is not a reflection of your worth as a human being.

Mark, a department head in a hospital, described Edna, an employee who had a severe Critical Judge. "I'm really at my wits' end," said Mark. "When I try to pass on information regarding her work or pointing out a mistake, she immediately becomes defensive. I've tried being nice, firm, stern, everything. Nothing works. You can't imagine how she reacts."

A typical exchange between Mark and Edna would go like this:

"Good morning, Edna. I wanted to talk to you briefly this morning. You left the respirator on again last night. It's not a major calamity, but it's happened twice this week. I just wanted to make you aware of the situation, because it's easy to forget."

"It may be easy for others to forget, but not for me. I didn't do it."

"Well, you were the last to leave. No one else came in after you. And the respirator was still on when I made my nightly rounds."

Notice how Mark has moved to the courtroom, and the real issue of how Edna could be helped to remember her job duties has been pushed to the background.

"I can't help that. I didn't do it. Besides, lots of other people leave the respirator on all night."

"Yes, I know. It's a problem for all of us, and that's why I'm addressing it."

"I don't understand why you are singling me out. You even do it yourself."

"Yes, I've done it. We've all done it, and we all have to learn to turn the respirator off when we leave."

"I do turn it off when I am the last to leave."

Now Mark loses his cool and yells at Edna. "You did not turn off the respirator! Please pay attention. That's all!"

"I don't like to be yelled at when I did nothing wrong. Why do you always yell at me?"

By this time, everything is in shambles. Mark feels like strangling Edna, and the respirator issue is never resolved. The stress level has reached the boiling point and nothing has been accomplished. Edna would not acknowledge that she made a mistake. When Critical Judge is this strong, it's too devastating to listen to criticism, no matter how gently applied. Edna's only relief was to throw up a defensive wall, but she still won't have protection from Critical Judge, who will get her one way or another. It might be on her way home when she'll hear, "You fool. You know you left the respirator on. You're always fouling up somewhere." And she'll be miserable.

Critical Judge can make your job miserable. Audrey, a department store clerk, described how Critical Judge kept her from developing her career potential.

"I have worked as a secretary-clerk for a department store buyer for five years. Recently, a job was posted for a buyer's assistant in a competitor's store. I've always wanted this type of job, but our store is too small to have such a position. I wanted to apply, but Critical Judge told me that the job required more experience than I had. I was concerned that I would have to bluff my way through. I ended up so intimidated that I threw away the application. About a week later, my boss asked me if I had applied for that job. He said that the department agreed that it would be the ideal job for me. By the time I heard those encouraging words, it was too late. The job had already been filled. To make matters worse, when I heard that, Critical Judge said, 'See, you're never going to amount to anything. Your timing has always been bad.' "

Under the guise of being helpful and protective, Critical Judge's fear of failure keeps you from reaching your goals. Without risk you become a prisoner of boredom. Although any promotion will generate some stress, if you're prepared and enthusiastic about it, the stress level will even out as you make strategic adjustments. Don't let Critical Judge transform a promotion into a crisis. You'll end up feeling incapable or unwilling to make the necessary commitment to the new responsibility.

The learning process involved with a new job is stressful too. There is always more information than you can absorb right away. With Critical Judge, you believe you should know everything from the start, and you feel stupid asking questions. Naturally, if you don't ask questions, you'll never learn. Setting realistic goals is crucial. Choose one or two aspects of the job to concentrate on each day, and keep asking questions until that aspect is mastered. Find models to emulate, but don't use their examples to show up your inadequacies.

Give up your belief that Critical Judge is a benevolent motivating force. Tom, a carpenter, confirmed the experiences of many of our workshop participants.

"I'm not gentle when I criticize myself. I really get mad at myself. I used to think it would make me work harder. I'd say to myself, 'You stupid idiot. You're not doing it right, fast enough, or carefully enough.' I figured the more criticism, the more output. Well, I can tell you it doesn't work. I got so preoccupied with what I'd done wrong that I'd lose my concentration and make more mistakes, slowing me down further. It was a vicious circle."

A typical round with Critical Judge starts as soon as you feel the least bit unsure of your work. You start checking and rechecking for errors, and when you find one, your confidence is shaken further and your work flow grinds to a halt. One highway patrol officer responsible for sending morning dispatches across the state describes this very process with respect to written reports.

"Some mornings I can barely live with myself. I'll write a dispatch and then Critical Judge will take a look. 'You can't send that all over the state. People will think you are illiterate.' So, I'll throw it in the wastebasket and start again. By the time an hour has gone by my wastebasket is full of dispatches that were unreadable — according to Critical Judge."

This same preoccupation with perfection hinders speechmakers. You become so self-conscious that your preoccupation with perfection blocks your ability to reach out and touch the audience. Concentrating and focusing on the needs of your audience will help still Critical Judge's running commentary on your performance. If you are prepared and allow yourself spontaneity, you'll connect with your audience, and mistakes will go relatively unnoticed.

Those with Critical Judges feed each other to no productive end. Envision this coffee break.

Maggie: "I hate this place. I can't believe I'm still working here. Management is so stupid, I'm surprised we haven't gone under by now."

Ann: "Did you see the cost-of-living raise they gave us? I almost laughed in my supervisor's face when he told me. That won't even cover the rising cost of toilet paper!"

Karen: "Why don't we all quit?"

Ann, giving Karen an incredulous look: "That's fine for you to say. You don't have any children. Do you know this cheap place only pays for half my kid's dental work? What am I supposed to do, tell the dentist to fill half of his teeth?"

Maggie: "Really! Well I'd better get back to the grindstone. My desk is so loaded with work, they would do me a favor to have a bulldozer come in and plow the whole thing under; desk, papers, and me, too, for that matter."

Maggie, getting up to leave: "Well, only two more weeks until vacation. That's the good news. I can hardly wait. Of course, the bad news is I have to come back."

Karen, feeling terrible now: "I guess I'll get back to my desk."

Ann: "You haven't taken your full fifteen minutes. You still have five minutes left. The way they treat us around here, I sure wouldn't give them five extra minutes. Hey, meet us here tomorrow morning again. At least we can cheer each other up."

Karen: "Sure."

After a R&R period like this, who wants to return to work. Employees who think they are relaxing by bad-mouthing their jobs are fooling themselves. On-the-job griping can be a substitute for acting to improve the situation since Critical Judge has people convinced that there are no alternatives to their situations. The "trapped" sensation is ever-present, yet they never learn to see how they are helping to create that situation. When you are on a job you don't like, you have two choices — to stay or to leave. If you choose to stay, accept responsibility for this choice. This will immediately reduce the stress you feel that is created by your belief that you are helpless to do anything about your situation.

Job stress is one of the most widespread causes of health problems among American workers. Because employment is essential to our economic survival, it demands much of our time and efforts. Start thinking about ways you could make yourself happier at work. Talk to others who seem to enjoy their jobs, and ask them what they like about them. Maybe you can change your attitude, or maybe you need to change jobs.

CRITICAL JUDGE AND HEALTH

Imagine standing in line for a bus when the man in front of you draws back his fist and prepares to hit you. What would your body do? Cringe, tighten muscles, and grimace in anticipation of the blow. Critical Judge produces a similar effect each time it delivers its punch. "You looked like an idiot giving that presentation," or "You made an absolute fool of yourself today." Your body reacts to each criticism as if you were receiving a physical blow.

Last year when we were in a hospital doing stress therapy with a patient, a nurse asked us if she could look at our workbook. That precipitated a discussion about Psychosomatic Illness. She began to tell us about her interest in holistic health.

"My mother went to see a holistic physician about a pain she had had in her neck for years. And do you know what she found out? The pain in the neck was my brother!"

We loved this example of how the mind can influence the body. Notice the next time you have an ache coming on. What were you doing? To whom were you talking? Had your Critical Judge been on duty? Just identifying this Stress Personality and making a few adjustments can help relieve stress-induced pain, but you need to learn your Stress Points. When you constantly berate yourself with negative criticism, when you dwell on the bad features of your job and your relationships to the point of losing interest, when you live with persistent feelings of depression and hopelessness, when you refuse opportunities for advancement or heightened responsibilities because of low self-esteem, or when you can't accept anything less than perfection in yourself and others, you have reached Critical Judge's Stress Point.

If left to run rampant, these Stress Points will drag you down the Stress Continuum. Critical Judge induces Personal Discomfort states including backaches, neck aches, general stiffness, stomach pain, lethargy, apathy, and fatigue. Depression, however, weighs heaviest on the Critical Judge Stress Continuum.

Mood swings, despair, weepiness, pessimism, discouragement, a sense of failure, and low self-esteem all point to Critical Judge's depressing influence. It's not surprising when you examine the process. How can you be cheerful if you believe you're a failure? You'll feel emotionally drained, lethargic, uncreative, and bored. Such self-punishment will leave you exhausted. Emotions like these are potentially hazardous, especially when they persist day after day, week after week, month after month.

The Critical Judge process is a death process in that it is the opposite of life-affirming. It warps your outlook and can lead to suicidal feelings. Suicide permanently stills the voice of Critical Judge, but what a price! Less fatal but still serious, depression limits your natural immune system, and repairing or correcting physical malfunctions becomes more difficult.

The effects of Critical Judge behavior are cumulative. The more that negative voice from within censures your every deed, scorns your competency, and sours your disposition, the more likely you are to contract a physical illness. An example of this is Will's story.

Will was a middle-aged foreman. A widower, he had raised his only son since his wife's death when the child was eleven. In his senior year of college, his son suffered massive brain damage in an auto accident.

"It took more than six months before he emerged from his coma. After that, I cared for him at home," Will said. "For twelve years, I tried everything I could to nurse him back to health. I spent a great deal of money, cried buckets of tears, but I couldn't bring him back to a normal state. My beautiful son now resides in a home for the brain-injured. I recognize Critical Judge when I remember the tremendous guilt I lived with because I couldn't cure him. I felt responsible. I wanted to do more. I was deeply depressed for years, and every time I looked at my boy in that hospital, I wished it was me. As a result, I came down with cancer of the thyroid. After extensive medical treatment, including psychotherapy, I began to recover. Finally I realized that I had done all that was humanly possible for my son. I accepted God's plan and not Critical Judge's. Your explanation of the Psychosomatic Illness process and the Stress Continuum really hit home. I had lived with it but never saw it clearly until now. In a recent thyroid scan, all my tests for further cancer were negative. I see my son twice a week and he is doing well. I love him just as he is, without any more guilt."

Will's Critical Judge put him through a merciless ordeal of recrimination, self-abuse, and guilt that deepened his depression. The depression caused severe stress that over the years moved Will down the Stress Continuum. When his resistance level bottomed out, his immune system failed and he became ill. This self-consuming process that results from Critical Judge's punishment can be fatal. Cancer consumes you physically, but Critical Judge consumes you emotionally. That is why you must come out of your depression as Will did and free yourself from guilt in order to fight back.

Critical Judge is a major contributor to health problems because it sets you against yourself. Your natural drive for health and survival is impeded by your negative self-criticism. Conflict with your body is bound to result. Recognition of this Stress Personality — what it means and how it affects you — is the key to countering the negative health effects of Critical Judge. You don't need to join the legion of people who live their lives unaware of the connection between the way they perceive the world and their physical health.

Pay attention to any illness you incur when you're depressed. Conversely, if you catch cold frequently, ask yourself if you're depressed often. Be aware that you are more accident-prone after a nasty bout with Critical Judge. This Stress Personality can and must be controlled if you want to avoid depression and the havoc it wreaks on your health.

CRITICAL JUDGE GAME PLAN

FAULTY PERCEPTION:	Constant negative self-criticism will point out your deficiencies and motivate you to try harder to perfect yourself.
HANDICAP:	You are excessively critical of yourself.
RESULT:	You are often depressed and easily discouraged.
NEW PERCEPTION:	You can be motivated more effectively by positive self-assessment.
FIRST MOVE:	Each time Critical Judge gives you a negative, identify and write down three positives about yourself. This positive self-talk will help retrain Critical Judge.
PITFALL:	Critical Judge will use criticism to compare you unfavorably with others as a way of pointing out your deficiencies.
COUNTERMOVE:	Start actively seeking criticism from those you like and respect. Give equal weight to the positive as well as the negative criticism. Seeking out criticism will take away the sting of Critical Judge by challenging its hold upon you.
FAULTY PERCEPTION:	If you don't succeed when you take a risk it means you are a failure.
HANDICAP:	You are reluctant to take risks in your

career.

RESULT:	You fail to acknowledge your assets and hesitate to develop your career potential.
NEW PERCEPTION:	If you never fail at something, you're not taking risks often enough.
FIRST MOVE:	Focus attention on the positive attributes and skills you can bring to a job. Start investigating new career options — the more the better. Find out what your knowledge gaps are and take steps to improve.
PITFALL:	Critical Judge will constantly tell you why you're not marketable and try to convince you to play it safe and not change jobs.
COUNTERMOVE:	Seek out career counseling. Get advice and suggestions from those you respect and admire. Take action instead of holding back. Focus on the positive side of risk-taking: new challenges, career changes, and new opportunities.

Take yourself through this Game Plan by writing down a Faulty Perception and one Handicap caused by your Critical Judge. What is the Result? Identify a New Perception for this situation. Determine what your First Move will be. Acknowledge and list a Pitfall you might encounter when you put your First Move into practice. Then

Figure out a Countermove to outmaneuver your Critical Judge.

FAULTY
PERCEPTION:

HANDICAP:

RESULT:

NEW
PERCEPTION:

FIRST MOVE:

PITFALL:

COUNTERMOVE:

Any problems that occur while implementing your Game Plan might be a subject for a dialoguing session with your Critical Judge. If so, you now have a specific problem to deal with and focus on.

NEW BEHAVIORS TO RETRAIN
CRITICAL JUDGE

What to do . . . *Think Positive*

- Ask for positive feedback if you're not getting any.

- Accept compliments at face value and feel good about them.

- Evaluate criticism: keep what's helpful, discard what's unproductive.

- Encourage yourself to try new things by telling yourself, "I can do it."

- Allow yourself to accept mistakes.

- Take ten minutes each day list your accomplishments no matter how great or small.

- Don't let Critical Judge compare you to others.

- Speak up in public settings and tell yourself, "My input is as valuable as anyone's."

5. STRIVER
Why Can't I Ever Be Satisfied with My Achievements?

*Y*OU'VE just sat down to read a brochure on a physical fitness program that arrived in the mail. Unfortunately, Striver is reading over your shoulder. The program looks great — the running exercise includes three twenty-minute periods twice a week for the average person. Not bad.

"I bet I could do that," you muse.

"At least," says Striver, "you really do have to get in shape. Everyone at the office has some kind of exercise program. Even that jerk, Fred, runs five miles a day. You earn more than he does; you're more creative than he is. It's humiliating to see him strut around the office acting like Bo Jackson."

"I know. I'll have to catch up. But the classes don't start for another two weeks."

Striver joins in. "Start a program right away!"

"You mean a sort of pre-program program?"

"Exactly. We'll have you running five thirty minute periods in the first week. By the second week, you should be running ten miles and by the time you start the class you'll be the best."

"I'll be in shape before I start," you say rapturously. "I'll be number one."

"Right," says Striver. "You'll be the leader."

"Wait a minute. I know who you are! You're Striver. You're the part of me that pushes harder and harder until I fail."

"Ridiculous," says Striver. "I'm just trying to help you set goals."

"But your goals are impossible to reach. No, I am sticking to the program as recommended — running three times a week for twenty minutes."

"You'll never get in shape that way."

"Yes, I will. Three times a week for twenty minutes, and that's that!"

Striver pauses. "Would you consider running uphill?"

With Striver, you will continually run uphill to win one thing, succeed at another, or accomplish the impossible. Striver is the part of you that provides constant assurance that you are not like all the others who are satisfied with puny achievements and humdrum lives.

"Stick with me, and you'll be somebody," tempts Striver.

Of course, Striver overlooks the fact that you already are somebody. Striver has no internal yardstick for measuring self-esteem; who you are is not good enough — you must have tangible proof of your worth. Hence, self-worth is measured by external standards: how much money you make, how many miles you run, your golf score, the price you paid for your house, or the relationship of your income to the national average.

Your conversations with friends will tend to resemble the six o'clock news. When you talk about work, which is all of the time, you will hear yourself describing how you sold 1,800 widgets, which represented an overall increase of forty-five percent over the same three-month period last year, or how you plan to meet three-year goals in two. This topic may be appropriate when talking to your boss or when making a presentation at the annual sales meeting. Unfortunately, Striver can't distinguish between people and settings and will gleefully report these statistics to your daughter's teenage friend who happens to get stuck next to you at the Thanksgiving dinner table.

In your mad dash up the achievement ladder, your relationships may become problematic. Friends and family will not be exempt. Striver's blind ambition will convince you that family takes too much time, that those in lesser positions can't help you, and that those above you are your competition. As a result, when you board Striver's express rocket to the stars, anything that is not work-related will be dropped, and anyone who gets in your way will be left in the contrails. Striver assumes that the only way to succeed is to push and drive yourself relentlessly, using everything and everyone you can to propel you toward your goal. Unfortunately, this obsession with success will never be satisfied, even after you've attained the impossible dream. Striver's basic belief — that you will never be quite good enough — will remain and will not be squelched by mountains of achievement.

How does self-worth become tied to achievement? It could be through parents who exhibit this behavior and reward their children for following their model. On the other hand, when parents don't provide well financially, the children may vow, like Scarlett O'Hara, "I'll never go hungry again." Some people may not even be aware that they've tied self-worth to achievement until they face a competitive situation in high school, graduate school, or at work. Then they launch a lifelong struggle of trying to prove their worth with objective success.

Striver behavior can be found in anyone, blue collar or white collar worker, student or retired person, housewife or husband, and its origins are just as diverse.

If, for example, you were the child of parents who had Strivers, you may well have been seen as one of their achievements, an extension of them and therefore judged by their Striver standards. Perhaps your mom dressed you straight out of McCall's whenever the family went on an outing. "Such a lovely family," the neighbors said. "How does she manage to keep all those children spotless?" The early message to you was, "Watch how you look, what you do and say — remember, you are a Snodgrass." Just what a Snodgrass was, other than your last name, was not clear, but you could tell Mom and Dad considered it something very special, and certainly a cut above the average. In fact, to be average *anything* in your family was looked at disdainfully. Report card time was a perfect example. Striver's grading system went into effect and a "C" was equal to an "F." An "A" was to be expected, and a "B" brought a scowl to Mom's and Dad's faces as they asked, "What happened here?" If Striver runs your life, this grading system is probably still in effect. With Striver in charge you will hear, "What happened here?" every time you do not come out on top.

Grades are one unit of measurement that bring positive rewards in such a family; accomplishments are another. Children of Striver parents often feel compelled to bring home trophies in exchange for admiration and love. Such heavy pressure causes a great deal of stress in children. It is no secret that many parents push their children to excel in order to reap some ancillary benefit themselves. Any outstanding accomplishment by the child reflects well on them and proves that they are "good" parents.

In a few lucky cases, the interaction between parents and child causes serious enough problems that the behavior is recognized and addressed in time to break self-defeating patterns. An attractive woman in her mid-thirties told us how hard it was for the Striver part of her personality to admit defeat when her son refused to compete any longer in swimming competition. He was a swimming champion at the age of twelve. He was competing for the California Junior Swimming title when he came down with a bad case of flu. Even though she made him rest and stay home from school longer than the physician recommended, he did not fully recover. She said she pumped him full of vitamins, health foods, and pills — all to no avail. He just seemed to lose interest. She brought him news of the other contestants and their progress. She even got his coach to come to the house to give him a pep talk." Finally, one day," she said, "he told me he was not going to compete in swimming anymore. I just sat down and cried. Somehow I knew that no amount of coaxing would change his mind. My Striver sure did hate to admit defeat." This decision brought about a long needed discussion between her and her son in which he talked about how angry she made him and how tired he was of swimming for her. She came to see how her Striver had taken over his swimming career and was partially responsible for his collapse.

Not all people who made straight "A's" or competed in sports successfully as children are driven by Striver. The distinction seems to be found by looking at the goal. If you love what you are doing and feel joy and strength in your accomplishment, you are following your life's path. Your attitude will not overstress you. In fact, it may reduce stress. However, if you push yourself in areas in which you're not interested in order to win someone else's love, Striver is interfering. Stress walks in and robs you of choices, just as it robbed you of your autonomy as a child.

If your parents gave you attention and affection primarily when they were proud of you, you probably have come to believe Striver's Faulty Perception that your worth as a person is measured by your accomplishments. This leads you to believe if you are highly successful, you will be loved even more. Conversely, Striver believes, "Nobody loves a failure." Teachers tend to reinforce this belief by praising scholastic or athletic achievement. Of course, the more you achieve, the more people expect of you and identify you with your achievements: a scholar, go-getter, basketball player, or you name it.

Average performances become disappointments. Your parents may push you by fostering a little family competition: "Remember, your sister was class president in both her junior and senior years. You'd better get hopping if you want to live up to her record." If you have several older siblings with Striver personalities, the pressure is even greater. Often the air of competition inhibits you from asking for help from other family members. Soon your self-esteem and your achievements are almost irrevocably linked, and you feel it's a point of honor to do whatever you do all on your own. By the time you're an adult, you find it hard to share work projects with others. Your relationships are crippled because you don't think you need anyone.

To develop a Striver Stress Personality, you don't necessarily have to come from a Striver family. If your family ambition quotient is close to zero, Striver behavior may spring from another need — that of disassociating yourself from your roots. This was true in Grover's case. Grover came to our workshop because he had developed a serious case of stress-related hypertension at the age of thirty-five. He was an installment buyer totally hooked on the American dream. He played, lived, and breathed his work. As Grover put it, "I've got too much invested in my career to get sick." He described his life as a long struggle to pull himself up by the bootstraps. "I had nothing but contempt for my father. He was content to spend his life in front of the television in a drunken stupor. I vowed as a teenager never to be like him, and I'm not. To get myself to buckle down in graduate school I used the image of my father to remind me of what could happen. This technique worked, too," he said somewhat defensively. "I am successful, but I guess there's something wrong or I wouldn't have this high blood pressure at my age."

Grover, like most who let Striver run their lives, developed this behavior as a survival mechanism to deal with his childhood environment. It was his ticket out of his father's world, but even after he attained his goal of independence and success, he still let Striver drive him relentlessly.

Managing Striver requires a change of perspective. You need to get ahead? What's wrong with setting high standards? What's wrong with wanting to be number one? Someone has to be! Isn't it natural to aspire to goals higher than you can reach?"

Setting such goals is fine if your striving does not result in excessive stress, which can cause health problems and job dysfunction and can destroy your primary relationships. Stress does not arise from your goals — it arises from your approach to those goals and the underlying needs that make them so important to you.

Assessing Your Striver Behavior

Answer honestly, choosing one of the five responses below and placing the corresponding number in the box opposite each question. Add up the score and place the total along the Stress Behavior scale. Pay special attention to those questions on which you scored a 6 or 8. If your total score is 48 or greater, you're engaging in Striver behavior to the extent that it can be significantly disruptive to your life.

(Almost always=8)   (Frequently=6)   (Sometimes=4)
(Occasionally=2)   (Never=0)

1. ( )   Do you follow the axiom, "If you want the job done right, do it yourself?"

2. ( )   Is it hard for you to leave your work and take a vacation?

3. ( )   Does achieving your goals give you only momentary satisfaction?

4. ( )   Do you use numbers and quotas to measure to your accomplishments and self-esteem?

5. ( )   Do you put increasingly high standards on yourself to succeed?

6. ( )   How often do you make sure your opinion prevails in group meetings?

7. ( )   Are you so absorbed in work-related activities that you haven't enough energy left for your family or friends?

8. ( )   Do you lose motivation when your ideas are passed over for someone else's?

9. ( )   When playing recreational sports with friends, is it essential that you win?

10. ( )   Do you bring conversations around to areas of self-interest?
11. ( )   Do you usually work more than an eight-hour day?
12. ( )   Do you abhor the thought of being average?

     ( )   TOTAL

0	48	96

STRIVER FRIEND

As you walk to your desk on Monday morning, you see a coworker whom you've wanted to get to know better. This seems like a perfect opportunity to strike up a conversation.

"How was your weekend, Terry?" you ask.

"Oh, we took a lovely hike into the hills for some bird-watching and had a picnic."

"Really? I love picnics. A little french bread, cheese, a bottle of wine, good company."

"Well, actually we didn't take any wine or much food. We were mostly interested in bird watching, and . . ."

"Beaujolais!" Striver forces you to interrupt.

"What?" asks your friend, looking puzzled.

"Beaujolais!" you repeat under Striver's influence. "It's the perfect wine for picnics. Fruity, young Beaujolais."

Terry tries to proceed despite the interruption. "Oh, well, if you say so, but we were really more interested in the warblers, and . . ."

There's no stopping Striver now. "I bought four cases last week. Outstanding value. Say, did you know wine is an excellent investment?"

"No, not really. Besides, I don't drink." Terry begins to edge away.

"So who has to drink? You don't drink the stuff, you invest

in it," continues Striver. "Listen, I know a guy who has a basement full of 1968 Cabernet. He's willing to let go of some at a good price. If you want, I can get you a good deal. I'll bring you a bottle to sample tomorrow."

By now it's too late. Striver is in control. "Hey, Seymour," Striver calls out. "Come over here. We are discussing wine as an investment."

"Actually," Terry mumbles in a disgruntled tone, "I was discussing warblers."

By this time, Striver is completely oblivious to the goal of the conversation, and it ends up a flashy display of your knowledge rather than a starting point for a new friendship. With Striver you have a tendency to talk "at" people rather than with them, believing that you always have to prove yourself or show how much you know. This does not allow much opportunity to explore other people's interests or to find a common ground. If you're thinking, "Well, it's just that most people don't interest me," stop and think about that for a moment. Have you really made an effort to get to know other people? Have you ever stopped to consider that because Striver can be such a bore others may react to you in kind? In other words, you may well be getting a dull reaction as a result of your constant name-dropping, one-upmanship, or flagrant self-interest.

Striver's arrogance makes you insensitive to other people. Many of those whom you dismiss as boring may just require a little more reaching out before you get to know them.

Just as arrogance keeps you from getting to know people who are beneath you in social or professional status, competition prevents closeness between you and those above you. Striver believes there is only so much to go around — so many good jobs, top positions, merits, and rewards. If someone else gets one, there's automatically one less for you. Everyone, including coworkers, friends, and relatives, is viewed as a rival through Striver's eyes. As long as you view people as stepping stones or roadblocks, you rule out closeness.

Striver's choice of friends is others with similar Striver philosophies. These people are usually business cronies, but they may be drawn from other competitive arenas like golfing, jogging, or tennis. You'll probably never know any more about them than their handicap, how many miles they run, or the incredible topspin they put on their serve.

Run through your list of friends and check off the ones you could and could not count on if the chips were down. Compare the basis of friendship for the two. Chances are the friendships you can't count on are based on superficial interests you have in common like similar businesses, cars, or club memberships. If you decide you want more friends you can count on, you'll have to start reaching out more. Give people your undivided attention when you talk to them and keep quiet about yourself for a while. Take time for someone you'd like to get to know, and ask him to share his thoughts with you. Make an effort each time to share an experience or a thought you feel is appropriate to his needs or interests.

Leash Striver's obsession with winning everything from arguments to sexual encounters. Sexual gamesmanship is a common way for Striver to add points to your scoreboard. A potentially genuine friend and lover is turned into an object by Striver. All personal, humanitarian, and intimate considerations are ignored when your interest is strictly sexual. You'll say things you don't mean, and give only out of self-interest. Once you succeed in the sexual conquest, your Striver will lose interest, and your general feeling of dissatisfaction will grow. It's not just men who take Striver along on sexual conquests. One young man told us about a date he had.

"I couldn't believe it. She was very nice, but after we made love, she sat up in bed, yawned, kissed me on the cheek and said, "I'd better get going; I have to run a marathon this morning."

I said, "What about our picnic in the wine country?"

"She looked at me vacantly as if she'd already forgotten who I was and replied, 'Some other time, OK?'"

Whether conquistador or conquistadora, these exploits can only reap short-term benefits at best. You need to learn to see people as a source of warmth and nurturing, not as checkers to be jumped on your way to the top. Life moves too quickly when you live only to achieve at the expense of activities that enrich your soul.

STRIVER MATE

Striver loves wooing over elegant dinners in sumptuous surroundings. Glamorous soirees and exotic gifts, flattery and attention are at first de rigueur. However, when the adulation and praise continue, Striver's prospective lover may well end up drunk on the convincing words and extravagant props before there's time to assess their sincerity. Soon Striver will hear lover say, "I love you and I can't live without you." That's Striver's cue to cut out. Camelot has ended. The thrill of the chase is over and it's time to seek new prey.

In an intimate relationship the Striver Stress Personality causes more anguish than any other Stress Personality. In one workshop, a physician's wife told us how frustrated and angry she felt at her husband's lack of interest in her and the family.

"He just won't sit down and talk about anything. All he's interested in is his work. He leaves the house at seven o'clock in the morning and comes in at midnight. He is always on call and will leave in the middle of a family gathering even if his beeper doesn't go off. It seems as if he's avoiding us. The children miss him and are beginning to show behavior problems. The other morning when I finally got him to slow down long enough to talk to me, he reacted with irritated impatience and finally said, 'Look, I don't know what you are complaining about. Do you know anyone else who makes $15,000 a week?' With that he walked out."

Striver tries to convince you that money and prosperity solve everything. More than likely your family won't agree. Your children can't understand why you work late every night. All they know is that you are never around when they need you. Your spouse gets the extra burden of single-handed childrearing even though parenthood had begun as a dual proposition. Striver can't give your family what it needs most: your companionship and affection. Striver's myopic vision makes it easy for you to lose sight of the value of vacations, Sunday concerts at the park, or backpack trips with the family. Those things will always be postponed.

Have your family and friends encourage you to take time off for non-work-related activities. Schedule at least one day a week that you will devote to sheer pleasure, and be sure to plan at least two weeks of vacation a year, as far away from the office as possible. Don't allow Striver to make you work-addicted. Recently we had an executive in one of our workshops who was unable to enjoy even three days off. He spent the first two days of his trip to Hawaii in his hotel room on the phone to the office. On the third day of his two-week vacation he became so anxious at being away from work that he had to fly home, leaving wife and kids to sand and sea.

With Striver, it is not only the quantity of your time that will be affected, but the quality of it. When you do find time for your mate or family, one of two things is likely to happen; either you will be too exhausted to go out, or you will have planned a day so full of activity that any one thing will be hard to enjoy. Even a simple hike often turns into an extravaganza. The family will need all the latest gear, you'll have to pick the most challenging hiking trail, and you'll pack a gourmet picnic complete with crystal glasses, imported wine, and cheese. This production misses the point. Your focus should be on the people with whom you're spending time, and not the trappings of the activity. It can be very stressful for your mate and children to have to live up to Striver's standards.

One woman told us how her husband practically dressed her every time they had to go somewhere that "counted." "I felt like one of those Pekingese that are paraded around in dog shows. He inspected everything, even the color of my nail polish. If my dress wasn't to his satisfaction, I had to keep changing until he was satisfied."

A man told us how his wife picked out all his clothes, right down to his shoes and socks. "She has a certain way she likes me to look, a bit flamboyant, but in good taste. She likes it when we walk into a room and everyone turns around to look at us."

Obviously pride in appearance isn't a bad trait, but be careful that your efforts aren't made in order to validate or establish your worth. In a solid relationship, your spouse will be more interested in you than in what you're wearing.

Striver will make it difficult for you to think in terms of caring for another person. "We" is a word that's tough to incorporate into your vocabulary. When you talk about joint possessions like house, car, or children, do you hear yourself refer to them as "my house," "my car," or "my children?" If you do, Striver is talking. This attitude can have far-reaching effects on a relationship, especially when both of you are vulnerable to this Stress Personality.

Ann and Scott are musicians in their early thirties. In the six years of their marriage, they have been intensely involved in their careers. She plays the concert viola, and he plays the violin. Although they are in the same profession they don't like working together. When one gets a break, the other is jealous, although it isn't openly acknowledged. Both have strong Strivers.

One summer, Ann was offered a European tour. She wanted Scott to travel with her, but Scott refused. His excuse was the strenuous schedule he had set for himself. For awhile, their relationship maintained the electricity that had brought them together in the beginning. However, as their careers became more and more enveloping, the relationship deteriorated until one day Ann told Scott she wanted a separation. They stayed in touch with each other, sharing their triumphs, but it was almost as if they were trying to prove they were getting along better apart.

About six months after their divorce, Scott saw Ann running in the park. He ran with her for a while and they talked. Ann informed him she was doing beautifully, had more European tours ahead, and was swamped with job offers. Scott told her about his bachelor apartment on Nob Hill and how he was being courted by a major symphony orchestra. Each felt a twinge of sadness. They were two terrific people who somehow had just missed each other, even when they were living together. As they parted, Scott wondered briefly what would happen if they got back together again. Just then he heard Ann's voice calling to him.

"How many miles are you running?"

He turned and called back, "Eight!"

She was some distance away by now, but he heard her as she countered, "I'm running ten." Scott's thoughts about reconciliation vanished, and he turned toward the hill, picking up his pace.

It wasn't their careers that ruined Ann and Scott's relationship. It was Striver. When Striver takes over, giving consideration and love to your mate is next to impossible. It is hard to give each other assurance, praise, or encouragement when you're both competing for the same blue ribbon. No one should be keeping score. You should work toward common goals and support each other. Focus as much on the process of working together as on your goal. Ground yourself in the present. You can never relive these years.

STRIVER BOSS

So now you're the boss. You've passed up all the other contenders for the job, and now they work for you. You've moved into an impressively decorated office and are officially among the best and the brightest. You can sit back, relax, put your feet up on the desk, and give yourself credit for a job well done. Right? Wrong! As long as Striver is around, there is no time for applause or congratulations. "You don't think it's going to be easier up here, do you?" warns Striver. "You're going to have to work twice as hard. We have records to set." And the beat goes on. Now you're running faster than ever, and your employees had better be, too.

As boss, you will expect the same unrealistic standards from your employees that Striver expects from you. To Striver, competency means total devotion to the job. To you, employees are your front-line soldiers, but they may not agree. Just because Striver has hoodwinked you into believing there is nothing more important than your career, your employees may not have bought the same philosophy. Be aware that Striver will have the tendency to be suspicious of anyone who does not approach the job with the same vim and vigor that you do.

Your Striver will be absolutely galled by employees who are less than 110% devoted to work. Even if they are responsible, handle their jobs well, and are dependable, you may find provocation to fire them just because they don't take their jobs as seriously as you do. You will also hesitate to promote people who don't share your dedication. What Striver fails to see is that your unspoken attitudes will still be perceived by your employees, and morale will break down. Absenteeism will increase. Don't let Striver fool you into thinking that your high standards will necessarily bring you respect. You may be resented instead of respected.

When Striver runs the office, work becomes an ordeal. Striver never knows when enough is enough. Anna told us how a Striver-run office affected her.

"I couldn't believe it when I started to work here. I had never worked any place like it. Not only did we have weekly quotas, we had daily ones too. If you didn't meet your quotas, you were out of a job. We were pitted against each other like gladiators in the colosseum. The dog-eat-dog atmosphere and cut-throat tactics finally got to me. Nobody was willing to help or trust anyone else. Because we didn't exchange information we often duplicated each other's efforts. Each person seemed totally caught up in his little cog in the wheel, but it seemed to me we'd all lost sight of the wheel. My husband finally pointed out to me that I needed five cups of coffee and a reminder of how much money I was making to gear up for work every morning. I decided it was not worth the wear and tear on me — I'd be old before my time, so I quit."

Managers under Striver's influence rely heavily on employees with Striver personalities, and tend to create an unhealthy imbalance between work and personal life. This approach can backfire. One Striver employee put it very succinctly:

"I, like my boss, used to work for the glory of it. One day I was talking to a coworker about how tired I was and how guilty I felt that I might not be as dedicated as our boss. My friend's response startled me. 'The boss ought to work longer hours than you. He gets all the recognition and makes ten times more money than you do.' "

When Striver takes over your workplace, you'll focus only on the production side of the business and tend to ignore the human side of the work arena. Striver will look at your staff as just part of the machinery. This attitude fosters a tense, competitive, and unhappy work environment with high stress levels. In the long run, absenteeism, production shortfalls, and increased accidents will result. Get to know your employees on a more personal basis. You'll never go wrong with an encouraging word or a simple, "Thank you." They both go a long way in terms of boosting employee morale.

You've certainly come a long way, too, come to think of it. From rags to riches, a genuine American success story. Your biography may one day read like John D. Rockefeller I, or Andrew Carnegie. But the question is, will you know when to stop before you blow it all?

When Striver becomes overconfident, the effects can be deadly. You'll bite off more than you can chew. Success in one area doesn't automatically assure success in another. The temptation after repeated successes is to think of yourself as infallible. Striver's addiction to challenge eggs you on to higher and higher risks. Yet, unrealistic goals often result in what Striver fears most — failure. While small but steady gains may seem undramatic, they are often less stressful than gambling your energy on higher stakes.

If you go into business for yourself with Striver, be careful. At first you'll feel free of the incompetency of others. You'll have to start hiring other people and delegating responsibility, and Striver will be distressed. "No one can do it the way we can," Striver insists. Even though your business may be wearing you out, you will have difficulty letting go of any part of it since Striver doesn't think about your health.

You can reduce your stress by putting Striver aside and increasing the responsibilities of you staff. A boss is only as good as his/her employees. Specialize in areas of the business you're best at, and develop your employees so they do the same. Allow people the freedom to solve problems creatively, rather than allow Striver to rob you of their good ideas. You'll be surprised to see how much better you feel as you gain confidence in your employees. Delegation saves you from the pressure of carrying the business all by yourself, and you'll have time to develop your own ideas.

STRIVER EMPLOYEE

You're on a fast track. Your employer has recognized your talent and you've been earmarked for advancement. Your competence, dedication, and ambition make you an attractive employee indeed. An opportunist attitude, alas, can trip you up. From your first day on the job, Striver will be analyzing the lay of the land. Striver's information to you will include who's worth knowing and who is not, whom you'd better keep an eye on, and even the size of the boss's shoes and an estimate of how long it will be before you are wearing them. Striver is not interested in your finding a home at work, but a structure to temporarily house your ambition. One young woman described her reaction after getting a raise and a promotion. Her boss had just told her how he hoped she'd found a home in his company, and she had replied that she certainly hoped so, too. But inside, Striver was saying, "Bull, I'm on my way up and I could not care less about this place. One place is as good as another as long as it serves my purpose."

Striver's tendency to be outspoken and disdainful of others' abilities will put distance between you and your colleagues. It is true that as a salesperson you could sell flippers to a seal, but your inclination to oversell and exaggerate your exploits puts many people off and makes you hard to know. When you serve on committees or work on joint projects, your bright mind and capabilities will be an asset. Striver's willingness to take over every aspect of every part of every operation may not be. What Striver fails to recognize is that you need the collaboration of others to get the job done right.

Note in the following example how Jack, a soil scientist working for the Department of Agriculture, found this out the hard way. Jack was the only member of his department who had a doctorate and had published. He sent his articles to his colleagues to read with notes attached indicating that this was the calibre of work to which they should aspire. He alienated his coworkers with his pointed questions and less-than-enthusiastic appraisal of their work. Associates with years of experience, but less education, resented what they felt was a patronizing view. Jack constantly harped at the older workers about the outdated procedures they followed, and was perplexed as to why they didn't want his advice on how to update the organization.

"I told these people they were way behind the times. I simply know more than they do."

Things went from bad to worse, until he found it was almost impossible to maintain his high standard of work. His rapport with the research department was so bad that they would not cooperate with him when he needed their findings to substantiate his work.

"What's wrong with these people?" Jack asked one day in

exasperation. A man who had been around the office for a long time gave Jack his advice:

"People aren't going to change their views to suit you, especially when you try to shove your opinions down their throats. You'll probably get more cooperation from them if you are less self-righteous and more considerate. After all, what good are your ideas if no one is listening?"

Since Striver has you living in the "competitive zone" most of the time, your natural inclination is to compete with everyone including yourself. People think it's tough working with you, but they don't know what it's like to work for Striver as you do around the clock.

Nora was the top salesperson in a highly competitive brokerage firm. She saw herself as a pioneer in her field since she was one of the few women to have such a job in the early 1980's. Acceptance in this career meant she was really better than average, but Striver continually discounted Nora's efforts. She was never good enough. At thirty nine she had to quit her job, a victim of chronic fatigue and high blood pressure:

"I thought for years that I thrived on competition. I was proving something. My mom died when I was ten. I had two older brothers, neither of whom was as smart or as capable as I. My dad tried to get me to take over my mother's role as lady of the house, catering to the needs of three men. I hated it and set out to prove I could compete in a man's world and beat men at their own game."

She accomplished her objective with astonishing success but still didn't feel adequate. During therapy with us she learned about Striver but couldn't let it go. "I just don't know what I'd do without this part of myself." She dropped out of therapy and went looking for an even better job. Two years later, we ran into her eating breakfast in a hotel in which we were giving a workshop. We talked for a bit and asked how she was doing.

"Well, my Striver is still in high gear," she admitted. "I have a great job. I travel all over the country and I am still tops in sales."

She lowered her voice as she continued, "The only problem is I'm hitting the bottle. And I mean hard."

Nora, like so many Striver work junkies, just can't bring herself to let go of this most seductive of Stress Personalities. It may seem paradoxical that a person like Nora would accept self-destructive behavior patterns for the sake of proving herself to the world. The sad thing is, Striver wouldn't know success if it were staring her in the face. High blood pressure, heart disease, alcoholism, depression, and ulcers don't represent success. It's hard to believe that the part of Nora that is so capable can be blind to the damage it wreaks on her body and soul.

Most people with a dominating Striver are certain that they are successful only because of this work-obsessed part of themselves. Even when faced with the unpleasant side effects of this Stress Personality, people often say, "But I love my Striver. It makes me excel. Without it, I have no zest for life." However, you may not like yourself once you arrive at Striver's goal.

"I question my own integrity," said Roy, a salesman in the fast-food business. Roy had always been ambitious. As he put it, he was "hell bent to make a pile of bucks fast!" Roy maneuvered his way through the sales hierarchy in three years and seemed on the brink of getting promoted into the managerial position he coveted. Then Roy's old college roommate called him with a rosy offer from a different firm. Roy accepted, got promoted, and soon found himself in line for the same position his friend was vying for. Roy went for the post anyway, indifferent to his friend's career aspirations. Roy got the job, but he had betrayed his friend along the way.

About nine months after he leap-frogged over his former friend, Roy got the axe. He was stunned. "What's wrong with my performance?" he demanded of his boss, Chet.

Chet looked him coolly in the eye and replied, "Nothing, Roy, nothing at all. I'll see to it that you get a recommendation that gives an accurate appraisal of your work. It will say you are bright, energetic, ambitious — very ambitious, and technically competent. If they ask how you work with people, I'll tell them you are cynical, selfish, and unwilling to compromise. If you want to make it in the business world, Roy, I suggest you find a company that appreciates such attitudes."

Roy was shocked, not so much because someone saw those qualities, but because they were found unacceptable. Roy had attributed his success to those very qualities, and to find out they were detrimental was a blow. "You know, at first, I thought about taking Chet's advice and finding a company in which my attitudes would be welcome," said Roy. Then I got to thinking. Do I want to work in an organization filled with people like me?" He decided he didn't. Roy's ability to look at himself saved him. After much introspection, he saw the folly of believing people were less important than his career.

Ask yourself what Striver really does for you. It usually keeps you working more than forty hours a week, immersed in your career. It blinds you to your friends and the world around you. It keeps you striving for the sake of striving. You won't savor your life as it progresses, and worst of all, you'll never be satisfied. Striver is afraid that if you don't grab every chance, pushing every minute of every day, you'll be passed by.

The secret is timing. As the I Ching so wisely suggests, "The main thing is not to expend one's powers prematurely in an attempt to obtain by force something for which the time is not ripe . . . He who remains in touch with the time that is dawning and with its demands is prudent enough to find pitfalls."

Each step forward must be signalled by a message from Better Judgement that you are ready to proceed. If you push before you are ready, time and energy will be wasted. Listen more often to your Better Judgement and tell Striver you want to live life without jeopardizing your relationships, inner peace, good health, and prosperity.

STRIVER AND HEALTH

"I'm going to make you an offer," says the devil. "You're twenty-five years old, your health is excellent, and you're feeling strong. You can have all the success and money you want, you won't need to curtail work to exercise. You can ignore a good diet and eat fast foods because you're going places. You can have all the love you want without having to offer deep involvement."

"Well, what's the catch?" you ask.

"Just ten years off the other end of your life."

You think for a moment. "Hmmm — life expectancy is around seventy-five years. That means I'll have to cash in my chips around sixty-two. Sounds like a good deal to me. Sixty-two is an eternity from twenty-five. OK, let's go for it — FULL SPEED AHEAD!"

You have just made a pact with the devil, and you've hired Striver to meet the terms of the contract. Allowing these two to decide your fate is risky. For one thing, Striver can't guarantee you money, success, or sixty-two years of life. Furthermore, at the rate you'll be traveling, sixty-two will arrive faster than you think, and you may not be ready to leave this world when your time is up. Even more likely you'll push yourself into a major health problem even before you've reached your sixtieth birthday. It all seems so far away, though, when you're in your twenties, and you'll grow accustomed to living at the stress breaking point.

You have reached the Stress Point when you regularly take mood-elevating drugs, drink pots of coffee or use other stimulants to keep your energy from flagging, when you take a vacation and cut it short because you can't stand being away from work, when you push yourself to the point of exhaustion every day until you suffer from chronic fatigue, when you constantly feel anxious, impatient, and tense. Striver will head you down the Stress Continuum in no time flat. Tight muscles, neck aches, back-aches, and tension headaches are common Personal Discomfort states. Along with these symptoms — believe it or not — people with excessive Striver behavior complain of boredom, anxiety, and depression.

The boredom often results from losing interest once the conquest has been made or the goal achieved. The challenge is gone and with it your interest. Striver's anxiety shows up as increasing activity, much of which is done with grim intensity. Depression shows up as an escape from Striver's incessant pressures. This, in turn, creates more anxiety, since nothing will terrify Striver more than to see you slumped into a depressed glob of inertia. Striver will offer you a second wind to get you going and to free you from the shackles of depression. This, of course, adds to the stress. One part of you is dog-tired and wants to rest and can only rationalize it by getting depressed. The other, fearful that you'll never come out of the depression, is trying to drive you like a mule. Exhaustion combined with depression can be a lethal combination.

Marilyn, a widow in her early fifties, told us her husband's tragic story:

"My husband built his business from the ground up. Twenty years ago he had a tiny local operation. Now it's a state wide enterprise. By age fifty, he was on top of the world — a thriving business and all the money he could want. But, about a year ago, he became deeply depressed and no longer saw a purpose in living. He felt there was nothing to challenge him. I tried to get him to seek help, but he said he could work out his own problems. After a few weeks of this depression, he killed himself. Our friends were shocked. The company went into a tailspin, and I'm just beginning to get a handle on my life."

Marilyn's husband wasn't suffering from the absence of challenges. Someone as capable as he could have found new challenges. The real source of his depression was the disappointment he felt when he realized he'd reached the peak of his success and it didn't really matter. The rewards he expected in love, inner peace, and satisfaction failed to materialize. This is Striver's dilemma, and it is only sublimated by ever-increasing activity and new goals — different carrots dangling from different sticks.

Striver's behavior is so narrowly focused that it isn't possible to satisfy the craving for self-esteem. To be loved for who you are is an internal process. To be loved for what you are is external. Mountains of money or success won't fill the inner void and depression that results when you're not in touch with yourself. Intelligently handled, though, this depression can be an awakening rather than the forerunner of tragedy.

We all feel tired and vulnerable at times, but with Striver you'll often feel like that. Don't ignore the clues your body gives you. Listen to parts of you that need to take it easy, and when you feel depression, impatience, or irritability, or suffer a continuous headache, pain in the neck, arms, or legs, take heed. If ignored, such ailments can escalate into serious illnesses. If you look the other way and ignore the Personal Discomfort clues, you will render yourself vulnerable to chronic fatigue, muscle tension, high blood pressure, and coronary heart disease.

Ed, a hospital administrator, ignored his own body signals in his obsession with running the best hospital human energy could buy.

"I've always been a workaholic. In the medical setting such devotion to work is not uncommon, and maybe that had something to do with the way I pushed myself. The hospital I worked for encouraged all of us to push, because the board wanted it to be the best hospital in town. It wasn't all altruistic either. Our goal was to be the most highly endowed hospital in the city. I was hired to fill beds and produce revenue, the more the better. I was good at it, too. I sweet-talked foundations into endowments. I hired a staff of grant-proposal writers and a top-notch business manager, and I worked an average of sixty hours a week myself, including weekends. Our board of directors' meetings were like football team pep rallies. I produced statistics proving we were the fastest growing hospital in the community with the highest occupancy rate and the lowest number of staff.

"Two years after I took the job, our hospital, by all of the criteria we cared about, was number one in the city. I was fatigued most of the time but always put off my vacation. I suffered headaches almost every day and was tense and irritable. It seems crazy looking back on it — here I was working for a hospital and ignoring my health. Just before my heart attack, my staff and I were involved in one of our marathon budget sessions. We worked all weekend to prepare for a big board of directors' meeting on Monday. We finally finished, and I was sitting at home in front of the television with a drink when the pains in my arm and chest started. I'd had some pain earlier in the week but ignored it. My wife got me to the emergency room of our hospital, where I collapsed while being examined."

Ed's coronary was, as he put it, a "bad one." His rehabilitation has been slow and painful. "There's not much I can do now but take it easy," he commented ruefully. It has been over a year, and Ed is still not working. Had he listened to his body's warnings, his heart attack might have been prevented, and he could still be on the job. Striver can blind you to the realization that a few precautionary measures can make a great difference in the quality of one's life.

Heart disease, hypertension, and migraines are cardiovascular diseases you can develop if Striver dominates your life. The incessant competitive drive to achieve illustrated by Ed is typical of what is known as the Type A personality, isolated by San Francisco cardiologists Meyer Friedman and Ray Rosenman. Comparing Type A personalities with Type B (individuals with a much lower competitive drive than that of Type A's), they found the Type A individual more prone to developing coronary heart disease, but not necessarily any more successful in goal achievement. In one study of presumably equally healthy people, they found that 28 percent of the supposedly healthy Type A's already had coronary heart disease. "Indeed they had seven times as much coronary heart disease as their Type B countertypes even though their diet and exercise habits were almost identical." (Friedman and Rosenman, *Type A Behavior and Your Heart*, page 77.)

The tension from the heavy competitive drive generated by Striver takes a great deal of energy and requires your cardiovascular system to work overtime. The tightness you experience with Striver contracts all your muscles, including those of your arteries, adding to the strain of an already overworked cardiovascular system. It means being literally "uptight."

Striver can only drive you this far if you allow it to. You must learn to counterbalance Striver with a sensible exercise program or meditation. Meditation is particularly good because it requires you to sit quietly. It provides pleasure through relaxation and inevitably slows you down. An outdoor activity that you enjoy can provide another balance. Running can be good for you, but don't let Striver have you competing with yourself or your friends. Striver can turn even a healthy activity into an unhealthy one. One man we met told us he had been running 120 miles per week until he got sick and was forced to cut back to 90 miles per week. He only grudgingly conceded that too much running had anything to do with his becoming ill. Run to exercise, not to brag about it.

Striver and Vince Lombardi have at least one thing in common: "Winning isn't everything. It's the only thing." Success, in truth, is more than winning. It can be quiet self-satisfaction as well as razzle-dazzle. Success also means warm, loving, enriching relationships with your spouse, children, and friends. Success is being proud of your achievements, but not making your self-identity dependent on them.

STRIVER GAME PLAN

FAULTY PERCEPTION:	**If you want a job done right, you have to do it yourself.**
HANDICAP:	You end up doing more work than you need to and you don't develop the fine art of delegation.
RESULT:	You'll have difficulty sharing the workload with others, either at home or in the office.
NEW PERCEPTION:	You can become part of the solution and not be the solution yourself.
FIRST MOVE:	Share your expertise with others and take in their ideas as well.
PITFALL:	Striver will make you feel as if you're compromising your standards. Striver will try to appeal to your ego by making you believe no one can do the job as well as you. You've always been able to handle your work alone — why should you stop now?
COUNTERMOVE:	Even though others may have a different way of accomplishing a job, they may be doing just as good a job. Make a conscious effort to delegate authority and allow others to take responsibility for their work. Be careful that in Striver's

scramble to the top, you do not step on people's toes. Make a list of the successful people you know who got where they are but not at the expense of others. Put yourself at the top of that list.

FAULTY
PERCEPTION: **Your accomplishments will be more important to you than your personal relationships.**

HANDICAP: You'll minimize the value of intimate relationships.

RESULT: You'll feel lonely and alienated and lose contact with those who care about you.

NEW
PERCEPTION: Having enriching intimate personal relationships is an accomplishment.

FIRST MOVE: Put the person who is closest to you at the top of your priority list. Give that person the quality of time he/she deserves. Listen attentively and try to keep your conversations non-work-related. Be open about yourself, too.

PITFALL: Striver will try to put work back at the top of your priority.

COUNTERMOVE: Tell Striver that you can't talk or make love to your papers, properties, or financial statements. Start making time for romance. Make a weekly schedule of time you can spend with a loved one. Make sure he/she is in on the planning to help reinforce these new goals of yours. And remember, no excuses as to why you can't live up to your end of the bargain!

Take yourself through this Game Plan by writing down the Faulty Perception and one Handicap caused by your Striver. What is the Result? Identify a New Perception for this situation. Determine what your First Move will be. Acknowledge and list a Pitfall you might encounter when you put your First Move into practice. Then figure out a Countermove to out-maneuver your Striver.

FAULTY
PERCEPTION:

HANDICAP NO:

RESULT:

NEW
PERCEPTION:

FIRST MOVE:

PITFALL:

COUNTERMOVE:

Any problems that occur while implementing your Game Plan might be a subject for a dialoguing session with your Striver. If so, you now have a specific problem to deal with and focus.

NEW BEHAVIORS TO RETRAIN STRIVER

What to do . . . *Lighten Up*

- Spend more time with your family and friends.

- Go home at a reasonable hour.

- Listen to and value the opinions of others and compromise more.

- Ask yourself if 110% is always needed.

- Savor your accomplishments before you move onto another goal.

- Work toward specific goals instead of open-ended standards.

- As a manager, explain the results you want and let employees choose the process for getting there.

- Be satisfied with a "best effort" solution in an uncontrollable situation.

6. WORRIER

Tell Me Everything's Going to Be All Right

*I*T'S half-past eleven at night and you're just drifting into sleep when an unwelcome voice awakens you with, "Did you remember to lock the front door?" These are the unmistakable words of Worrier.

"OK, take a chance on getting robbed."

"What?" you say, startled slightly.

"Leave the front door unlocked. Give the burglars an open invitation," says Worrier.

You start out of bed to check the door and stop.

"No. The door is bolted firmly. I'm going to sleep," you tell Worrier. As you climb back into bed, Worrier starts up again.

"That's right, go to sleep. Don't worry about burglars stealing your money. Hah! What money? You'd be lucky to have money for a burglar to steal." The note of growing urgency in Worrier's voice jolts you. You start to feel uncomfortable at the mention of money.

"Will you shut up?" you say in exasperation. "I have to get to sleep! I have an early meeting tomorrow, and there won't be any money if I'm too tired to work."

"You're absolutely right," says Worrier. "You still have to earn a living. It's not as though you're ready for retirement."

"Retirement?" Back comes that nagging worry about the retirement benefits you don't have. By now it's three o'clock in the morning and you are staring wide-eyed into the darkness, imagining yourself as a washed out old bum on welfare. Worrier has once again succeeded in creating a sleepless night.

This type of worrier behavior is completely dysfunctional. The fact that Worrier wakes you up in the middle of the night when you are least able to plan a course of action is evidence. Like a bad habit or the ring of Pavlov's bell, certain subjects will set this Stress Personality into action. If you pay attention, you'll notice that not only do the subjects of worry repeat themselves, but even the wording in your mind will be the same. At the mention of inflation, you launch into worry spiel number four, in which your savings dwindle to nothing and you're stuck with a fixed income. If someone mentions a car accident, you go to worry spiel number twelve: is your teenager home or lying bloody on the freeway? Worrier seeks reassurances but can never be satisfied. You worry no matter which way things go. "What if no one asks me home from the party? What if someone does?"

You can recognize Worrier in others who issue constant warnings and dire predictions. World War III is imminent. An earthquake is bound to wipe out everyone in your area or, on a lesser scale, you're sure it's going to rain on the day of your family reunion. There may be justification for concern about any of the above, but Worrier can do little to change the circumstances of any of these fears. Like Chicken Little, Worrier arouses panic.

Worrier doesn't stick to rational issues, either. Worry material can be found almost anywhere. For example, a secretary in word processing has a sister whose brother-in-law was diagnosed as having a rare form of malaria. Worrier is sure there is danger of catching it from the keyboard, long after the secretary has resigned. A gruesome story about a murderer lurking around college dormitories 3,000 miles away will have Worrier warning all of the neighborhood girls to get home before dark. One woman told us that she was still worrying about the people who went down on the Titanic.

Worrier opens the door for panic. The following incident occurred in one of our workshops in Southern California. Mary Rose was conspicuous from the beginning. Before the workshop began, she was earnestly discussing where, when, and how her husband would pick her up after the meeting. She didn't drive to the workshop for fear of getting lost. At the first session, Mary Rose began fretting and asking questions. Would the meeting be in the same room every night? Was there more than one entrance? Would the workshop end at the same time every night? The questions continued as Mary Rose sought reassurance that her husband would be able to find her. After the second session, panic struck. Her husband was ten minutes late. "Maybe he's forgotten me. Maybe he's been in a car accident. I'd better walk around the block and look for him." We kept pointing out to Mary Rose that Worrier was causing all this havoc, but she couldn't stop herself. The third session ended with Mary Rose disrupting the relaxation exercise. Tiptoeing across the prostrate forms lying on the floor, Mary Rose whispered, "I think I'd better wait outside. The lights are dim, and my husband might think we finished early."

We worked hard to help Mary Rose. With the group's encouragement, she finally drove herself to the last meeting. She did ask whether we thought the traffic was going to be heavy and scrutinized the map her husband had drawn for her. Afterward, she left with the others, Worrier seemingly in hand — so we thought. She returned several minutes later in a panic.

"My key won't fit in the ignition. Something's wrong!" She exclaimed.

We told her to calm down and then go back and try again.

Twenty minutes later we found Mary Rose in the parking lot struggling with her key in the ignition. We tried to talk calmly with her. Then we were hit with a flash of insight. "Do you notice any other car in the parking lot, Mary Rose? There is one other."

"Yes, yes, but what about my car? I'll never get home," she sputtered.

"Mary Rose," we said firmly, "look at that car."

"Why?" she asked excitedly.

"Because, Mary Rose, it's your car, and you're trying to fit your key into the ignition of our car."

Worrier had snuffed out Better Judgement. Mary Rose smiled sheepishly and admitted it.

Worrier can create so much panic and confusion that you can't listen to good advice. You get so caught up in the process that pretty soon you see disaster lurking in every corner of your life. It is an exhausting process guaranteed to cause stress through anxiety, doubt, fear, and alarm. Worrier creates an abnormal amount of fear.

You may have learned to worry from your parents. Watching them worry seemed so adult, so serious and important. It seemed to be an important tool for survival. If your parents were possessed by Worrier, you were well prepared when you went to summer camp. You had your name, address, phone number, and where to find your next of kin stamped on everything.

"Well, kid, we have to take these extra precautionary measures in case you get eaten by a bear or drown in the lake."

As you were sent off to have a good time, the following instructions were read as though you were being parachuted behind enemy lines on a suicide mission:

"Don't forget to take three drops of your anti-poison oak medicine morning and night. Take one allergy pill after every meal. Don't swim where it isn't safe, and don't pet any strange animals."

"Strange animals?" you said to yourself. "Do they think I would be that stupid? Why do I have to be warned so much?

Maybe I'm not as good at taking care of myself as the other kids are."

As your parents leave you at the bus station, your father is telling the bus driver that you get car sick and should sit up front. Mother is waving a handkerchief and tearfully imploring you to be careful. Suddenly you feel worried. Summer camp sounds dangerous.

Worrier parents are well-meaning but they often inadvertently harm their children. Parents want children to be safe and secure in the world. They impress upon them the necessity to be careful in a world they view as a dangerous place. They constantly drum out warnings, presumably because no child has the sense to take care of himself. But how can you feel safe if you feel unable to take care of yourself? You won't develop trust in yourself, so you'll worry too.

What happens if you don't experience the world as the same dangerous place your Worrier parents do? Let's say, for example, your mother is afraid of the water and constantly warns you not to go near it. You've been near it and in it lots of times and you love it. When you swim out to deep water, Mom yells at you to come back with obvious fear in her voice. "Jimmy, you don't want to be swimming out there. It's very dangerous."

Your immediate response is, "I do too want to be out here. It isn't dangerous because I know how to swim." Can you believe in yourself? There is a trust issue between children without Worrier and parents with Worrier. If you believe your parents, you deny your own perceptions. If you don't believe your parents, you admit your parents' view of the world is untrustworthy. Since you love them and depend on them, you find yourself in a dilemma.

Jeff picked up the worry habit as a child listening to interchanges between his family members.

"I remember when my grandmother came to live with us. She was grave in appearance and always seemed to put a damper on the spontaneity and fun we had in the family. When she was there after dinner, we kids were always sent out of the room so the adults could discuss grown-up issues. I would feel a little scared, wondering what was going on behind those closed doors. One day I listened at the kitchen door. I heard Mom and Grandma discussing whether Dad could support us or whether Mom would have to get a job, too. I was about ten years old and I thought from the tone of their voices that we were going to starve! I was so worried I went out and picked apples from our tree and set up a roadside stand. I was going to provide for the family. I felt the least that I could do was worry along with them, so I did. I always thought that it helped, because Mom never had to take a job and there was still food on the table. Now, years later, I find myself doing the same things to my family. I worry about my job, I worry about my wife's car breaking down, and I worry about whether we'll be able to afford a bigger house by the time the kids are teenagers. I worry about the kids walking to school, I worry that we're too strict, and I worry that they'll get worried. I feel like a bundle of nerves!"

Viewing life through Worrier's eyes can create an anxious, fear-ridden world. You develop the Faulty Perception that worrying about something is the same as doing something about it. This is magical thinking. You superstitiously believe that worrying, not action, will ward off the problem, but worry becomes a substitute for action. In Jeff's situation, discussing the family problems behind closed doors led Jeff to imagine the worst. Had the family discussed it openly and without Worrier's influence, reality would have prevailed. Jeff really had the right idea when he tried to set up his roadside stand. He was trying to tackle the problem instead of just worrying about it.

We see children using magical thinking all the time. "Step on a crack and you'll break your mother's back," is an example. It is less noticeable in normal adult behavior. A client of ours came to us because of her fear of flying. She told us that once on an airplane, she didn't dare even get up to go to the bathroom. Worrier had her convinced that if she didn't move and concentrated all her positive thoughts, she could keep the plane in the air.

Worrier keeps you prepared for the worst so you won't be caught off guard when the sky caves in. But what if it doesn't? You've tortured yourself for nothing, and should the most drastic of events unfold, you will have put yourself through the stressful ordeal twice.

The anxiety and fear generated by Worrier is a misguided attempt at problem solving. Problems frequently clear up in time without your having to do anything. There are also times when there's nothing you can do about a problem. To decrease your stress, let go of problems until you can figure out what to do. The key is to develop an inner security and basic trust in yourself. You have to believe that you can take care of yourself and that life is to be lived, rather than worried about. With this inner confidence, there are no right or wrong decisions, only choices. When you can quiet Worrier long enough to listen to Better Judgement, your decisions will inevitably be the right ones.

Assessing Your Worrier Behavior

Assess your own Worrier behavior. Answer the questions honestly, choosing one of the five responses and placing the corresponding number in the box opposite each question. Add up the score and place the total along the Stress Behavior scale. Pay special attention to those questions on which you scored a 6 or 8. If your total score is 48 or greater, you're engaging in Worrier behavior to the extent that it can be significantly disruptive in your life.

(Almost always=8) (Frequently=6) (Sometimes=4)
(Occasionally=2) (Never=0)

1. ( )   When you make a mistake at work, are you afraid of losing your job?

2. ( )   Do you concern yourself with the pitfalls of a project to the point that it impairs your creativity and productivity?

3. ( )   Before an evaluation, do you experience fear and alarm?
4. ( )   When you think you've done something wrong, do you begin to mistrust all your decisions?
5. ( )   Do you "over-supervise" those you work with by looking over their shoulders?
6. ( )   In ambiguous situations do you expect the worst thing to happen?
7. ( )   Do you believe worrying about those close to you means you care about them?
8. ( )   When you warn your family or friends of potential danger, do you feel they don't take you seriously?
9. ( )   Does your fear of what "could happen" prevent you from partaking in activities you might otherwise try?
10. ( )   Do you seek constant reassurance from friends and family, even over small matters?
11. ( )   Does your preoccupation with worry make it difficult to listen to others?
12. ( )   How often do you wake up in the middle of the night worrying?

   ( )   TOTAL

---

0   48   96

WORRIER FRIEND

You're not a lot of fun when Worrier monopolizes your thoughts, limits your risk-taking, and controls your actions. Although you may be a very loyal friend, you'll be less than the spirited adventurer most people like. Worrier can limit your adventures to a once-a-week potluck at the neighbors. Any thing more exotic is turned down. "You never know what could happen away from home," says Worrier. "At least when something goes wrong here, you know whom to call." If you're planning a trip to Europe, you'll worry about the language barrier, losing your luggage, the devaluation of the dollar, and the cost of airfare. When you are invited to a party, you'll fret about who is going to be there, how you're going to get there, what to wear, and what you're going to talk about. Worrier lives in the future and is always more concerned about what could happen than what is happening. The "what-if's" of a situation become so insurmountable that cancelling is a lot easier. Such a solution may quiet Worrier, but you'll turn into a bore.

It's not easy to maintain a friendship with someone who is dominated by Worrier. It takes the patience of Job to support someone who always seems to be coming apart.

"I have a friend named Ellen with a Worrier problem you wouldn't believe," says Lori, a librarian. "She's always talking about how lonely she is, so last summer I invited her to join me on a camping trip with a bunch of people. From the onset, I could see the weekend was going to be a disaster. When my friend Marisol and I arrived to pick her up, she was pacing back and forth in her living room. She was only half packed and she'd had a change of heart. She had so many reasons why she shouldn't go that Marisol just said, 'OK, see you later.' I knew how lonely Ellen was and thought if she could loosen up, stop worrying and come on the trip, she'd have a good time. Finally I convinced her to go. I ended up driving her car, following my husband and Marisol, because Ellen said she got nervous driving on freeways.

"By the time we arrived at the campsite, our friends were already there swimming, sunning, and having a good time. We left to change into our bathing suits. When we returned and I started to introduce Ellen to the rest of the group, I couldn't believe my eyes. There she was in a wide-brimmed hat, white sun cream smeared all over her face, and she was even wearing gloves! She told us she was allergic to the sun. It was as if she had forgotten that one of the reasons she wanted to come on this trip was to meet some men. Nobody in his right mind would ever be attracted to her after this first appearance.

"That afternoon some of us decided to take the five-mile walk around the lake. Ellen decided she wanted to go with us. After about a mile she told us she felt dizzy. She had hypoglycemia and had forgotten to bring any high protein along. She made it, but she didn't add a lot to the party. That night we got out our sleeping bags to sleep under the stars. My little boys put theirs next to my husband's and mine. Pretty soon my eight-year-old son came over to me and said, 'Somebody moved my bag away from you, Mom. My bag is at the edge of the woods!' I went to look and sure enough, Ellen had moved her bag next to ours. She was afraid to sleep anywhere but in the middle. The sad part of this story is that while I had really liked this woman for her many endearing qualities and respected her abilities at work, it was so difficult to relate to her worry that I gave up. I don't know if she ever saw how difficult she had made it to socialize with her. It was little wonder that she was having a hard time making and keeping friends."

Another Worrier drawback is that Worrier feels threatened, uncomfortable, or out of place around people who are "different." Worrier will limit your friends to people just like you. Often they belong to the same church, share the same political views, or do the same kind of work. Because Worrier always opts for the known and familiar, you will feel awkward in any out-of-the-ordinary circumstances. "Play it safe," cautions Worrier, "so nothing bad will happen." If you frequent the same places and see the same faces, you will miss chances to meet many interesting people. Many older people identify with Worrier. Some report that worry immobilizes them, confining them to their homes in fear, unsure of their health, finances, or security.

"It's not that I'm scared to leave my house," one woman said, "It's just that I don't have anyone to see. Most of my friends have passed away."

"You don't know anyone?" we asked.

"Well, I do have friends two states away, but I'm afraid to fly, and I feel nervous on long car trips."

Don't let Worrier tell you, "You can't go because you're too old. What if you had a heart attack or a stroke on the golf course?" Such things are out of your control. All you can do is try to maintain the best possible state of health and keep right on living.

What happens if you're well-adjusted but you have a friend whose Worrier drives you up the wall? How can you help? You need to let your friend know straight out how his/her behavior affects you. Since no amount of reassurance helps a person with Worrier, don't try. The hat out of which Worrier picks its worries is bottomless so you have to try another approach. Try setting limits on your friend. Refuse to discuss topics that are out of anybody's control. If the problem is something your friend can solve, put the responsibility where it belongs — on your friend. Explain why you are being so direct and make your rules clear.

If you're the one plagued by Worrier, encourage your friends to call you on this behavior. After all, what are friends for?

WORRIER MATE

"Do you love me? Are you sure you still love me? How do you know?"

"I told you I loved you yesterday. It hasn't changed today, and as far as I know I will love you tomorrow."

"As far as you know? Why, what is going to happen tomorrow?"

With Worrier, the need for reassurance is so great that the number of times your lover says, "I love you," will never equal the number of times you need to hear it. Worrier is afraid love is transitory, so you hound your lover for words that should spring from joy. With Worrier flinging doubts faster than anyone can field them, your mate will feel defensive. Spouses and lovers don't like their sincerity questioned and they get tired of continually having to prove their love. Worrier crowds out spontaneity. How can your mate express feelings impulsively if Worrier has already forced the words right out of his/her mouth?

If Worrier is interfering with your love life, it's time to change. Do not allow intimate moments to be taken up with worry. If any issue is outside your control, let it go. Focus on the moment and shelve your worries. When the timing is right for you to act, take them off the shelf and do something, but don't take any down that you can't handle constructively. Keep your worries under lock and key as if they were addictive drugs. Both are dangerous habits and can endanger the relationship you regard as nearest and dearest.

Ernest described how his wife's attachment to her Worrier parents increased her problems and added stress to their relationship.

"Sally and I, although extremely compatible, had one sore spot — her parents. Living with her Worrier was bad enough, but when her father's came in, it was unbearable. To make matters worse, her parents lived next door to us. They all got together and worried about our five-year-old handicapped son, Michael. Michael went to a school for exceptional children, and the bus would pick him up and drop him off right in front of our house. That didn't make any difference to my wife. She'd continue to worry that Michael would fall out of the bus and get run over. Sally's father would call her with every story about a school bus accident. She'd call me at work, nearly hysterical, and though I'd tell her not to listen to him, she couldn't block it out. Instead, she would accuse me of being indifferent to Michael, and then we'd start to argue.

"A year ago we moved away from her family after living next door to them for nine years. It was hard on Sally at first because she had become so dependent on them. When the long-distance phone calls started, I put my foot down. She'd call from 1,000 miles away to ask her mother's advice on the simplest matters. After a lot of talking, she began to see my point and gained confidence in her own decisions. Now she calls her family just once a month, and she worries much less. In fact, the last time they were late calling, she decided to go out with friends instead of waiting. Now that she's standing on her own two feet, it's been better for all of us."

A trusting, intimate relationship can be a supportive place to try out new behavior. Talk to your spouse about Worrier, and have him/her point out to you when this Stress Personality comes on the scene. The next time you talk about your worries, look for solutions instead of reassurances.

Blowing events out of proportion is another way Worrier seeks assurance. One of Worrier's greatest fears is not being heard. When nobody believes Worrier's daily predictions of Armageddon, you will escalate the seriousness of a situation in order to get a reaction. The more excited you become, the more your mate will turn a deaf ear. Then Worrier goes into a full-blown panic. When you finally succeed in stirring up your mate, Worrier gets temporary satisfaction. "Thank heavens," says Worrier, "someone else finally sees how serious this is."

Gloria and Clifford play this game. Clifford has just come home from work and Gloria greets him at the door.

"My goodness, look at your coat. It's all covered with snow. You'll catch your death of cold. You didn't take your gloves and hat either, did you? I've been worried sick about you all day."

Clifford comes back with his usual response. "Forget it, will you? I'm all right."

Gloria returns from the kitchen saying, "I felt like committing suicide after the hospital reports I got back today."

Clifford is all attention. "What hospital reports? What's

wrong with you?"

"I had some tests taken last week, and it doesn't look good."

"What doesn't look good? What did they find?" asks Clifford, beginning to sound concerned and confused.

"That's just the trouble," says Gloria. "They didn't find a thing, and they don't know what it is. That's what doesn't look good."

Now Clifford begins to get agitated. "You probably paid hundreds of dollars to have tests taken to find out there is nothing wrong with you."

"Not hundreds, Clifford. Fifteen hundred. I told you this was serious."

Now Clifford is up from his chair, his face purple with rage and the veins standing out in his temples.

"You spent $1,500 to find out there is nothing wrong?"

"Calm down, Clifford. You know this isn't good for your high blood pressure."

"CALM DOWN?!! YOU SPENT $1,500 AND I'M SUP-POSED TO CALM DOWN?"

Some people with dominating Worriers marry someone who is much calmer, at least on the surface. It's as if some survival instinct guides one toward a balancing force. Worrier, however, can drive your partner crazy. Instead of working your mate into Worrier's frenzy with you, model your mate's low-key nature. Learn to soothe your mate as he/she soothes you. If you want to avoid the discomfort that anxiety and panic cause, don't jump to Worrier's conclusions. Stick with reality and Worrier's hold will loosen.

Worry is often a substitute for other more appropriate emotions. It can even be used to mask anger. Sometimes it seems synonymous with caring, whereas anger doesn't.

As an illustration of this logic, imagine that your wife comes home two hours late, and you greet her in this way:

"Where have you been? I've been worried to death about you. I had you pictured dead somewhere along the highway."

Now she feels contrite for causing you so much grief. In truth you probably had been feeling jealous, imagining her having a good time somewhere without you, but you masked your anger with worry. Had you expressed your anger directly, you and she could have had a much more honest exchange and cleared the air.

If you become identified as the family Worrier, others will be careful not to tell you things that other family members are privy to because you'll "just worry." Knowledge that your daughter and her husband are on the brink of divorce, Junior is flunking out of school, or your wife is considering getting a job will be withheld from you. This puts stress on your family, because not only do they have to go to great lengths to keep the information from you, they also miss out on your support.

In order to stop being kept in the dark, tell your family that you want to know what is going on, that you understand why they have kept information from you in the past, but that you are turning over a new leaf. No longer must the bearer of bad news feel guilty for setting off your alarm. If you get bad news and need help, ask for it. Get a second opinion before you accept Worrier's. Often, just discussing the realities of a situation can point out Worrier's subtle distortions. For the next couple of months, set a goal of disproving Worrier every time it comes on the scene. Find the facts, not the suppositions.

If you do not take charge of Worrier, you'll never know peace. For example, you'll always worry about your children, even once they're reared, educated, and out on their own. This problem was particularly nettlesome to Loretta, who described how worry turned into a full-time job.

"Sue, our oldest daughter, aged twenty, moved into her own apartment. First I worried that she was living alone, and then I worried when a young man moved in with her. He was twenty-eight, divorced, and had a son. He was not well off financially and didn't seem to be too responsible. I spent more than a few sleepless nights worrying about Sue. We had so hoped that she would find a man with a bright future. Then my husband brought home a video called 'Looking for Mr. Goodbar,' and I began to worry that Sue would be mistreated or worse. My husband reminded me that the two women had nothing in common, but I worried anyway. As it turned out, the worry was for naught. Sue eventually lost interest in her friend and told him there was no future in their relationship. I should have known she'd use her good sense, but it's hard to stop worrying after all these years."

After taking a long hard look at Worrier, Loretta decided she wanted to live her life differently. She and her husband were free, having raised their children the best they knew how, and now it was time for the children to be responsible for themselves.

"Everyone has problems. It's better for my kids to work out their own," Loretta finally acknowledged. "I can't be there to protect them. I'm going to start focusing on my own problems, like taking care of Worrier. I'm doing some relaxation exercises and taking yoga. I'll offer help when they ask for it, but otherwise I'll stay out of things and remain calm. If my stomach knots up, I'll pull up a chair and have a good talk with Worrier."

So many people believe that the only way they can maintain a relationship with their children is to worry about them. It really is a wasted effort. Worrier will only rob you and your children of happiness. Let Worrier know that, children or no children, you are going to spend your life enjoying it, not worrying about it.

WORRIER BOSS

You are looking in the window of the foreign auto dealer for the fourth time this week. Should you or shouldn't you walk in and make a down payment on that BMW and drive it away? Maybe you should reconsider, and weigh the facts some more.

"Why shouldn't I buy it?" you argue with yourself. "In just two weeks I'll be general manager with a good raise. For once in my life I want to throw caution to the winds and splurge."

"I wouldn't be so hasty," advises Worrier. "You never know what may happen. You don't really have that raise and promotion yet. This car could drive you to bankruptcy."

"Why wouldn't I get promoted? The formal announcement has already been made!" you say, slightly irritated.

It's starting to get dark. The salesman in the window is smiling at you, motioning you to come in. You shake your head indicating you are just looking.

Worrier kicks in again. "Even if you do have the job, won't everybody think a BMW is pretty pretentious? They'll probably think you're trying to outclass them or something."

You hesitate, "That's right, too. I hadn't thought of that. I guess I'd be overstepping my bounds, wouldn't I?"

You begin to believe Worrier and decide the BMW is much too ostentatious. You're worried it will affect your relationship with your new staff, so you leave the lot, shoulders slumped, and get into your battleship-grey Chevy and drive home to the suburbs. Your image as the dashing sports car rake disappears and in its place is Worrier.

As boss, you won't have only your mistakes to fret about. You'll have to worry about what others do as well. Worrier erodes trust.

A supervisor of an alcohol rehabilitation program confessed, "When an employee hands me a completed report, I go over it a thousand times. I worry so much that I'll get blamed for a staff error. I feel totally responsible for anything that goes wrong. If someone catches a mistake I let slip by, I can't concentrate for the rest of the day, and, of course, I take my work worries home with me."

Employees recognize a boss with a Worrier instantly. He's always looking over their shoulders and they resent it. They feel as if they can't be trusted. You'll stifle employees' creative ideas if they have to provide proof of success before they've even been tested. While they can offer facts, figures, and hunches, they can't give you any guarantees before the idea has been tried. Your original thinkers will leave or dry up.

"We had a kid who worked in our ice cream parlor," said

Vernon, the owner of a confectionery business. "He was full of bright ideas, but my Worrier thought they were too far out. During the Bicentennial, he came up with the idea for red, white, and blue ice cream. I told him I didn't care how patriotic the ice cream looked, nobody was going to eat a combination of blueberry, marshmallow, and strawberry. Well, darned if one of our competitors didn't come up with a red, white, and blue ice cream that sold like crazy. Shortly afterward the boy quit and went to work for my competitor."

The Worrier boss is ambivalent, and this upsets office equilibrium. One employee who caught on to her boss's Worrier said, "Around our office, you're damned if you do and damned if you don't. When business is slow, the boss is worried we'll go broke. When business picks up, she's worried we won't be able to handle it all."

Accurate information combats Worrier and leads to accurate perceptions. A young woman who was part owner and manager of a theatrical company told us how Worrier almost lost her business.

"I loved my work and the troupe's enthusiastic attitude. We started small and when we began to grow, it became apparent we needed someone to manage the business affairs. I hated bookkeeping, so I hired a bookkeeper and told her I didn't want to know anything unless we were ready to go broke. Every time she'd tell me our funds were low, I'd panic. I'd tell everyone that it wouldn't be long before we'd have to close our doors. We'd always managed to make it, but our shaky financial status was making me very fearful. I would try to look over the books, but they'd scare me. I finally realized that I was being hurt more by not knowing. I decided, at the suggestion of my Better Judgement, to take charge of financial reporting and bill paying. It's funny, but ever since I took over this job, Worrier has let up. Numbers really take the guesswork out of financial planning. Now I know months ahead how to organize our bookings so that we can meet our projections."

Challenge Worrier's beliefs and the lights will come on to

dispel the ominous shadows of worry. You must force yourself away from ambiguity. Make your position clear to your employees on every issue, including their performance. Ambiguity is one of the worst drawbacks of Worrier behavior. Your employees will feel anxious and stressed when they leave your office with instructions like "Go ahead with the project, but exercise extreme caution. Don't make a mistake, and bail out at the first sign of trouble." Conditional confidence is the worst possible form of stress for employees to handle. Challenge that Worrier, and trust your staff and yourself.

WORRIER EMPLOYEE

Once Worrier is under your skin at work, you won't have a problem that isn't laden with disaster. Insignificant events will be blown out of proportion, mole hills turned to mountains. Worrier fever spreads like wildfire and destroys office morale. Rumor escalates to panic. Observe Shirley as she passes on unsubstantiated information to Lionel, who has just returned from vacation.

"Lionel, where have you been? I thought you got fired."

Lionel laughs off the remark. "Fired? No, no, I just got back from Tahiti. I've been on vacation."

Shirley looks disapproving. "You flew over there? You're lucky the plane didn't crash."

Lionel ignores the comment and replies good-naturedly, "No quicker way to that beautiful sunshine."

"I hope you remembered your sun screen. You can get skin cancer from too much sun, Lionel."

"Nonsense. It's relaxing, and I'm as mellow as Jello. So what's been going on around here?"

Shirley leans forward and in a confidential tone says, "Didn't you hear about the layoffs?"

Lionel jerks upright in his chair, heart pounding. "Layoffs! What layoffs?"

"I'll tell you what layoffs. I saw Chris from personnel coming out of the boss's office. She had red eyes. Obviously she'd been crying, and that means layoffs."

Lionel starts to feel panicky. "Well, I'm OK," he assures himself, "I've got ten years of seniority."

"I heard seniority doesn't mean a thing."

"Oh, no! I just borrowed a lot of money. How did you find out about this anyway?"

"Well nothing's for sure — I mean I'm low on the totem pole around here, but something's up — something big."

"Well, who does know about this? Where did you hear it?" Lionel is agitated. His Tahitian tan is paling. Shirley begins to back away as others in the office start to notice their intensity.

"Relax, Lionel," Shirley says under her breath as she glances about the room.

"Relax?! I'm getting laid off after twelve years and you say relax?"

By now Shirley has turned to her work, dismissing Lionel. Lionel wanders off in a daze. Then, after a moment, she calls back over her shoulder and says, "Nice to have you back, Lionel."

Worrier behavior can be a real nuisance in uncertain times. Whether it be layoffs, company reorganization, change of personnel, or a merger, the experience is stressful. Worrier will always make the transition worse. Anything uncertain will be replaced by imagined "facts" or rumors. Since you can't work effectively when you're worried, get the facts.

Panic is an inhibiting emotion. It curbs your ability to handle crises. At the very time you need to think with a clear mind, Worrier will cloud your Better Judgement, interfere with your ability to sort out the facts, and paralyze your ability to act. Worrier brings doubt and divides your energies. Speculating on what could happen instead of solving the actual problem is nonproductive. Christopher illustrated this in the following incident involving his friend, Sue.

"It was three o'clock in the afternoon when Sue called. She was absolutely frantic. The television studio had some electrical blow-out, and her crew was stalled with no power. All the other studios in the area were booked, and her show had to be filmed that day to get on the air as scheduled. We were old friends, so I intervened at our studio, got the boss to switch another client around, and cleared three hours for her. Just before we set up, she called back to say she had changed her mind. The electricity had come back on, and she was going to take the chance that it would stay that way. Ten minutes hadn't passed when she called again. The lights were still flickering over there, and she didn't want to risk another power failure. She would be right over.

"When she arrived with her entourage, she had them all upset with her constant worry. What if they couldn't finish? What if the lighting wasn't right in our studio? Should she have stayed in the other studio? I told her that if she settled down, things would run smoothly. We finally started the taping, and naturally there were unavoidable delays. We were making progress until halfway through when Sue decided to move the whole project back to the original studio. She decided the power failure had been corrected and she trusted her own facilities more than ours. There was no reasoning with her. She paid us in full, packed everyone up, and headed back to the other studio. I felt as if I had been blown over by a hurricane with all this frenzy. And damned if she didn't call back an hour later. The lights had gone out again. Did we have any time to spare? Of course, we didn't, and Sue was out of luck. It wasn't the confusion that got to me, but her indecisiveness. Most of her time was spent worrying instead of concentrating on getting the job done."

Worrier prevented Sue from sticking with her decision. Because of Worrier, she managed to snatch defeat from the jaws of victory. As Christopher said, "Either studio could have met her needs had she stayed long enough to iron out the wrinkles."

Any work situation requires that you make decisions and some will turn out better than others. You can't hit a home run every time, but with Worrier you're more likely to strike out with the bat on your shoulder. Act decisively without looking back.

Make the decision as best you can, and move to the next item on your agenda. You won't get experience unless you stick your neck out. Another word of advice — before you make a final decision, take a couple of minutes to unwind. Breathe deeply, sit alone, and get your thoughts together. This will reduce your panic and make you feel stronger.

Try to avoid accepting other people's opinions. Since Worrier makes you indecisive and unsure of yourself, you'll feel others are better qualified to make decisions than you. You'll be continually wondering, "Is this really what the boss wanted? Am I doing the assignment correctly? I wonder if it's good enough. Maybe I should ask someone else."

Helen, a woman who works in the electronics business, told us how she sought reassurance from others to avoid taking responsibility for her own job. "Worrier continually has me asking questions of others that I should be able to answer myself. Often those I ask are less knowledgeable than I. Many of their suggestions I have already thought of or implemented, yet I persist in asking for their advice. Why do I keep asking?"

The answer lies with Worrier. "If you just play dumb, you won't have to take any responsibility."

Helen didn't like this answer. "I have a good record here," she said, "and there's a lot of room for advancement. But not with Worrier. I realized this behavior wasn't helping me. I was passing the buck. It's not only time-consuming to rely on others, but I'm sure they don't appreciate the nagging questions, either."

Next time you ask a colleague for guidance, ask yourself, "Do I really need information or am I doubting my own judgement?" If your answer is the latter, you can bet Worrier is on the scene. Reassure yourself that you are the most qualified person to make the decision because you understand best the subtleties of the problem.

If Worrier dominates you at work, you probably are overly meticulous. Milt worked for a large printing company. He operated a four-color press that produced a large volume of work.

Coming from a much smaller printing shop with fewer orders, Milt felt unsure and Worrier stressed him. After six months he had to quit.

"I like to take time and pride in my work," Milt said. "It's very important to keep the machines clean and working properly. One slip-up can cause a bad registration and the entire job is wiped out. My supervisors kept telling me I wasn't fast enough. I guess it was true, because I always had more work to catch up on than the other printers did. When I tried to work faster, I always worried about making a mistake. If I did make one, I'd forget what I was doing and revert back to may old habit of stopping the press every few minutes. Jobs would stack up and I'd get further behind. If my union had allowed it, I would have stayed after hours. I started losing sleep at night and worrying about everything. But worst of all was the anxiety. The more anxious I got the more mistakes I made. I got so upset I finally had to quit. I'm a good printer as long as I don't make a mistake, but one mistake triggers Worrier, and I slow up, petrified I'm going to make another one."

Milt learned that Worrier slows down not only your work but your advancement as well, because the higher you go, the more is expected of you. Worrier has more fuel for sleepless nights. If you are content with a dusty little room in the rear of the building doing the same tedious job at the same careful pace, year after year, you won't need to deal with Worrier. If you want advancement, get rid of Worrier before you lose points with a boss who likes quick decisions and high output.

WORRIER AND HEALTH

Traveling in a remote mountainous area of eastern Nevada, we stopped in a small town to have breakfast. The restaurant was in an old dilapidated saloon, and a few cowboys and miners were eating at the counter. The waiter had a cast on his arm and was explaining it to the man next to us.

"When I was a small boy, my parents read me a story from the newspaper about a child who had a rare disease that prevented his body from metabolizing calcium. He couldn't drink milk or eat dairy products, and calcium deposits were causing his bones literally to turn to stone. That story had such an effect on me that I quit eating anything that contained dairy products. The weird thing is, a few years ago, I began having the same problem. I've had several operations for calcium deposits on my bones, and my doctor told me the disease is incurable. Now my body is literally turning to stone."

Was it mere coincidence, or did this man's preoccupation with his childhood fear contribute to the development of his disease? We'll never know, but we can speculate. Self-fulfilling prophecy is powerful stuff and so is the ability of our minds to imagine the worst.

Another example comes from a PBX operator who told us, "When worry takes over, I imagine the worst things happening. Then everything seems to go wrong at once and I can't function. With me, worry tends to snowball. As the day proceeds, Worrier predicts disaster wherever I turn. By five o'clock I'm so upset I could scream. My nerves are shot, my head is pounding, and I feel completely exhausted."

Morris, a truck dispatcher told us, "I startle easily. When someone comes in the room, even if it's someone I work with, I jump every time. I'm already feeling anxious by midday. I worry about sending the wrong truck to the wrong place. Sometimes I get panicky. My wife says I'm restless and jerk around in my sleep. I often sit bolt upright in bed with no real reason."

Morris is describing his Worrier. This Stress Personality sends his body into paroxysms of high excitation as he prepares for the hourly catastrophes that Worrier insists are inevitable. Worrier causes your body to react as though you were facing mortal danger. Your body is unable to distinguish between that which Worrier interprets as danger — like being late to work — and real danger. Worrier can trigger your body's alarm system at the slightest provocation, causing your heart to pound, your head to pulsate, and your anxiety to increase. The physical trauma Worrier generates because of a broken Xerox machine or a spouse who is half an hour late stresses your body countless times a day. In order to reduce the emotional and physical damage Worrier causes, you must pay attention to the Worrier Stress Points.

When you feel daily anxiety resulting from vague fears you can't put your finger on, when you constantly seek reassurance from others for even the most simple decisions, when you suffer from insomnia or wake up in the middle of the night worrying, when you are chronically excitable, jumpy, and easily overwhelmed — you've reached the Stress Point.

Insomnia affects about 30 million people in the United States and is the principal stress disorder caused by Worrier. The debilitating effects of insomnia are evidenced by your feeling tired all the time, less resistant to pressure, and less able to cope with daily demands. Of course Worrier becomes more worried because you're not sleeping and that causes a chain reaction, making chances of sleep even more remote. Exhausted by anxiety and sleeplessness, you can easily become a nervous wreck, or the victim of a bona fide nervous breakdown.

Look at the Worrier Stress Continuum. Note the Personal Discomfort clues Worrier sends out. Anxiety is number one. It is a self-perpetuating emotion. The more anxious you are, the more anxious you become. Feelings of panic, fear, and alarm often accompany anxiety.

If you suffer from allergies or asthma, Worrier's emotions can trigger an attack. In an asthma attack, the bronchial tubes become constricted, making it difficult to exhale completely. This erratic breathing pattern causes fear and panic. The body tightens, further constricting the bronchial tubes. In dealing with asthma it is vital to understand the roots of your anxiety and your fears before you reach this point.

Asthma, insomnia, and a multitude of phobias can be found on the Psychosomatic Illness end of the Stress Continuum. And, if Worrier dominates your life, watch out for the tendency to blow your symptoms out of proportion. You are often rewarded for being sick. People are more solicitous of you. Remember, this is a trap. You can really make yourself sick.

Hypochondriacs are stereotypical Worriers. Some really believe they are more vulnerable to disease than others. To them, life is capricious and untrustworthy. They'll come up with diseases known only to three doctors in the world. If you are a hypochondriac (and you know if you are), be careful you don't worry yourself into some illness you might otherwise never have contracted. Make sure Worrier isn't dumping you into some hospital bed so that you can be dependent on others. If this description fits you, ask yourself why you would want to be a passive recipient of illness. If you are, it is your choice. Excessive worry is an affirmation of your helpless victim status.

You have the ability to maintain a high degree of good health, which is your normal state. Take an active role in health maintenance. Nothing is a better insurance policy against ill health than a close watch on Worrier. When you learn and institute specific steps to maintain good health, the positive routine makes you feel better and eases Worrier's fears at the same time.

WORRIER GAME PLAN

**FAULTY
PERCEPTION:**   Worrying will keep you from unforeseen disasters.

HANDICAP: You will worry about decisions instead of making them.

RESULT: You will sound, act, and be unsure of yourself with a tendency to undo decisions you've made.

NEW
PERCEPTION: You've made good decisions in the past and you can trust yourself to make good decisions now.

FIRST MOVE: When making a decision, allow yourself a specific time period. List the options available to you within that time. Eliminate the options one by one in the amount of time you've allotted. Then congratulate yourself on your thoroughness and carry out the decision.

PITFALL: Because Worrier is afraid your decisions are wrong, it will try to make you change your mind and reopen the decision making process with: "Yes, but what if you've made the wrong decision?"

COUNTERMOVE: Allow yourself monthly reviews of your decisions. After making a decision, give yourself one-month during which you will experience the result of the decision, without questioning it. Then, sit down and review what has happened. Do not let Worrier preoccupy you during the one-month period.

FAULTY
PERCEPTION: **Worrying about those close to you means you care about them.**

HANDICAP: You alienate those close to you by worrying excessively.

RESULT: Family members will not tell you impor-
                           tant information because they fear it will
                           worry you. This "protection" will inter-
                           fere with their ability to communicate
                           and share intimate information with you.

NEW
PERCEPTION: You can have more intimacy in your rela-
                           tionships when they are not clouded by
                           worry.

FIRST MOVE: You have to give up the notion that wor-
                           rying about someone is an act of love.
                           Worrying will not protect you. Discuss
                           your Worrier traits with those close to
                           you and encourage them to tell you how
                           your worry affects them.

PTIFALL: Worrier will be reluctant to give up the
                           control over others that worry gives you.
                           This Stress Personality will tell you that
                           if you don't worry about people, you don't
                           care about them.

COUNTERMOVE: Don't let yourself worry about other
                           people's problems. Either do something
                           or let go of the worry. Those who look to
                           you for guidance will develop more self-
                           confidence when you show them you trust
                           them.

*Take yourself through this Game Plan by writing down the
Faulty Perception and one Handicap caused by your Worrier. What is
the Result? Identify a New Perception for this situation. Determine*

what your First Move will be. Acknowledge and list a Pitfall you might encounter when you put your First Move into practice. Then figure out a Countermove designed to outmaneuver your Worrier.

FAULTY
PERCEPTION:

HANDICAP:

RESULT:

NEW
PERCEPTION:

FIRST MOVE:

PITFALL:

COUNTERMOVE:

Any problems that occur while implementing your Game Plan might be a subject for a dialoguing session with your Worrier. If so, you now have a specific problem to deal with and focus on.

NEW BEHAVIORS TO RETRAIN WORRIER

What to do . . . *Trust Life*

- Concentrate on what is happening not on what could happen.

- Keep your eye on the "big picture." Better Judgement can help you do that.

- Instead of fretting, move to action whenever feasible.

- Worry about situations when they arise, do what you can, then let it go.

- Consider and accept change as positive and exciting.

- Trust yourself and stop checking your work over and over.

- Practice compartmentalizing problems to prevent them from becoming overwhelming.

- Acknowledge rumor as just that, and don't regard it as fact.

7.
INTERNAL CON ARTIST
Why Do I Say One Thing and Do Another?

$\mathcal{T}$ODAY is a new day. You've just awakened from a good night's sleep. You take a shower and look at yourself in the mirror. "All right, that's it. I've put this off long enough. I've got to go on a diet." You start your day with half a grapefruit, unbuttered toast, and black coffee. At lunch you have cottage cheese. You return to work feeling virtuous. That evening you go to a movie with friends and end up at your favorite pizza joint. Since you're dieting, you decide on tea with lemon. Knowing people are bored with hearing about another new diet, you practice in your mind what you're going to tell the waiter. "Tea with lemon," you say to yourself. When the waiter reaches your table, you're still reciting it in your mind, "Tea with lemon, tea with lemon." When the waiter finally asks for your order, you hear yourself say, "I'll have a small pizza with everything on it."

What happened? Who said that? It wasn't you. It was the part of you we call Internal Con Artist. If you are frequently frustrated because you don't follow through when you try to establish new behavior patterns, check to see if Con Artist isn't talking you out of them. "Eat, drink, and be merry, for tomorrow you may die" is the motto of this Stress Personality.

Internal Con Artist refers to conning ourselves. When we deny, ignore or minimize serious issues because we don't want to deal with them, it's an attempt to cope with stress. It's a form of nurturing. That the behavior is widespread is not surprising. Not everyone seeks psychotherapy for depression or to soothe hurt and anxiety. "Eating pizza, while not as healthy, is easier and cheaper to obtain," says Internal Con Artist. However, the bulge of excess weight is an obvious message from your body to find another form of nurturing. Feeling helpless is one feature of depression that evokes powerless feelings we felt as a child. By eating treats we're giving ourselves goodies forbidden by our parents. Since we're big now, no one can stop us . . . so there. This illustrates a major feature of the Internal Con Artist process, the internal battle for control of your impulses.

If you're eating because you feel bad, it's important to figure out what you're feeling bad about. One woman in our workshop discovered that because of a recent move she was lonely, "Hungry for relationships" was the way she put it. She had taken the hunger literally, and, eating her blues away, had gained thirty pounds. No amount of eating could substitute for friendship. Her Internal Con Artist eased up on the craving when she got to the real source of her problem.

If you're trying to curb sugar intake or stop impulsive behaviors like binge buying, you control Internal Con Artist by saying "Yes" but doing "No." For example, you're passing the frozen yogurt store. The inner tempter says, "Let's have a double cone, yogurt's good for you." So you apply willpower like a club and say to yourself, "No, absolutely not, we can't have sugar." Internal Con Artist interprets your "No" as a permanent ban on all comforting indulgences. A feeling of deprivation sets in. This increases the urge to splurge. Instead, say to yourself, "Yes, we can have yogurt or ice cream, but not now. We'll have it later." Then you add, "There's plenty of frozen yogurt in the world." This gives a message of self-indulgence which Internal Con Artist considers nurturing, and the desire diminishes. Do this every time your Internal Con Artist asks for something you're trying to abstain from.

This is the addictive part of your personality and the voice of procrastination. Con Artist believes things that don't come easily aren't worth the effort. Difficult projects are better avoided or conveniently forgotten. Con Artist is indisciplined and seeks immediate gratification. If you're susceptible to impulse buying, overeating, excessive drinking, gambling, or stretching the truth, check to see if you're not headed down Easy Street with Con Artist leading the way.

It is not hard to spot Internal Con Artist behavior in others once you become aware of it. Witness the person who conveniently "forgets" to pay debts, or your friend who has been putting off finishing her Master's thesis for eight years. Perhaps it's that personal friend who always has a new way to make a million, but is constantly broke. Another example is the woman who falls in love every week, swearing that this time "it's the real thing." The easiest to recognize are the ones who announce that the next time you see them they will have quit smoking or lost ten pounds, but it never happens. There is a little Con Artist in each of us. But when your procrastination and overindulgence become habitually self-defeating, it is time to take a serious look at this most elusive of Stress Personalities. People who were never able to trust the limits their parents set for them have difficulty developing self-control. Self control is the issue that becomes the primary focus of the internal struggle between you and your Internal Con Artist.

Internal Con Artist behavior develops in a variety of ways, but often a conflict is involved between parents who don't back up their demands and a child who resists having to follow orders. In Timmy's family, this conflict can be seen clearly:

"Timmy, this is the third time I've asked you to get up from that television and return Mr. Kaiser's garden tools."

"Not now, Mom, the movie's just started, and I don't have my shoes on."

"All right, you can do it later, but don't you forget."

Mom's Pleaser has encouraged Timmy's budding Con Artist behavior. Of course, later never comes and the garden tools lie rusting in the yard. When Mom discovers them, she gnashes her teeth and tries to think up a plausible excuse to tell her neighbor, who will not be happy to have his tools returned covered with rust. She may blame Timmy's negligence on his being a "scatter-brained kid with his head in the clouds" or his being too young to be responsible. Mom may just dismiss her inevitable guilt feelings by believing that since Mr. Kaiser is a grouch anyway, he deserves to have his tools rust.

Mom's inconsistency in enforcing rules is a model for Timmy's irresponsibility. On Monday she makes him clean up his room, but on Tuesday he sees her swearing in frustration as she does it herself. On Wednesday, she has quit checking on the condition of Timmy's room, thinking that it is too much bother. "He'll learn to be neat when he goes to college," she rationalizes.

If Mom's credibility is gone, Dad seems to be her opposite, but actually he has an equally ineffective way of dealing with Timmy. Although he pretends to rule with an iron hand, Dad is just hiding his disinterest in discipline. Timmy can see that Dad is mainly absorbed with himself, showing concern only at Mom's insistence that he "do something about that boy." Dad is frustrated that he can't get through to Timmy, thinking his position as father earns him respect, if nothing else.

Dad gets tough. "All right, Timmy, you will keep your room picked up every day and do what your mother tells you, or else . . ." For Dad, it is easier to tell Timmy what to do than to set a good example. Since Dad never follows up what he says, Timmy ignores his empty edicts and goes on about his business. Timmy soon learns that Mom is a pushover, softhearted, inconsistent, and easily manipulated. Dad's rigid posturing, moralizing, and attempts to foster responsibility by fiat can't be taken seriously.

Timmy will soon grow to resent his parents' attempts to pretend they are something they are not. "Do as I say, not as I do."

Parents who try to put forth an image that they can't live up to will not be trusted or believed by an impressionable youngster. Such a situation can create fertile ground for the growth of Internal Con Artist behavior, because in the future, anyone who imposes limits looks as if she is using unfair authority. Since your parents could be manipulated by your Internal Con Artist behavior, it is easy to draw the conclusion that so can anyone else, especially in stressful situations. Both you and other people will suffer from the lack of self-discipline that will haunt your adult life. Internal Con Artist will keep urging you to try to have your cake and eat it too.

Healthy adults exercise authority over themselves and develop their own standards. Internal Con Artist will limit self-control by associating self-discipline with punitive control. Because discipline has always had negative connotations, Internal Con Artist will avoid it at all costs. The Faulty Perception develops that self-indulgence should be the norm and self-denial the exception.

Because Tim has never learned to moderate the two excesses of self-indulgence and self-denial, as an adult he will be blind to the fact that other people see through his manipulations and don't approve.

This may prove especially true of women with whom he tries to form relationships. He will be baffled that women don't fall for his charm and manipulations the way Mom did. He will have trouble following through on commitments, taking the easy way out whenever possible. He will spend more energy figuring out how to avoid responsibility than accepting it. He will struggle constantly to control bad habits, and as he grows older they will take an increasing toll on his health.

As a parent, Tim will find his own children disturbing and troublesome. They will constantly test him and demand attention. They will seem irresponsible and unwilling to do what he asks. Tim will know he ought to be more strict, but it isn't easy to set standards when his own are inconsistent, changing from situation to situation. Instead of getting a grasp on his life and his children's, Tim will listen to Internal Con Artist, who assures him, "Hey, don't worry about it. Things always work out somehow."

Stress occurs when the anarchy in your life gets the better of you. The habit of denying reality when it is unpleasant and inconvenient takes more energy in the long run than facing it and dealing with it. If your Internal Con Artist is dominating you, it will be tempting for you to take the Easy Street option. If you do, you'll only be postponing responsibility until you eventually have to face facts.

Our survival skills are honed by challenge, struggle, and adversity. A Sufi wise man, so it is told, was explaining to a child the wonders of life. As the child watched the struggle of a butterfly to escape its cocoon, the wise man said, "Watch. It's strengthening its wings as it struggles. This is necessary, for without strong wings it can never fly." But the child, upon later observing this same scene alone, out of pity could not resist helping the butterfly escape the cocoon. He helped the butterfly before its wings were strong, and it fluttered to the earth, unable to fly.

The easy way out seldom helps you learn. Facing up to difficulties, working to change unhealthy habits, and assuming full responsibility for your actions will increase the immediate stress in your life, but the stress that results will gradually diminish as you become more and more adept at handling problems. The potential for harmful stress will be much greater when you let Internal Con Artist dominate your life. You can fool yourself only so long, and you can't fool your body.

Assessing Your Internal Con Artist Behavior

You can assess your own Internal Con Artist behavior by answering the questions below. Answer them honestly, choosing one of the five responses and placing the corresponding number in the box opposite each question. Add up the score and place the total along the Stress Behavior scale. Pay special attention to those questions on which you scored 6 or 8. If your total score is 48 or greater, you're engaging in Internal Con Artist behavior to the extent that it can be significantly disruptive in your life.

(Almost always=8)   (Frequently=6)   (Sometimes=4)
(Occasionally=2)   (Never=0)

1. (   )   How often do you put off until tomorrow the things you could have done today?

2. (   )   How often do you hold back from becoming fully involved in your work by telling yourself, "This job is only temporary, so why give it my best?"

3. (   )   Do you tell yourself and others, "Oh I don't need to jog; I get plenty of exercise walking from the parking lot to the office?"

4. (   )   Do you ignore regulations at work by saying, "Nobody follows these rules anyway, so why should I"?

5. (   )   How often do you have "one more drink" or "one more helping of food" than you intended?

6. (   )   Do you deny the existence of problems until it's too late to take corrective action?

7. (   )   At parties, do you tell yourself, "I'll be more relaxed and have more fun, once I start drinking?"

8. (   )   Do you eat, drink, or smoke when feeling sad, depressed, or angry?

9. (   )   Do you risk money impulsively in hopes of a windfall return?

10. (   )   Do you find yourself unexpectedly buying goods you don't really need?

11. (   )   How often do you talk yourself out of your decisions to quit smoking, go on a diet, or start an exercise

         program?

12. ( )   How often does procrastination keep you from accomplishing your goals?

    ( )   TOTAL

0	48	96

INTERNAL CON ARTIST FRIEND

"I don't understand it," laments Louise, a thirty-year-old secretary. "I just can't seem to get a relationship going with a man. As far as I can tell, I'm psychologically ready. I just don't know what gets in the way." What gets in the way is the extra sixty five pounds of fat she carries around. What Louise says she wants and what her appearance will attract are in direct contrast. When confronted with this fact Louise retorts, "But if a man really loves me, he should love me despite my fat." That's a tough enough request in a sexual relationship, but it is especially tough in this case because a man will have to love Louise despite both her fat and her Internal Con Artist, the real culprit.

Internal Con Artist not only leads her astray when she tries to lose weight, but prevents her from finding out that she may not really want to get involved. Louise's husband died of cancer three years ago, yet she still has not really let herself experience the pain and sadness she felt over her loss. Internal Con Artist had let her soothe her pain with food and then encouraged her to challenge conventional standards that say fat is ugly. There is nothing wrong with wanting to challenge convention, except that in this case, it's a bogus issue. It is Internal Con Artist urging her to avoid looking at the stress and pain she's suffered.

Internal Con Artist encourages self-defeating behaviors other than overeating, and such habits often lead people in the opposite direction of their real goals. For instance, Internal Con Artist may let you blame your loneliness and lack of friends on your job, your city or neighborhood, or the social climate of the times.

It is important that you start looking beyond Internal Con Artist's solutions. If you want friends, what can you do to develop them? Do you belong to organizations in which you meet people with interests similar to your own? Do you volunteer for civic activities that put you in touch with those who live near you? Do you make yourself available to friends when they need a helping hand? Internal Con Artist can hoodwink you into believing that you should change your life-style when you may be able to find happiness in your own backyard. Examine your own needs clearly in the light of day. Maybe you really enjoy spending most of your time by yourself and only get lonely occasionally. On the other hand, maybe you're reluctant to reach out for relationships for fear they'll require too much involvement. Internal Con Artist causes stress when it prevents you from taking a good look at yourself and your behavior. You feel dissatisfied but don't do anything about it because you don't know the roots of your dissatisfaction. This often occurs when Internal Con Artist prevents you from hearing things about yourself you don't want to face. If you're lucky, a good friend may be willing to warn you of behavior that's becoming a problem.

Mike's friend, Allen, tried to help, but Mike didn't like to listen to anything that didn't fit his easygoing view of the world. Mike and Allen used to play basketball at the YMCA every Monday night, but Mike began to cancel their games, going out for drinks instead. They gradually drifted apart. Allen made some attempts to get together with Mike, but it wasn't until they accidentally saw each other at a wedding that they made firm plans to meet. Mike, who had put on weight and was pouring down lots of booze, suggested they meet at a bar. When Allen arrived, Mike was already half loaded. They talked for a while until Allen finally cleared his throat nervously and said to Mike, "Uh, I've been meaning to talk to you but what I have to say isn't easy. It seems as if whenever we get together or talk on the phone, you're loaded.

Are you — ah — having any problems — with drinking, I mean?"

Mike was taken aback and a little embarrassed, but his Internal Con Artist quickly replied, "Why, no, not at all. I mean I'm not an alcoholic if that's what you're driving at. I do drink more than I used to, but then I've gotten in with a crowd from the office who like to drink. There's really no harm in it. I've never been a Puritan — you know that. Anyway, I like to party. It runs in my family," laughed Mike.

Allen felt a little sheepish and apologetic, saying that he didn't mean to bring up a problem where none existed. Mike quickly laughed it off and changed the subject with a joke. They finished off the evening with some good-natured bantering and solemn promises to get together "real soon." But it never happened. Allen was bored with Mike's drinking and Mike switched his allegiances to his drinking buddies. For Mike, it was easier to let a friendship go than deal with unpleasant realities.

Internal Con Artist believes friends are a dime a dozen, and it chimes in, "Statistics say there are at least thirty thousand people in the world at this moment with whom you are potentially compatible." If you believe this, you may never stick with any relationship too long. You'll never experience the fulfillment that comes from sharing both good times and bad.

Internal Con Artist will not be content with merely conning you. You will have to be on guard to make sure this part of you isn't a bad influence on your friends, too. Have you ever been with a friend who has to go study, and you hear yourself say, "You study too hard. Why take life so seriously? Let's go out and have some fun." Friend may even comply, but the next day when friend has to face her negligence, you will not be remembered fondly. Be careful when you try to get friends to do something "for their own good" that your motives aren't selfish and ruled by Internal Con Artist.

Another way Internal Con Artist affects your friendships is in urging you to take advantage of friends whenever you want something. Although it's true you take advantage only of those who allow it, friends will give you the benefit of the doubt, at first, since part of the role of a friend is to offer support. But if you have an Internal Con Artist, you will be tempted to prevail upon people more often than is good for the relationship. They end up feeling hurt and skeptical, and if you continue with this behavior, you lose their trust and friendship. Friendship cannot compete with your Internal Con Artist, but, more importantly, not even the best of friends can save the Internal Con Artist dominated person from self-defeat.

INTERNAL CON ARTIST MATE

Internal Con Artist loves the game of subterfuge in a marriage. People who make a habit of hiding things from their mates but who confide in friends are playing this game. A common example is "Now don't tell the wife, but . . ." Your mate probably suspects you are not always open and lives with a nagging suspicion that you are dishonest or even unfaithful. Internal Con Artist believes that what your spouse doesn't know won't hurt him or her. It is similar to the logic a child uses in keeping the truth from parents so he won't get into trouble. While children love secrets to help them maintain some autonomy, it is a dangerous way for adults to relate.

This juggling act your Internal Con Artist uses to manipulate the truth causes unnecessary stress and erodes your mate's trust. Let's say you've been going out a lot with the office gang after work. Although your wife hasn't said anything or shown any displeasure, Internal Con Artist urges you to avoid any potential hassle by covering up your real whereabouts. Convinced she'll be perturbed, you claim to have been working late. Murphy's law guarantees that before long your wife will call to ask if you've ordered the ballet tickets and someone will tell her you're at Sweet Freida's Hole-In-The-Wall bar next door and you're not expected back until next morning.

Now your wife is perturbed. Could there be something

going on? If you're escaping home for any deeper reason, then it's time to discuss the problem openly and honestly. Don't let Internal Con Artist talk you into believing cover-ups prevent problems. If you don't believe that, ask Richard Nixon. Cover-ups and lies are addictive and they too often come back to haunt you.

Internal Con Artist is your accomplice when you actually are up to something. If you have a tendency to cheat on your spouse or lover, you have probably lied about it more than once. That's what happened to Chad. Chad, forty-one, is an engineer for a computer firm.

"I don't know what's the matter with me. I'm happily married. I have a great wife and two terrific kids. I even like being married and having a home life. Yet I continually put my marriage in jeopardy. My wife had caught me cheating two or three times and the last time it happened she warned me she was leaving if I did it again. I behaved myself for almost a year, but then I met a woman I was attracted to and started seeing her. Boom, I was back in the old pattern of deception and lies, intrigue and secrecy. Finally I made a really stupid mistake. I gave my secretary a number at which I could be reached, and my wife happened to call. Naturally, as luck would have it, my girlfriend answered the phone. I had forgotten to tell the secretary not to give the number to my wife. My wife moved out with the kids and left. I no longer see the other woman. I could kick myself for having started the affair. I've promised my wife I will change and she's considering coming back, but deep inside I wonder if I will repeat the whole damn thing again."

Chad is caught in a typical Internal Con Artist cycle of resolve followed by breakdown. He then makes himself miserable with self-recriminations. Next he feels remorse, begging forgiveness and promising not to repeat the behavior. A new resolve follows, including claims to "stick to his guns" this time. But the guns get rusty, temptations appear, and the cycle begins again. One way Chad can interrupt the cycle is to avoid the trap. Remorse allows him to feel guilty and convince himself he's paid penalty enough, so Internal Con Artist steps in again and breaks down his resolve. Internal Con Artist tells Chad that it is worth taking a risk for the excitement of winning over a new woman and the intrigue of lies and subterfuge that can allay his fear that life will become boring. Chad's stress and that of his family is never-ending. If it were just he and his wife involved, the implications would be serious enough, but the children also suffer from this turmoil. They, too, are Internal Con Artist's victims.

In primary relationships, such as marriage, beware of the self-con game created by this Stress Personality. Here's how it works. You'll send out the hidden message to your mate that you can't handle yourself. You do this by subtly asking your mate to assume some of your responsibility. Maybe you ask, "Will you remind me to call my mother tomorrow? I keep forgetting."

Tomorrow comes, and your mate obligingly reminds you, "Don't forget to call your mother."

"Oh yeah, I've got to do that." You put it off. Your mate really should stop there, but since your unspoken message has been sensed, your mate is beginning to assume the responsibility of getting you to call your mother.

"Have you called your mother yet?"

"No, I forgot. Besides, I haven't had time."

All day you are being reminded by your dutiful mate, "Your mother's probably home by now."

"I'll call her in a minute as soon as this program is over."

An hour later you hear, "If you're going to call your mom, you'd better do it before she sits down to dinner."

"Yes, yes, I'll call her in a minute." Now you're irritated. This is where the game reaches its climax. Someone else has taken on your problem and you're starting to resist. Now you are replaying the childhood game you used when your parents tried to get you to do something and you resisted their authority.

Finally you blow up at each other. "Damn it, I'm not your father. You asked me to remind you to call your mother, and that's what I'm doing."

"Well, then stop acting like my father and stop bugging me."

You are back in the old family scenario, this time with new players. Now instead of experiencing the Internal Con Artist stress by yourself, you've dragged your mate along. The best thing your mate can do for you is to refuse to take any responsibility for your behavior. You have to shoulder your own responsibilities. Internal Con Artist lets you foist them off on your mate and it's instant trouble.

When you finally do decide to undertake substantial behavior change, Internal Con Artist will make matters worse by trying to blame others for your lack of success. For example, it will convince you that other people aren't supportive of your new efforts. One man told us how his wife was undermining his diet "She's always making rich Italian pasta dishes. She knows I'm on Weight Watchers, yet she cooks things I can't eat." It sounded like cruel and unusual punishment until we found out that Internal Con Artist was selecting the facts. His wife had supported his Weight Watchers' diet about 200 times over the last five years. As it became obvious that he had no intention of staying on it, she lost interest and returned to cooking what she liked. Be careful that you don't let Internal Con Artist blame your lack of self-control on someone else.

When one partner has a drinking problem, Internal Con Artist behaves the same as in the dieter's example. Internal Con Artist will get your mate to participate in the problem. First, the drinking partner pleads with his mate to hide the liquor. When his resistance lowers, he begs, cajoles, or terrorizes mate into revealing the hiding place. The next day the raging hangover is blamed on the mate who didn't care enough to help the drinker resist. Stay clear of this form of manipulation. It is the alcoholic game. It is also the Internal Con Artist's game, which involves constant effort to avoid responsibility for lack of self-control.

When you become aware of Internal Con Artist's behavior and decide to change it, you will start to change your life. Change, even for the better, is threatening. You may be afraid your relationships will change when you do. They will. Relationships are living things and when one person begins to change, the result will inevitably affect the other person. If your partner also has an Internal Con Artist, don't expect support as you begin bringing this part of yourself under control. You may hear your mate say, "You're not any fun since you quit drinking." "You're going to die of something, so it might as well be good food." If that doesn't work, your mate may try to discourage you by telling you, "You can't change. You're always going to be this way."

If this describes your relationship, it's time for a frank discussion with your mate in which you declare firmly that you are finished suffering from Internal Con Artists, whether your own or mate's. If your mate is also interested in changing, you can help each other by pointing out Internal Con Artist behavior whenever you hear it. If the problem involves drinking, you may need professional help. If it's food, there are organizations like Weight Watchers that can help. However, the primary responsibility is yours for controlling your Internal Con Artist's impulsive needs. It will take all the energy you have to break this self-destructive behavior pattern. But it could also mean opening a new chapter in your life and your relationships.

INTERNAL CON ARTIST BOSS

Just because you've made it to a management position doesn't mean you're free of Internal Con Artist. It simply means Internal Con Artist shows up in different ways. Since you have ultimate responsibility for your decisions now, Internal Con Artist may allow you to put off making decisions in the hope that better answers will come floating through the window. You may be used to having backup help or sources of advice in another role, but as manager you need to face issues squarely. There may be a temptation to cut corners or employ questionable ethical tactics since there's less chance of being found out by a superior. Although

Internal Con Artist hasn't been a serious enough threat to keep you from getting where you are now, it may start to interfere once your responsibilities have been expanded. One thing that often happens is that you take advantage of your power. This will eventually lead to a breakdown of the trust and respect you need from your employees. No matter what Internal Con Artist tells you, a manager can enforce "right of rank" for only so long before mutiny occurs. Keep listening to your employees rather than becoming intoxicated with your own power.

Ravi, an investment analyst for a fast-growing electronics firm, found himself caught in a classic squeeze play, brought about by a boss whose Internal Con Artist got carried away. Profits had led to a large cash reserve, and the board of directors was anxious to find some investment opportunities. When the president came up with an idea, he asked Ravi to develop a feasibility plan to show the board. Ravi's conclusions led him to advise against the president's idea.

"The president called me in and gave me a long talk about loyalty and how during his tenure as president the company had come up from nowhere to its current lucrative position. He said that the stockholders trusted him to make these decisions because of his nearly flawless track record. It took a while before I realized he was asking me to change my recommendation and produce evidence that would validate his point of view. I thought it over for a few days. I really stewed about it. Finally I came to the conclusion that it was unethical to change my point of view. He kept telling me how good I would look once the deal paid off and that there would undoubtedly be a promotion in it for me. His power and flattery went straight to my head, so I rewrote the report to his satisfaction. Well, as you probably guessed, the deal went sour and the company lost a bundle on his bright idea. Worst of all, I was fired. It turned out that in order to cover himself, the president used me as a scapegoat."

Ravi's boss's Internal Con Artist dealt the final blow to Ravi, but not before Ravi's own Internal Con Artist had taken over and put him through a great deal of stress.

When others, especially those who outrank you, break the rules or exhibit dishonest behavior you may be tempted by Internal Con Artist's conclusion that "Everybody else is doing it, so I will too." This is ultimately an untenable moral position. A value system based on what you can get away with will be stressful because of its lack of consistency and sense of purpose. Managers are very visible. Many of your employees will be paying close attention to what you're doing, waiting for a slip-up so that they can rationalize a drop in the quality of their own work. You will find that employees tend to do what you do, not what you say. If you are lax about company rules or policies, they will be, too. If you take two-hour lunches, your employees will stretch their breaks. Whenever Internal Con Artist talks you into bending rules, you can count on the fact that others will do the same.

If you are self-employed, it is vital that you control Internal Con Artist. Procrastination here is lethal. Karen, a freelance writer, tells about her struggles with Internal Con Artist:

"Since I am self-employed, I have to keep myself motivated. Many days I do fine. But on too many occasions Internal Con Artist diverts my energy from my work. I decide to clean up the kitchen before I start to write. Then I do a load of laundry. I may start some work project that isn't due for months, but fail to work on pressing deadlines that seem like awesome tasks. Some days I manage to stall writing until five o'clock. I'll decide to work until midnight and find myself spending half the evening on the phone talking to a friend. I have never missed a deadline but the agony I put myself through to finish is getting to be a strain. I'm having a very hard time changing this pattern. Maybe I don't exert enough willpower or have enough self-control."

Indeed, self-control is at the heart of dealing with Internal Con Artist. Karen should set goals and take charge of her progress from a more responsible position. Like so many others, she may see self-control as being too tough on herself. She needs to redefine it as a benevolent, helpful trait.

Along with learning self-control comes paying attention to details. This will be a nettlesome problem with Internal Con Artist urging you to ignore such pettiness. In contrast to Internal Timekeeper, who creates problems for you by keeping you so busy you become inattentive to details, Internal Con Artist always looks for ways to save effort and thus never does a completely thorough job. Although not all of Internal Con Artist's effort-savers will trip you up, in the long run some will, and the damage can be serious.

A carpenter told us about a housing contractor he once worked for who thought he was saving money by building houses the easy way. "This guy was unscrupulous," Jake told us. "We had a contract to build a large number of housing units on an air base. He took all kinds of shortcuts, but one day he went too far for me. When you frame a house, there has to be a certain ratio of two-by-sixes to other structural supports. These houses were all alike, so the formula was the same. But this guy, in order to cut costs and beef up his profits, wouldn't put up the required number of two-by-sixes and other lumber. He figured out a way to fool the building inspectors, so those units were going up in violation of code, not to mention ethics and safety. I finally quit, but I should have blown the whistle on him first. He finally got caught when one of the other carpenters told the inspector. The rest of them were furious when the job got shut down and they were laid off."

Awareness of Internal Con Artist behavior frequently offers enough motivation to start controlling this Stress Personality. Internal Con Artist's voice may not go away, but you can start saying no. Internal Con Artist behavior stifles your innate ability to find effective solutions to problems. An effective leader plans and directs action. When you realize that all you're doing is reacting to situations, it's probably a result of Internal Con Artist-induced failure to plan. Remember, Internal Con Artist likes to avoid responsibility at all costs. If you are asking for increasing responsibility, you have to control Internal Con Artist if you are to succeed.

INTERNAL CON ARTIST EMPLOYEE

Literally millions of people hate their jobs. For many, the jobs are truly unrewarding or boring. If you count yourself in this number, it may be time to take a look at the attitude you bring to your work. If it's influenced by Internal Con Artist, your unhappiness may well stem from Internal Con Artist's disdain for any disciplined endeavor. Perhaps your Internal Con Artist is preventing you from getting totally involved in your work with the excuse that you are really destined for something different and better. In either case, Internal Con Artist views work somewhat like punishment. Until you bring this Stress Personality under control, no job will be satisfying for you and you will spend eight hours a day disliking your work and causing yourself stress.

This Internal Con Artist attitude can put you at a decided disadvantage when you're working in a large organization that requires some self-motivation. Suppose you're newly employed and scheduled for orientation sessions the first two months. Internal Con Artist, ever alert to ways of circumventing orders, hears that nobody checks to see who actually attends the orientation meetings. You figure you can learn all there is to know by osmosis and so you skip the first session. The following week you listen to Internal Con Artist again and sneak out early from the next two sessions. You miss the last session entirely. If you feel a little uneasy, there's good reason. Internal Con Artist has already created a stress problem for you.

Because Internal Con Artist is more interested in having you look prepared than be prepared, you may find yourself in an embarrassing situation at staff meetings for which you are supposed to have done your homework. The evening before, when you decided to watch television instead of read up on T-Bills, it didn't seem it would matter much the next day. "Who pays attention to what you do anyway; no one will even notice," Internal Con Artist had assured you. This morning, however, as you see everyone getting ready to go into the meeting you begin to feel the panic of unpreparedness. Five minutes before the meeting you are pumping everyone you can corner for information. ". . . and for that reason the market trend in T-Bills is showing an upward surge," Smith, a colleague, tells you earnestly. At the meeting the boss throws out the general question: "What does the high interest rate portend for passbook savings accounts?" The boss looks right at you. Before you can stop yourself, Internal Con Artist jumps into the breach volunteering, "Sir, it is my opinion that we'll see an upward trend in the T-Bill market." The boss smiles and nods. You keep your face averted from Smith's and hasten out of the meeting the minute it adjourns.

Not only will you lose the respect of colleagues with this Internal Con Artist behavior, but you tend to give the impression you know more than you actually do.

Eventually the boss will dig deeper and ask you to substantiate what you say and you will be caught with egg on your face. Throughout your career you will dance along the edge of credibility always aware of the risk of last minute or incomplete preparation. Anxiety and guilt build up and you experience stress. Better Judgement may warn you that you may get away with it this time, but that you can't be lucky all the time. Stay in touch with Better Judgement, because if you don't you'll lose your conscience completely and careen through life taking advantage of others.

One of Internal Con Artist's favorite on-the-job delusions is to make believe your current job is only temporary and that your real career waits just around the corner. This con robs you of job satisfaction and your employer of his or her money's worth. You'll feel bored because you're not really involved and you avoid as much work as possible. Internal Con Artist can think of many ways to put off work in which you don't feel involved. The salesman who spends the afternoon at the movies instead of making calls and the programmer who habitually takes three-hour lunches, daydreams, and pretends to look busy when she's not, are both Internal Con Artist victims.

Several years ago we were introducing our stress program to a trainer in a company and in the middle of our presentation he told us, "Well, it's OK with me for you to train our staff, but I doubt that I will be here. My brother and I have been planning to sail around the world for years and I suspect this year we'll do it." We did present our program and this man was still there. We came back the next year and he was still there, bored and feeling uninvolved in his job. Evaluate the reason you may be taking a mental vacation from work. If you can find a more exciting job, go out and do it, but beware of the self-con game where everything is temporary and the grass is always greener on the other side of the fence.

Internal Con Artist behavior can also be a sign that you're burning out on your job. If you are normally a highly motivated ambitious employee and notice a loss of interest, boredom or weariness with your job, those are tell-tale signs of burn-out.

Be careful not to let this part of yourself use that as an excuse however. Evaluate your job periodically. Are you getting what you want? Is there a future in it? Have you lost the fire? You'll have to squarely face those issues by setting Internal Con Artist aside. You don't want this Stress Personality making your career decisions.

On most jobs there is enough potential for stress without your creating more. Lots of people go to elaborate efforts to avoid investing themselves in their work. This effort only adds to the stress of being dissatisfied with your job. Internal Con Artist defeats you by not allowing you to take yourself seriously as a worker, whatever your position. When you let this stress dominate you, you're leaving your economic fate in the hands of a part of you that is still waging a childhood war against being responsible.

INTERNAL CON ARTIST
AND HEALTH

A recent survey by pollster Louis Harris, sponsored by the Pacific Life Insurance Company, revealed that "Americans know what's good for them, but haven't the willpower to change their habits towards better health." In this survey, which represented a cross section of American public opinion, sixty-seven percent of those questioned said they would be healthier if they changed their eating habits. Sixty-two percent said they knew that lack of regular exercise was harmful. An equal number were overweight and knew the extra pounds were unhealthy. Seventy-one percent agreed with this statement: "Like most people, I just go on doing the things that make me less healthy even when I know I shouldn't." (San Francisco Chronicle, December 1, 1979)*

This poll shows the prevalence of Internal Con Artist and its detrimental effects on America's health. Internal Con Artist behavior is irrational. Why, for example, do hospital X-ray technicians who spend their days photographing diseased lungs, smoke? Why do long-haul truck drivers risk driving thirty-six hours without sleep, relying on amphetamines to keep them awake and alert? Why do people suffering from obesity keep stuffing themselves? The answer to these questions is denial, a major feature of Internal Con Artist behavior. This Stress Personality carries a memory eraser and denies obvious analogies between past experience and present behavior. Blinding you to your behavior, Internal Con Artist helps you deny that your habits are harmful so that there's no pressure to change.

If you have ever convulsed, wheezed, or hacked your way through a cough caused by smoking, ending the cough with a resolve to quit that never is carried through, Internal Con Artist was at work. You may light up another cigarette, vowing that pretty soon you're going to quit. Maybe you do quit for a while but go back.

Mort took a no-smoking class to help him through the first

* This survey is done every year and the most recent 1991 survey indicates that people haven't changed much in the last twelve years.

few days of quitting. It wasn't long afterward that Internal Con Artist convinced him the withdrawal symptoms he was suffering were worse than the smoking, so he allowed himself three cigarettes a day. Then five. Soon he was back to his old habit. The denial process had taken over.

Internal Con Artist also uses denial by underestimating or ignoring signals from your body. Internal Con Artist will tell you that going to the doctor just because of a few chest pains is the sign of a hypochondriac. Be wary of that con also. Chest pains can be a serious warning of cardio-vascular disease. Coronary patients often deny or fail to recognize symptoms of hypertension. One of the most difficult problems in cancer treatment is caused by people who ignore or deny warning signals until it is too late for effective treatment.

Again, you need to pay attention to the Stress Point. At work, if you habitually feel balanced on a tightrope, bored by doing just enough to get by without getting fired, you've reached the Internal Con Artist Stress Point. The same is true if you consistently refuse to face up to daily problems in the hope that they'll go away. If you drink regularly to help make it through the stress of your days or if you are chronically moody, irritable, and depressed because you cannot get your weight down, you've reached the Internal Con Artist Stress Point. If you are unable to muster the self-discipline to control impulsive spending or if you are convinced you need to drink, smoke, or use drugs to make you lovable, interesting, creative, or successful, you've reached the Internal Con Artist Stress Point.

Your Internal Con Artist will help you ignore the frequent hangovers or memory blackouts that are the first clues of alcoholism. Alcoholism is promoted by Internal Con Artist behavior and at the same time, in its turn it promotes Internal Con Artist behavior. Internal Con Artist first involves itself in creating the denial system that starts you drinking. Then, the toxic effect of alcohol creates the addiction that stimulates more Internal Con Artist behavior to help you find ways to keep drinking.

The process is similar for obesity. Internal Con Artist weakens your willpower and you overeat. Soon you become depressed and disgusted by your fat, and you'll soothe the pain with more food. One woman told us in a seminar, "I feel so bad about being overweight that the only thing that makes me feel better is to eat something. At least it tastes good." The popularity of diet books attests to the extent of the obesity problem in this country. Yet while a diet can be helpful, it only treats the symptom. The real problem lies in the Internal Con Artist process. This Stress Personality confuses psychological nourishment with physical nourishment. When you feel deprived, Internal Con Artist fulfills you with food or drink, but the process gets you in trouble. Your real deprivation is emotional. It might be anything from unhappiness over a love affair to the loss of a job or a child leaving home. Internal Con Artist doesn't understand that you can nourish yourself better by abstaining. This is where you can utilize the services of your Better Judgement, the part of you that knows what it is you're actually being deprived of. The deprivation is only part of the issue. The main issue is how you are handling the deprivation.

Even those who really want to take an active role in keeping themselves healthy can be stymied by Internal Con Artist. Getting back into shape after an illness created a struggle for Inga with her Internal Con Artist.

"Two years ago I went from an extremely athletic person to a virtual invalid. I was thirty-three years old and developed a chronic debilitating illness while traveling in Africa. Prior to my illness I'd been an avid runner, averaging about forty miles per week. It took nearly two years to recover, and my doctor suggested I might get well faster if I returned to running. I started over again. As I worked my way up to three miles a day, my body rebelled. The sore muscles, creaky bones, and achy joints made me want to give up. I started finding excuses not to run. Either it was too hot or too cold or I was too busy. Finally I gave it up entirely. A month or so after I quit, my friend Hal challenged me."

'Why did you quit?' he asked. I told him it was too hard to get back in shape and I was afraid I might get sick all over again. Hal knew there was no real reason I couldn't make it and said so. 'Nonsense,' he said, 'there's no easy road to physical conditioning, Inga. You know that. I think you're babying yourself.'

"My Better Judgement told me Hal was right, but I didn't realize Internal Con Artist was helping me baby myself. Once I figured it out, I asked Hal to start running with me since I knew he wouldn't put up with my Internal Con Artist excuses. Now I'm back to running thirty miles a week and I feel great."

The most important Personal Discomfort symptom associated with Internal Con Artist behavior is the frustration that results from Internal Con Artist thwarting your efforts to improve yourself.

"I've been trying to lose weight since I was a teenager," says Loretta, a nurse. "For twenty years I've been fighting this battle. All I have to show for it is a sense of overwhelming frustration." When this frustration becomes a daily feature of your life it causes feelings of defeat, unworthiness, and hopelessness. These feelings, in turn, trigger overeating, excessive drinking, or whatever other self-defeating behavior is familiar. In order to fight Internal Con Artist, you need to begin some systematic communication with your Better Judgement. We describe a dialogue with Better Judgement in the dialoguing section. Read that section; then sit quietly, take some deep breaths, and let yourself relax. Clear your mind and visualize your Better Judgement sitting opposite you. If you're trying to control your eating habits, for example, ask your Better Judgement what need your eating is substituting for.

Once you begin dialoguing with your Better Judgement, listen for its answer. Then write down the answer on a tablet. Do this once a day for as long as it takes you to begin following Better Judgement's advice.

INTERNAL CON ARTIST GAME PLAN

**FAULTY
PERCEPTION:**   Self denial is punishment.

HANDICAP: You rationalize your self-defeating patterns.

RESULT: You feel frustrated and discouraged about your inability to change your stress behavior.

**NEW
PERCEPTION:**   Self discipline can give pleasure and satisfaction and enhance self-esteem.

FIRST MOVE: List all Internal Con Artist rationalizations as to why you can't change.
(a) "I can't lose weight because I'm too set in my ways."
(b) "If I quit smoking I'll be a nervous wreck."
Next to each rationalization list one exception.
(a) "In college I played sports, ate balanced meals and weighed fifty pounds less."
(b) "There was a time when I didn't smoke and wasn't nervous."

PITFALL: Internal Con Artist will resist by saying, "Let's start next week." "You'll never have any more fun." Or, "Food, drink and cigarettes help you relax."

COUNTERMOVE:	Begin substituting a New Behavior for each rationalization in the First Move, e.g. (a) Begin a diet program you know will work and give yourself a thirty-day trial. (b) Attend a stop-smoking class. (c) Start exercising moderately by walking whenever and wherever you can.
FAULTY PERCEPTION:	**If you ignore problems, they'll solve themselves.**
HANDICAP:	You don't face up to serious problems.
RESULT:	You resist dealing with tough issue until it's too late to take corrective action.
NEW PERCEPTION:	By dealing with issues, you control your life instead of leaving it to the whims of fate.
FIRST MOVE:	First, squarely face up to the fact that you have an issue to deal with and choose your first action step.
PITFALL:	Con Artist will try to convince you that it's going to take too much time and trouble to deal with this issue.
COUNTERMOVE:	Start immediately taking active countermeasures against Internal Con Artist's rationalizations. Decide on some goals and

outcomes you want to achieve and move toward them.

Take yourself through this Game Plan by writing down the Faulty Perception and one Handicap caused by your Internal Con Artist. What is the Result? Identify a New Perception for the situation. Determine what your First Move will be. Acknowledge and list a Pitfall you might encounter when you put your First Move into practice. Then figure out a Countermove designed to outmaneuver your Internal Con Artist.

FAULTY
PERCEPTION:

HANDICAP:

RESULT:

NEW
PERCEPTION:

FIRST MOVE:

PITFALL:

COUNTERMOVE:
    Any problems that occur while implementing your Game Plan might be a subject for a dialoguing session with your Internal Con Artist. If so, you now have a specific problem to deal with and focus on.

NEW BEHAVIORS TO RETRAIN INTERNAL CON ARTIST

What to do . . . *Shape Up*

- Be accountable for your actions to yourself and others.

- Change situations you don't like.

- Curb eating "bad" foods by having a food plan six days a week. Let ICA choose the foods on the other day.

- Make your own decisions and be wary about the influence of others' Internal Con Artists.

- Be results oriented.

- Replace smoking with healthy nurturing.

- Be honest about your mistakes.

- Don't rationalize non-productive behavior.

DIALOGUING

*Talk to Your Stress Personalities —
They Are Talking to You.*

Stress Personalities act out of our conscious awareness. Once you're familiar with these parts of yourself, you are ready to go a step further and contact the Stress Personality directly. You can do this through guided dialoguing, a systematic method of carrying on a conversation with your subconscious. Most of us do this all the time as we slip into deep thought as we walk, ride, or do odd jobs. By engaging in direct negotiation with your Stress

Personality you can actually conduct stress-reducing therapy on yourself. Confronting yourself constructively will enable you to reduce your own stress. You will, in effect, negotiate a contract with your Stress Personality to change its behavior, become more cooperative, or cease and desist.

Dialoguing needs to provide for a give-and-take process. Because your Stress Personality has been with you a long time, it won't be easy to let it go. Negotiation is the key. When you stop to think of it, you negotiate contracts every day when you agree to perform a service, make a date to meet someone for lunch, or pass along information from one person to another. Use the same methods you use in everyday negotiations to negotiate a contract with your Stress Personality. Since it is a part of you every bit as real as another person, you can treat it just as you do another person. Don't be afraid to question, demand, and compromise.

There's no better way than dialoguing to get to know your Stress Personalities, and until you know them you can never be sure you have the upper hand.

How to Dialogue

The best way to begin dialoguing is to set up two chairs or pillows facing each other in a room where you have some privacy. (Later, after you are familiar with the technique, it can be done in writing, while walking down the street, or jogging — virtually anywhere.) Sit in a chair and imagine your Stress Personality in the other. Engage the Stress Personality in conversation by asking it a question such as: "Why are you so strong in my life right now?" Or, "What is your purpose in being here?" Then change positions, moving to the other chair or pillow and reply as the Stress Personality would: "I'm here because you need me right now, and I'm very important to you because I keep you striving (or making people happy, or whatever)." Continue this conversation back and forth. Whenever a question is asked, switch positions and respond. The goal of this conversation is to clearly separate you from the Stress Personality and to establish the nature of the relationship between the two of you. This way you can begin to resolve the conflict you have been experiencing. Sometimes powerful self-realizations emerge. When you switch chairs and respond as your Stress Personality, posture and voice changes may occur, and you may be startled to hear what you are saying to yourself. Don't be alarmed. It does not mean you're schizophrenic. You are, instead, finally acknowledging the warring factions within you that are operating at cross-purposes and causing you stress. Because the Stress Personality developed many years ago when you were a different person, you may be surprised to hear yourself acknowledge aloud attitudes and beliefs you thought were part of your past, not your present. Expressing these feelings, attitudes, and beliefs promotes release of stress and motivates you toward health.

When you dialogue, there's nothing you are *supposed* to say. There are no right or wrong responses. When they first dialogue, some people feel insincere, as if they are play acting. It may seem awkward, like anything you try for the first time, but stick with it. In time you'll find the self-revelations so profound that you'll become an enthusiast of the technique. The more you do it, the easier it will become. Remember, there is no way to be "unreal" when dialoguing. Whatever you say or do is real because you are doing it. This process brings a structure and purpose to self-conversation in order to help you reduce stress.

When you dialogue with your Stress Personality, start by expressing your feelings. Feelings often give better clues to the cause of your inner conflict than does your rational mind. Expressions of feelings include "I feel angry, hurt, scared, depressed." Expressions of feelings do *not* include "I feel I should get ahead." "I feel that you never consider me." These are opinions that mask underlying feelings. Stress Personalities act against you because you are estranged from these parts of yourself. Communicating feelings closes the gap between you and the Stress Personality and allows the true nature of your problem to emerge. Feelings don't lie. They come out for a reason, and when you pay attention to them, underlying problems can be uncovered.

You may be surprised to find that the Stress Personality actually has feelings different from the ones you think you are experiencing. When you recognize this, you will have established the separation between you and your Stress Personality. This is an important step in gaining control over your Stress Personality. Now that you see each other's points of view, you can begin to resolve your differences, just as you would with a person with whom you are in disagreement. In the following pages, we'll provide some examples of dialogues. Read them over to get an idea of how the process works. Then try dialoguing yourself.

Self-Guided Dialoguing

The results of dialoguing sessions vary. Sometimes you will find that your Stress Personality is reluctant to cooperate with you. Even though a behavior is causing you stress, the Stress Personality will be convinced that it is acting in your own best interest, and its convictions may be too strong for you to alter at that given moment. Here is an example of dialoguing in which John is trying to be an effective supervisor, but he can never satisfy Critical Judge.

John: "You always have me apologizing to my boss for the kind of job I do. I hear you telling me I'm not prepared or that my unit thinks I'm incompetent. Whenever I think I've done a good job. I hear you say, 'You could have done better.' I just sink into despair when you do that. You make me feel depressed and my neck feels stiff."

(John switches chairs and responds as Critical Judge.)

Critical Judge: "Well, what's wrong with doing better? You can always improve. You never live up to your capabilities. You're really lazy."

(John switches chairs and responds as himself.)

John: "I feel pressured when you tell me I'm not living up to my capabilities or that other people do so much better than I. When you tell me I'm not as good as I should be, I feel sad, frustrated, and angry that I cannot live up to my own expectations."

Critical Judge: "Well, I feel the same about you. Here I am trying to help, and you are angry at me. Why if it weren't for me, you'd never get anywhere."

John: "I get tired of hearing what I should and could be doing and what I'm doing wrong. Is there anything you do like about me"

Critical Judge: "You need so much improvement that it's hard to like you. Look at the way you dress. You're far too lenient with your staff. They're never going to learn anything unless you consistently and continually point out their deficiencies."

John: "I want you to let up, Critical Judge. You don't help me with your negative attitude. I need to feel better about myself."

Critical Judge: "I don't think I can do that. Without me you'd be an utter failure."

John: "Does that mean you're not going to let up?"

Critical Judge: "I can't, you need me."

John: "Maybe I do, but then maybe I don't. I'm going to start paying more attention to your constant put-downs. We are going to talk some more."

In this example, John's Critical Judge has stated clearly that it will not give up its role in his life. At this point he is unable to negotiate a contract. But he has begun the process of challenging his Critical Judge. He is aware of how this Stress Personality creates stress for him, but is not sure that he can get along without its pushing him. More dialoguing will eventually bring about some compromise between John and his Critical Judge.

Contract Dialoguing

In the following example, we'll show you how one person did negotiate a contract with her Stress Personality. Lois, a high school teacher, is working hard to make the debate team she coaches the best in the state. She wants to slow down, but Striver is reluctant.

Lois: "Striver, you are pushing me so hard I'm worn out. I'm exhausted and feel resentful that this job has become my whole life."

Striver: "You have to do your best and be the best. It's the best or nothing, and I don't care if you're tired."

Lois:	"I don't feel I need you anymore. I've pushed hard enough for the last twenty years. The debate team's standings are higher than I ever expected. I feel I've done my job."
Striver:	"But the community, school administration, and students expect you to perform at a certain level. You've got to improve on last year's performance."
Lois:	"Maybe we can, but I'm not working Saturdays anymore."
Striver:	"You can't slack off. We were fifth in the state last year. If you push a little harder, we could be first."
Lois:	"I don't have that extra energy to put out. I've given enough to this debate team. I have to save some energy for myself and my family. If fifth is as high as we finish, it's OK. The competition is stiff and fifth is more than adequate."
Striver:	"Yes, but first is higher and almost within your reach."
Lois:	"I mean it, Striver. I have to slow down, with or without your cooperation. Are you willing to cooperate?"
Striver:	(Reluctantly) "Well, we could be first, but I do see what a toll it is taking on you. Besides, when I push you it just seems to make you more tired. OK, I will cooperate."

Lois: "Here's the contract. The New Behavior
                     I'm proposing is that I will be taking Satur-
                     days off for the next three months. We'll
                     see how it goes and then renegotiate for
                     more time. I'm going to start next Satur-
                     day."

Striver: "Three months seem like too long. How
                     about two months?"

Lois: "Ok, two months it is. But we definitely
                     renegotiate after two months. Let's estab-
                     lish a cue word, because I know that from
                     time to time you will forget I mean business
                     and go right back to pushing me. I'm going
                     to use 'fifth' because fifth place is good
                     enough. When I say 'fifth,' I want you to
                     back off. Do you agree?"

Striver: "Yes, but I may not like it."

Lois: "You don't have to like it. You just have to
                     back off."

Use any cue word or phrase that is meaningful to you. Cue
words can be used with any of the Stress Personalities. If your
Stress Personality doesn't stop pushing you when you use the cue
word, dialogue again. Find out what's getting in the way. Listen
to the Stress Personality's position, but stick with your convictions. The art of compromise can help modify the behavior of
your Stress Personality. Compromise takes patience. You may
want to get rid of a behavior overnight, but since your Stress
Personality has been a part of you for so long, it is unlikely that it
will disappear altogether after one self-revelation. As you con-

tinue to dialogue and work on your behavioral changes, it will be easier to keep annoying Stress Personalities in line. Continually point out to your Stress Personality that it isn't helping you. You may even miss this part of you once its voice is stilled, but as you begin to live free of its influence, you will wonder how you ever allowed it to dominate you so.

Better Judgement

We all have Better Judgement, but frequently we forget to call on it. Sometimes we just don't want to listen. During your formative years, Stress Personalities develop. Often they become so dominant they blot out Better Judgement. But just as you can use dialoguing to get in touch with Stress Personalities, you can also use it to reach Better Judgement. If you are unable to resolve a problem you are having with a Stress Personality, sometimes just talking to Better Judgement can set you straight and point you toward a healthy course of action.

Better Judgement is an inner gyroscope, guiding us every day often without our awareness. Insights which come in a flash, are from Better Judgement. New Perceptions are an example of these insights. For instance, when you're plagued by self-doubt over an important decision, you may have an "ah ha" experience that Worrier is preoccupying your thoughts. This realization comes from Better Judgement. The ability to recognize that you have Stress Personalities and step out of yourself to objectify your behavior, is a quality of Better Judgement.

Better Judgement is definable only in subjective terms yet it's wisdom is unerring. Here are some statements which serve as both description and definition. They come from participants of our programs.

*"Common sense. My Better Judgement is non-reactive,
and considers alternatives."*

*"A part of myself that encourages me to take the time to
evaluate prior to acting."*

*"An inner sense that makes me stop and pause when I'm too busy to
smell the roses. It just takes a moment and
so much good comes from it."*

For some people Better Judgement seems to emerge from a logical
or rational part of themselves. For example:

"A logical reasonable part of myself that asks me questions."

*"A calm, logical, part of myself that helps me step back when needed,
and view the situation objectively."*

For others, Better Judgement seems to rise from a more mystical
source.

*"A gut feeling that tells me to take a course of action
contrary to the standard."*

*"It's the part of my inner self that emerges from the unconscious.
It urges me."*

*"Mostly an intuitive feeling. I'm not always sure when
it comes in but afterward I know it was there."*

"A sixth sense. When I'm relaxed it gives me answers."

*"Reminds me that my immediate problems are not important
in the outcome of my total life and they will pass."*

We worked with a man dominated by Pleaser who got himself into a stressful ordeal and couldn't see his way out until he talked to Better Judgement. He was having an affair with a client and although he wanted to break it off, he couldn't bring himself to do it. His client was unstable and manipulative and threatened suicide every time he suggested ending the affair. Pleaser wouldn't let him take the risk of breaking off the affair, nor would it let him tell his wife. Pleaser was afraid that she would leave him and take the children and, of course, he would be helpless to do anything about it. He was trapped into trying to keep everyone happy. His dialoguing session was going nowhere because Pleaser gave him no options. We suggested he put Better Judgement in the opposite chair. What would Better Judgement suggest he do?

Carl: "I can't tell my wife. It would hurt her and she would probably want a divorce. If I tell my lover, she'll do something drastic — maybe even kill herself. I'm torn up over this. I can't sleep and I'm anxious and fearful. What should I do?"

When Carl changed chairs and talked from his Better Judgement, an amazing thing happened. His hapless manner and woeful demeanor vanished. He sat up straight and in a clear, firm voice replied:

Better Judgement: "All right, first you've got to tell Marla (his wife) about this situation and take the consequences. The deceit has got to stop. You'll have to deal with the issues in the marriage that got you into this mess in the first place. It may as well start now."

Carl: "But I'm afraid of what will happen. Marla will be hurt and angry and may want a divorce."

Better Judgement: "Yes, that may happen, but at least you will bring the whole thing out into the open. It may be the catalyst that will get you and Marla into family counseling. Your marriage has been in serious trouble long before this affair began and you know it. Next, you've got to break off this affair, pronto."

Carl: "But if I end the affair with Debbie (his lover), she says she will kill herself."

Better Judgement: "Debbie is manipulating you. She's using blackmail and you can't let her continue. She's not going to commit suicide any more than she's going to fly to Mars."

Carl: "What a relief! I know the right thing to do now."

Everything worked out for Carl even though he went through a lot of stress. He ended the relationship and his lover backed down. He and his wife went through a crisis that included a separation, but they got into family therapy and, after a year, worked out their problems. Now they're living together again in a much more stable relationship.

Better Judgement is always there, but you have to quiet the voices of your Stress Personalities in order to hear it clearly. Until that happens, present your problems to both parties; e.g., if you have an Internal Timekeeper and are suffering bouts of exhaustion, dialogue with both Internal Timekeeper and Better Judgement to determine for yourself who has the most sensible solution.

You: "I am overwhelmed with so many things to do. There isn't enough time to do them all and I feel anxious, scattered, and exhausted."

Internal Timekeeper: "Well, you could get up earlier and get more done. You could also get more proficient at doing more than one thing at a time. You could cut your lunch break in half and spend the extra time getting things done that you need to do."

Better Judgement: "What you really need to do is cut out some of your unnecessary activity. Make it a rule never to have a dinner party on the same day you have a hectic schedule. Learn to delegate some of your responsibilities. Build in some periods of relaxation, even if only for five minutes. What is the point of those precious projects if you don't enjoy them and you get headaches all the time? Why don't you start by finding someone else to drive the carpool? Ask Jim to share in cooking dinners, and don't take on any new projects for the rest of the month."

Better Judgement is interested in the quality of your life, not the quantity of things you require of yourself to prove you're a worthwhile person. Better Judgement will be as specific as you want it to be about the best way to handle your life and deal with stress. When you do hear from Better Judgement, listen. When you follow its advice, you will feel much calmer, stronger, and better able to cope with stress that does occur. No one is better able to handle your problems than you.

Stress is a personal issue. Self-knowledge is essential to learning how to reduce your stress. In this book we have presented a model for learning about yourself in order to be happier and healthier. We know it works, because many thousands of those who have used this method have found it a useful tool in managing their Stress Personalities. If you dialogue, you'll enhance the usefulness of our model in your life. Take the time and have the patience to try it.

BIBLIOGRAPHY

Dempcy, Mary & Tihista, Rene, *A Guide to your Stress Personalities,* workbook, Focal Point Press, Bolinas, CA, 1978, 1982, 1990.

A step by step guide for utilizing the Stress Personalities Model as a self-help program for stress management.

Dempcy, Mary & Tihista, Rene, *Conflict at Work,* workbook, Focal Point Press, Bolinas, CA, 1986, 1987.

A conflict workbook utilizing the Stress Personalities Model with assessments and expanded sections on Faulty Perceptions and New Perceptions.

Friedman and Roseman, *Type A Behavior and Your Heart,* Alfred A. Knopf, New York, NY, 1974.

A milestone book, linking behavior and personality patterns to cardiovascular disease. Recommended for help in understanding Internal Timekeeper, Striver, or Sabertooth Stress Personalities.

Kohn, Alfie, *No Contest: The Case Against Competition,* Houghton-Miflin, Boston, 1986.

Kohn reviews the literature on the effects of competition and the stress it produces in children, adults and in corporate settings. Read this book to get another perspective on your Striver.

Lewis & Lewis, *Psychosomatics,* Pinnacle Books, New York, 1975.

Easy-to-understand information on psychosomatic illness for the lay person.

McQuade & Aikman, *Stress,* A Bantam Book, New York, 1974.

Good general book on stress and its relation to psychosomatic disease for the lay person. Easy to read.

Ornstein, Robert & Sobel, David, *Healthy Pleasures,* Addison Wesley, Menlo Park, CA 1989.

Pleasurable reading. A review of the many common activities available to us all that can reduce our stress and improve the quality of our lives.

Pelletier, Kenneth, *Mind as Healer, Mind as Slayer,* Dell Publishing Co., Inc., New York, 1977.

Excellent sourcebook for those interested in learning about stress, psychosomatic disease, personality and illness, and stress reduction methods. Some sections are technical but understandable for the lay person. A fundamental book for anyone interested in stress.

Perls, Fritz, *Gestalt Therapy Verbatim,* Real People Press, Lafayette, California, 1969.

This book describes Gestalt therapy and is included because of its verbatim Gestalt dialoguing. We developed guided dialoguing from this method as a form of self- therapy. This book can give you a perspective of this process as therapy.

Satir, Virginia, *People Making,* Science and Behavior Books, Inc., Palo Alto, California, 1972.

An excellent, easy-to-read book that describes the development of human behavior within the family system and communication styles that we grow up with. Recommended for parents and children alike.

Selye, Hans, *Stress Without Distress,* Signet Books, New American Library, New York, New York, 1974.

Basic sourcebook on stress by the foremost research pioneer on the subject.

Smith, Manuel, *When I Say No I Feel Guilty,* Dial Press, New York, 1975.

The assertiveness training manual by its originator. An excellent book that is must reading if you have a Pleaser or Sabertooth Stress Personality. A practical how-to book.

The I Ching, Bollingen Series XIX, Princeton University Press, 1950.

The ancient book of Chinese wisdom has advice that is not only applicable to modern Westerners, it is foundation wisdom. More than just a book, it is a life-long source of learning. It is full of Better Judgement.

Wilson, Colin, *The Mind Parasites,* Arkham House, 1967.

This book is a science fiction tale about how our minds are preyed upon by elusive and mysterious parasites. It is a marvelous tale that fits our view of the human personality having many parts. If you have a Critical Judge stress Personality, you will recognize the symptoms of the mind parasites.

.